CRUEL BRITANNIA

CRUEL BRITANNIA

Reports on the sinister and the preposterous

NICK COHEN

VERSO

London and New York

First published by Verso 1999
© Nick Cohen 1999
Paperback edition first published by Verso 2000
© Nick Cohen 2000
All rights reserved

Verso
UK: 6 Meard Street, London W1V 3HR
USA: 180 Varick Street, New York NY 10014–4606

Verso is the imprint of New Left Books

ISBN 1–85984–288–7

British Library Cataloguing in Publication Data
A catalogue record for this book is available from the British Library

Library of Congress Cataloging-in-Publication Data
A catalog record for this book is available from
the Library of Congress

Typeset in Perpetua by The Running Head Limited,
www.therunninghead.com
Printed and bound in Great Britain by Biddles Ltd, www.Biddles.co.uk

to Anne-Marie

CONTENTS

CONTENTS

INTRODUCTION

I joined the *Observer* in 1996 and was anxious to make a good impression. Alas, my first task was to help compile a seemingly dreary news feature about the zero tolerance of crime in the United States, which offered few opportunities to impress my new employers. 'News feature' is a deceptive label given by editors to articles which are neither. In this instance, the New York police's tactic of reducing crime by pouncing on the smallest disturbers of public order – beggars, graffiti-spraying boys, street vendors – had been chewed over so often by the British media it could be dolloped on the page with a flick of the wrist. Mainstream journalists had applauded the American authorities for 'proving' that clearing nuisances created districts that repelled hardened criminals. More curious souls had gone further and examined the treatment of the homeless, the transformation of the land of the free into the penal capital of the Western world and military policing. Anything new to say would be said by a colleague in America whose eye had been caught by a demand that week from the unteachable opportunist Bill Clinton for curfews on teenagers out after dark. I was left with the task of reporting what zero tolerance tactics were being practised in Britain and, after rudimentary inquiries, discovered that the only example was a ban on boozing in the centre of Coventry. Derelicts were moved on and settled in a suburban park. Their squawks and belches annoyed the neighbours, but everyone else agreed the city centre was a better place for their absence. There were no Swat teams or helicopters with searchlights; it was all very modest and rather English, as we like to say.

For want of anything better to do, I phoned Jack Straw. At that time the hatred of left-of-centre journalists and their readers for the Conservative government bordered on the irrational. Condemnations of its immiseration of the poor, plumping of the rich, quangocracy, subservience to American foreign policy, corruption and banality fell easily from our lips because they had been repeated through a generation of defeat. The imperative to get rid of them by any means necessary overrode worries about what Labour might do when, and if, it at last managed to defy history and win an election. Few of those who flattered themselves into thinking their opposition to Thatcherism was based on a considered critique of the consequences of Conservative policy wondered if they should also oppose Blair when he was singing every song in the Tory songbook, and composing new numbers of his own. For what turned out to be the last time I therefore approached Straw as a comrade in a common project and dropped a helpful hint that his words would be put in a liberal newspaper whose readers, I fondly imagined, would be more likely to vote for his party if he dwelt on helping the poor rather than arresting them.

'Now, Jack, obviously you don't hold with teen curfews and all of that,' I said with unwarranted confidence.

He gave the idea two, maybe three, seconds' thought and found, on the contrary, that curfews were 'a sensible way to deal with the issue'. He had heard 'a lot of complaints from the constituencies about youngsters out on the streets'. He saw them himself when he drove 'back from the Commons' and wanted to know what had happened to their parents. I put the phone down and stuck my head round the door of the editor's office to tell him New Labour was planning to impose martial law on children. After taking a deep breath and – or did my ears deceive me? – howling with the pain of a dying timber wolf, he cleared a gratifying large space on the front page. Straw called back an hour later. He had not been authorised to talk off the top of his head about curfews. Would I mind forgetting about our conversation? I most certainly would. I had interviewed him on the record and he knew the rules. It was unthinkable that a member of the free press should be censored by a politician, and so on. Because we published Straw's ramblings we forced Labour's majestic policy-making machine to begin the grave and careful task of constructing a legal framework for the arrest of children who had committed no crime. Plans were scrawled on the back of a fag packet by Sunday lunchtime. If I had killed the article, there may well have been no curfews. (Sorry.) Yet the outcry Straw appeared to anticipate was strangely muted. Libertarians complained, but the press was largely satisfied. The Conservatives were reduced to envious mutterings and the Labour Party did not mutiny. A handful of Labour supporters may have assumed that Straw was lying to win the election and would reveal compassionate and democratic socialist credentials in office, but I guess that by then most realised that you cannot win the battle of ideas by stealth. It was taken as read that Labour would move ever further to the right, and that an acceptance of the squalor and authoritarianism of the Thatcherite status quo was not only necessary but, to use the cant of the time, modern.

I hope you will quickly pass over my disastrous contribution to criminal justice policy (*look*, I said I was sorry) and examine instead the nature of the modern political consensus. Even if you foolishly believe that an absence of conflict is possible or desirable, questions remain on the nature of the agreement. Ever since the growth of party discipline and the arrival of oligarchical control of the means of communication at the end of the nineteenth century, radical critics have argued that a consensus can be defined by what is wilfully excluded from debate: empire, the position of women, Ireland, nuclear disarmament (in the past) and the causes of poverty, power of big business and hollowing out of democracy (today). Yet a comforting assumption hums in the background that, given the chance, consensual politics will be benign.

George Orwell when he was all but a Trotskyist saw Britain as 'a family . . . a family with the wrong members in control' in 1941. In 1961, E. P. Thompson could describe the segregation of dissent, the conditioning of public opinion and the concentration of power but still regard Establishment defences as 'bland and fair-minded'. I don't believe it is possible for anyone to write like that today and be taken seriously. The Nineties – whatever happened to the Nineties, incidentally? – were meant to be a caring decade in a warm if doltish way. John Major talked of a nation at ease with itself, Tony Blair appropriated the language of One Nation Conservatism, and people cried for a while over a dim princess. If you are tempted to go along with them and regard Thatcherism as an aberration, consider what reply you might give to that perennially inquisitive Martian if it asked what made you proud to be British. A level of tolerance resting somewhere above zero? Or the decency and preference for quiet patriotism Orwell admired, rather than vicious nationalism? How about the national character: stoicism and a healthy suspicion of the motives behind public displays of emotion? Irony, self-deprecation, amateurism, sportsmanship, romanticism, eccentricity and an empirical respect for science and inventiveness? OK, concern for the deserving poor and refugees? Perhaps the strength of Parliamentary and local democracy, wisdom of the judiciary, fairness of the police, fearlessness of the press and quality of the television? You can find traces of a few of the above if you look hard enough, I suppose, but the envy of the world? Come, come now. Surely you won't be reduced to citing the grace of the House of Windsor?

It is reasonable to suspect that what we have is a consensus built around the prejudices of right-wing conservatism. On any issue apart from constitutional reform and Europe, you can predict what Labour ministers will do by imagining what their Tory counterparts would have done. For a journalist who was critical of the Conservative government, the election of New Labour presented few professional difficulties. The same themes kept being heard, the same vices were displayed, only the suits were different. But to say that Blair is a Tory tied to the prejudices of the Eighties only takes you so far because in England, if not Scotland and Wales, we now have conservatism without opposition or the possibility of change, and that difference takes us into a new world.

Talk like this and you are accused of being a cynical miserabilist who hates his country. Obviously, I don't hate Britain – if I did, I'd leave. Nor need current affairs journalism be miserable. The political class is preposterous as well as sinister, as my exchange with Straw taught me. Mockery and satire have a chance to be the dominant idioms of the next decade as we watch emotionally literate Pecksniffs sob as they comfort the powerful and each other, and apostates defend their perfidy with ever more desperate fervour. The new consensus is neurotic and bombastic and requires stern intellectual policing if it is not to be undermined by contemptuous laughter. The British elite may not govern wisely, but if you cover its absurdities it brings moments of exultant joy when, as Oscar Wilde wisely noted, it becomes more than a moral duty to speak one's mind. It becomes a pleasure.

What follows is a collection of articles and essays. They were written for the moment and because I write to earn my living. There are, to my surprise, common preoccupations behind a majority of them. Chapter One contains thumbnail sketches of members of the political class and shows – if you will forgive a journalist's trade unionism – that you do not have to be a satirist to capture our times, merely a reporter. (What wild mind, after all, could have invented Harriet Harman?) Chapter Two shows both the malign and risible sides of New Labour pedalling in tandem and examines the government's oxymoronic ethical foreign policy, one of the few initiatives that even battle-hardened cynics had faith in. Chapters Three and Six report on the uncontested assault on civil liberties and how fears of crime and alien invasion are used to keep the population nervous and compliant – a useful task previously undertaken by the Soviet Union and the IRA. Chapter Four discusses the forces that mould what little news we receive and Chapter Five looks at the related triumph of commercial values over all others.

No reporter can survive without newspapers who will back him, and it has been my good fortune to have worked for successive editors of the *Observer* who have given me the freedom to follow my whims and write without restraint, even when they disagreed with my conclusions. I thank the managements of the *Independent on Sunday*, the *London Review of Books*, the *New Statesman*, *Jewish Quarterly*, *Modern Review* and, particularly, the *Observer*, for their kind permission to reproduce articles that originally appeared in their pages. In compiling this book I have added paragraphs that were cut for reasons of space and tidied up ugly sentences I should never have written in the first place. In several cases – on the calamitous collapse of news journalism, for example – I have included material not available when the articles first appeared. Other pieces are presented as single essays – on the handing over of schools to business, or the boom in private prisons – but are the result of a merger of a series of reports written over weeks or months.

Journalism is a collective enterprise, although only the writer's name appears at the top of an article. It has been a pleasure to work with Euan Ferguson, the *Observer*'s inspirational comment editor, who read the proofs, and his deputy, Michael Holland, who has saved me from numerous solecisms. This book is dedicated to my wife with love and gratitude.

All errors of judgment and taste remain – as ever – the author's own.

London, January 1999

CHAPTER ONE

PORTRAITS FROM A NEW ERA

When David Evans, the Conservative MP for Welwyn and Hatfield, pushed liberal tempers to the limit by calling his Labour opponent 'a single girl with three bastard children' and demanding the castration of 'black bastard' rapists, worldly Conservative commentators lectured his detractors on the facts of life in the real world. The *Telegraph* did not doubt that its finger was on the pulse of popular feeling. 'It is not Mr Evans, but the prissy ideologues who express deep shock at his words who are out of touch,' wrote its old-Etonian editor. Richard Littlejohn, a millionaire journalist who affects to be the voice of the people, said in the *Mail* that Evans spoke for the 'great unwashed' who paid MPs' wages. 'While the incestuous worlds of Westminster and the chattering classes were working themselves into a lather of indignation, in saloon bars and supermarket queues the length and breadth of Britain most people must have been wondering what all the fuss was about. What really frightens the *bien-pensants* is that they know millions of people in Britain think in exactly the same way as Evans.' The unwashed voted on 1 May 1997, and Melanie Johnson, 'single girl with bastard children', thrashed the upright Evans. 'Perhaps prejudice does not have a home here,' she said. 'Hundreds of voters mentioned his attack on me and wanted to disassociate themselves from him.' People crossed the road to shake her hand. Churches circulated petitions defending her reputation.

In Exeter, which had not been seen as a centre of sexual experiment, the gay-and-frank-about-it Ben Bradshaw faced Adrian Rogers, president of the Conservative Family Institute and one of God's noisiest botherers. Rogers, who had described homosexuality as 'sterile, disease-ridden and God-forsaken', ran the nastiest campaign of the election. He implored Devon voters not to 'let the pink flag fly'. Exeter City supporters were assumed to be unreconstructed on the homosexual question and were given leaflets at home matches telling them Bradshaw was gay. Rogers's last tract was, Labour alleged, handed to children who were told to take it home to mummy and daddy. 'I ask every Exeter parent and everyone concerned about our country's children: Do you want an MP who wants to promote homosexuality in schools?' They did. Bradshaw won with the biggest swing to Labour in the South-West. 'I think the press fails to understand the decency and tolerance of the British,' he told me.

Gisela Stuart, Labour contender in Birmingham Edgbaston, was a target because she was born a German and did not move to Britain until she was a teenager. A local Conservative councillor warned the electorate 'not to vote for a Kraut'. 'I'm knocking on people's doors telling them to vote British, not German,' he said. 'She's wrapping herself in the Union Jack and it's a damned cheek.' The party of the family said she had misled the voters by losing her German and taking her English husband's surname. The wealthy suburb was one of the first seats to fall to Labour on election night and became the Basildon of the 1997 campaign.

To those who knew the West Midlands, Stuart's victory was nothing compared to the end of the career of Nicholas Budgen, the austere representative of the racism, Unionism, anti-Europeanism and monarchism which had dominated politics for 20 years. He had appealed to John Major to make an election issue of Labour's plans to relax a few immigration controls. To the surprise of jaundiced commentators, whose number included your correspondent, Major refused to play the well-thumbed race card. Once again, the tribunes of the far-right press knew that they and Budgen spoke for the nation. Simon Heffer of the *Mail* said Budgen's views 'were popular with the public' and added, without irony, that Tory MPs had 'winced with shame at Major's failure to see the importance of the issue'. Budgen defied his leader by running in Wolverhampton South West – the seat he had inherited from Enoch Powell – on an anti-immigration ticket. Powell sent a personal endorsement and the Conservative right consoled itself with the thought that although Major would lose, Budgen would triumph. Powell's support was 'ominously prescient,' the *Mail* said. Powell would be proved right and was 'now surely entitled to feel some wry satisfaction'. Powellism would, surely, survive in the old brute's former stamping ground and provide the ideas around which the Tories could revitalise themselves in opposition. Budgen lost on a 10 per cent swing to Labour's Jenny Jones.

A New Era, free from bigotry and fear, seemed to have dawned. 'Goodbye xenophobia,' sang the *Observer*'s lead headline. Six months later, Johnson, Bradshaw, Stuart and Jones pushed through Conservative cuts to the benefits of the poorest women and children in the country.

THE STEPFORD WIVES

They tripped out of Church House on a bright May day and lined up in the Westminster sunshine for the defining picture of the New Era. Blair's babes exploded with colour and promise. When Fleet Street's cameramen instructed them to surround the leader, only the sourest critics noted the similarities between their pose and the shots of Playboy bunnies encircling Hugh Hefner. The 101 New Labour women dismissed the comparisons as patronising. They did not trip – *thank you very much* – and weren't babes or bunnies for that matter, but serious, principled politicians. Their success was not merely a victory for a clique of courtiers on the make, but a triumph for all the women of Britain. They would modernise the macho Commons just by being there, and place women's concerns at the centre of the nation's affairs.

Maria Eagle, the newly elected Labour MP for Liverpool Garston, was confident that 'male-dominated' Westminster was dead: 'The fact that there are so many of us will change the way things are run in the House and in the country.' Shona McIsaac, MP for Cleethorpes, believed that the women's magazines *Chat* and *Bella*, where she used to earn a crust, were forces for emancipation. Cherie Blair read the glossies and through her they were influencing her husband's politics. 'If you look at Tony Blair's speeches, you will see that they're softer, more compassionate.' Who could doubt the feminisation of the Labour Party, when the previous year Tony Blair, Gordon Brown and Harriet Harman had promised to reverse an attack on the income of single mothers? The Conservatives had decided to cut additional income support (worth £4.95 a week per mother) and additional child benefit (worth £6.05). From the opposition benches, Harman developed the obvious but none the less reasonable argument that you do not help the poor by 'plunging them further into poverty'. She echoed Chris Pond, the articulate director of the Low Pay Unit. The loss of benefit, he said, 'was particularly spiteful, given that it only raises £300 million. This is small change for the Treasury, but will make it much harder for families to make ends meet.'

Labour's opposition did not survive election victory. Within weeks it embraced the doctrine that the poor were poor because they were stealing all our money. The feckless mares would have to live on less. Harman, as a female colleague said, 'made her career standing up for women and is now standing on their backs'. There is talk of the Parliamentary Labour Party rebelling. I'd sooner expect to see veal calves savaging butchers, but if a revolt takes place it will be too late.* Dissident MPs are objecting to a social security bill which will cut £40 million from the child benefit budget. Far greater penalties were imposed at a meeting of the Commons social security standing committee when Labour MPs agreed that from April 1998 new single parents will lose

* It did; it was.

special rates of income support and contributions to council tax and housing bills.

Joining New Labour is like joining the Mafia – you must kill what you love to prove your loyalty to the capo – and the MPs who had shouted loudest about the the triumph of women were put on the committee and ordered to fight the class war against the poor. Eagle and McIsaac were there. So was Caroline Flint, New Labour MP for the very Old Labour Don Valley, who had appeared alongside McIsaac in a fashion shoot of five 'sexy, stylish and spirited' politicians in *Elle*. It's 'time to get some glamour into politics,' she told the magazine. The whips also recruited Siobhain McDonagh, a new MP whose first recorded intervention at a Labour Party conference began: 'I'm a real *Cosmo* girl. *Cosmo* is more influential than the *New Statesman*.'

Now, I've bumped into members of the 1997 intake of Labour MPs over the years and would have said, even on election night, that no matter how right wing and unscrupulous they appeared, whatever else they did in the future, the remnants of their youthful feminism and egalitarianism would stop them picking on women and children. Here was a line in the sand, albeit a long way up the beach. I'm therefore likely to become a bit of a bore on this subject now that the hope that there are some things they wouldn't do, on principle, has proved a chimera. I don't think anyone who believed a Labour government would make life slightly better for the poor could read the record of the committee hearing without embarrassed disgust. New Labour's spirited representatives sat through a meeting determining the livelihoods of 1.5 million women like hirelings from an escort agency at a tycoon's party. They looked stylish – maybe even sexy – and said absolutely nothing. Pond, who is neither, was told to join them and could not find the words he found the year before or the courage to vote against the cuts he had previously deplored.

It was left to Damian Green – a Tory man, of all things – to ask if it was for this that they 'spent years in the political wilderness as Labour activists, hoping to become members of Parliament'. No one answered. Afterwards, shyness prevented many going on the record. I phoned Maria

Eagle's office on a Thursday. 'I had a word, she won't have time to talk to you,' her secretary said.

'Friday or Saturday, then?'

'She'll be in her constituency, she won't have time.'

'It'll only take a minute.'

'No!'

Eagle is clearly rushed off her feet. One New Woman did chat anonymously. She dismissed the evidence that two-thirds of single parents live below the poverty line with a remark that would be endorsed in the nineteenth holes of every Home Counties golf club: 'These aren't desperate people. Most of them have got men somewhere in the background.' She continued in this dreary vein, until my prodding about breaking promises and letting down supporters led her to say it all in two sentences. 'I appreciate there were some people who voted for us who thought we would make a difference. They didn't understand.' Silly of them, really.

Flint in public and others in private said they were happy to see cuts because Labour's plans to take the poor from welfare into work would counter impoverishment and forgot to add that Welfare to Work is not aimed at women with children under five. A single mother now on benefit who takes an insecure job will be £4.95 a week worse off if it falls through and she returns to the dole after April 1998, when the new regime begins. The government has given her every incentive to stay at home and carry on collecting the money because existing claimants will not be affected by the cuts. She will be in a classic poverty trap. Single mothers in low-paid work will be £10.25 a week worse off from June and may well decide to live on benefit instead. Labour has approved an absolute cut in the living standards of single mothers in low-paid jobs, of unemployed mothers who want to work after 1 April and of mothers who stay at home because – heaven forfend! – they love their children and don't want to dump them in slum nurseries.

Stephen Pound, an eager new MP, maintained at a private meeting of the Parliamentary party that women were foolish to complain about the loss of trivial sums: 'It's no more than the price of a couple of packets of cigarettes,' he said, neatly articulating the new establishment's distaste for fag-smoking slags without personal trainers. Denis MacShane did his chances of promotion no harm by saying that single mothers were recipients of 'state charity'. Only Old Labour MPs – Alice Mahon, Helen Jackson, Maria Fyfe and Ann Clwyd – said that £10 buys several meals, and that a party which professes to believe in 'inclusion' should not dismiss help for the weakest as charity. Their best friends wouldn't call them glamorous, and they will never appear in *Elle*, but they at least know the difference between politics and power-worship.

While Blair's babes sat silently as the cuts went through, a group of single mothers at the back of the Commons committee room forcefully compared them to the Stepford Wives. In the film, intelligent women were turned into robots, programmed to cry in ecstasy when their repellent masters screwed them. It is a faintly sexist comparison, but a simile does not fail because it will not pass in polite society. This analogy collapses because the babes will be fine. It's their constituents who are about to be shafted.

Observer November 1997

ALBION'S ALBANIANS

Imagine (if you can) being a New Labour MP. The party you thought gave voters a left-of-centre alternative has left the left and is taking a sharp right out of the centre. Your pager tells you what to do. The Prime Minister, whose wife once said she wouldn't have the *Sun* in the house, now ushers its proprietor to the easy chairs in the Downing Street study. The ministers you admire are impotent. Cabinet government has been replaced by a monarch's court.

Briefly, your glum meditation is brightened by a happy if paradoxical thought. The supposed control freaks are giving away control. Like Lear, they are dividing up the kingdom and handing out freedom to Labour MPs and party members; to the Scots, the Welsh, Londoners and anyone else who wants an elected mayor or regional assembly. There's a closing-down sale in Whitehall and every centralised power must go, gift-wrapped in boxes labelled devolution, modernity and choice. You start to cheer up, then the whips spoil it all. They send you a ballot paper where you can express your choice on who should sit on the National Executive Committee, Labour's ruling body. The form must have been printed in North Korea. Although you thought you might nominate any colleague who impressed you, the boxes where you were to identify your favourite MPs have been filled already by the Government machine with the pre-printed names of Anne Begg, Clive Soley and Pauline Green, two Westminster politicians and one Euro-pol. You make inquiries and discover that if you decide not to endorse the leadership's preferences you will have to fill in another form and make a dangerous public declaration that you are off-message.

Oh, well, what about ordinary, decent Labour Party members, surely they can pick who they want in the people's section of the NEC? After all, Tony has taken power away from union barons and given it to the party. But democracy has become a complicated business. A marketing company has been hired at great expense to cold call the members and tell them to vote for the leadership's favoured candidates. The rank and file will be told to dismiss Mark Seddon, the amiable editor of *Tribune* (who reminds you of your younger self) and his left-of-centre slate as Trotskyist wreckers who will bring back the division and poison of the Eighties. From the look of him Seddon must have been in nappies when Benn was in full flood.

Your eyes turn north to Scotland, where Labour men and women standing for the new Parliament must, you hope against hope, be able to free themselves from metropolitan fixers. They're a fierce bunch up there, who don't take kindly to English bullies. But, and your soul is numbed by yet another but, *but* even in Scotland a panel is vetting candidates, blackballing those whose bearing or views are not slick and correct. Murray Elder, a kind man who worked for John Smith (remember him?), has been banned, along with Dennis Canavan, a left-wing MP who supported devolution in the days when other comrades (memo to mouth: never utter that word again) were hostile.

You have heard in the Westminster bars about the case of Ian Davidson. Everyone knows his persona is non grata because he leads the trade union rights campaign in the Commons. Anonymous 'sources' – why don't they bloody come out in the open? – deny he's been blacklisted for being a leftie (the very thought!). Good grief, no. Davidson made an unforgivable political error. He arrived at his panel interview in a T-shirt. What a slob. Obviously unfit for office. The fact that his trousers were smart and, he assures you, the T-shirt was actually a polo shirt of which he is rather proud, could not save him. Nor could his plea that he was going on to play for a Labour team in a charity football match. It was Sunday – a scorching Sunday at that. You'd never have guessed that prized rarity, a hot Scottish day, could be used against you.

Is Wales safe? No. There are panels vetting candidates for the principality and for local council elections. The Mayor of London? It's been made painfully clear that the people will be allowed to vote for anyone they want, as long as it's not Red Ken. European elections? Ah, here you come to the mother of all buts. For Europe we have chosen a system of proportional representation the Stasi would have rejected as hopelessly biased. The party's 'closed list' will mean it is Millbank apparatchiks, not the electorate, who decide which Labour candidates win.

In your heart you know that Parliament will be next; that panels will soon be vetting Labour MPs, throwing out supporters of union rights and those who, wilfully pushing old ideologies to the extreme, insist on wearing polo shirts on Sunday. You realise that Britain will soon be a collection of truly weird islands. People will be voting almost monthly in referendums and on citizens' juries; in parish, local, mayoral, regional, Parliamentary and Euro elections. Yet the only Labour candidates the exhausted electors will be able to support will be Blairite.

The public will, you think, have all the freedom of choice of a shop-aholic in an Albanian supermarket.

You think. You don't say.

Observer May 1998

DeANNE JULIUS

In 1970 DeAnne Julius, a young and by several accounts bright American, left the University of California in Santa Barbara and joined the CIA during one of the ugliest periods in its history. Her career choice would not have disturbed far-right Americans with no qualms about the CIA-inspired massacres in Vietnam and their country's decision to create the conditions for Pol Pot's victory by bombing Cambodia 'back to the Stone Age'. What is surprising is that it has not prevented a Labour government from putting a former agent of a foreign power on the Bank of England's monetary committee.

Gordon Brown's decision to end democratic control over the setting of interest rates gave Julius her entrée into British politics. Ever since their elevation, Julius and her colleagues have decided what home-owners and businesses should pay for their mortgages and loans and, indirectly, set the rate of the pound for exporters.* Julius is 48 and is described by her friends as an open woman. She closes up when asked about her past. She confirms she did work for the CIA as an analyst based in the United States.

'It was just a civil service job,' she said. 'I was looking at the economy of Ceylon as it was then called.'

'Why? What was the CIA's interest?'

'I'm not prepared to discuss it.'

---

* Between June 1997 and the autumn of 1998, the Bank of England ignored a global recession and regarded the non-existent threat of inflation as an ever-present danger in an era of collapsing commodity prices. Interest rates were raised continuously and manufacturing industry was crucified by the high pound and dear money.

A CIA spokeswoman was equally vague. She described Julius's labours as 'classified academic research'. This meant, she explained, that Julius would have provided financial commentaries based on secret information. She was pleased to hear her former colleague was at the heart of British economic policy. Her job was 'a logical progression,' she told the *Scotsman*: 'a good assignment'. There is a faint possibility that Julius did mention her life as a spook before Brown appointed her. The Chancellor's aides say they knew nothing and there is no mention of her time with the CIA in the potted biography issued by the Bank of England. But now Brown knows, he says her covert past does not trouble him. 'She was just a number cruncher,' explained an insouciant Treasury official. 'It's very hard to find American economists who have not worked for the CIA. We wanted her because she's very good. She gives the bank credibility.'

The Treasury's justification was feeble to the point of infirmity. Our civil servant does not explain why an American is running monetary policy. Nor does he recognise that thousands of American economists would not work for the CIA. 'Credible' was not an adjective many would have used to describe the agency in the early Seventies, when its role in inciting the coup that overthrew Salvador Allende's elected government in Chile – and in the mass murder and torture that followed – was exposed along with its involvement in the Vietnam atrocities and the grotesque betrayal of the Kurds of northern Iraq. (They were encouraged to rise against Saddam Hussein and then abandoned to his tender mercies when he did what the US wanted and stopped troubling the Shah of Iran, America's client.) Even US legislators were troubled and ordered the first and only robust inquiry into CIA outrages. But Julius does not appear to have been bothered.

She moved from the CIA to the World Bank and by 1989 had a British husband, a home in London and a job at Shell. She was with the multi-national at the moment when the staggeringly corrupt Nigerian government was suppressing Ogoni protesting against Shell's pollution of their homeland. The company and its friends in the army received international condemnation when the Nigerian military executed the Ogoni writer and leader, Ken Saro-Wiwa. His death does not appear to have bothered Julius. Nor, as far as I can see, did the record of another organisation which liked its tricks dirty. In 1993 she became chief strategist at British Airways. When she arrived, the scandal about BA's tactics in its battle against Virgin was at its height. The names 'Mission Atlantic' and 'Operation Covent Garden' – BA's alternately sinister and ludicrous 'operations' to stop Virgin competing on trans-Atlantic routes – peppered the papers. To persuade Virgin passengers to switch to BA, the company hassled them at airports and called them at home. The addresses of Virgin customers were found by computer hackers. BA's managers assumed their opponents were equally creepy. They recruited a force of private detectives to run counter-surveillance operations against Virgin. A BA executive was wired for sound when he went to meet a 'friend' he suspected of being a Virgin spy. He wasn't. A journalist's bins were searched. Nothing was discovered. BA's employees were assumed to include Virgin moles. They were secretly monitored. No traitors were unmasked. Staff had a loyalty their company would not reciprocate.

While Brown was deciding Julius was a 'credible' director of economic policy, the BA management was trying to break its unions. Cabin crew threatened to strike against a new pay structure they believed would lose each of them £4,000 a year. BA took industrial relations to a post-war low by warning it would ruin strikers. They would not only lose their jobs, redundancy rights and cheap travel, but also their homes and savings in court claims for damages brought by the company. Once again, surveillance was used against the BA workforce. Employees on picket lines were caught by video cameras.

None of this appears to have bothered Julius, but it does not appear to have bothered New Labour either. Tony Blair and Jack Straw remained close friends of Bob Ayling, BA's chief executive.

As you would expect, Julius is a very conservative economist. Kenneth Clarke rejected Bank of England demands to raise interest rates because he wanted to protect manufacturers. As a Midlands MP, close to industry, he was well aware of the danger of an overvalued pound. It seems unlikely that Julius will show a similar concern for the needs of the Britain beyond the Home Counties. In an essay that won first prize in an economics competition sponsored by the American Express Bank, Julius and her co-author wrote that manufacturing industry was nothing special and should not be protected. Companies would have to shift factories from Britain and exploit the cheap labour of the Third World if they wanted to survive. 'It would be a critical mistake' for Western governments to try to stop factory closures. They should make the flight of capital easier by encouraging free trade. The only hope for the British was to find jobs, somehow, in services. 'We are asking politicians,' the authors condescendingly concluded, 'to do what they find most difficult: Nothing!' Oh well, there goes the industrial base. Julius has hinted she finds the idea of democratically accountable economic policy ridiculous. 'Even well-intentioned politicians are less able to make fine judgments about complex economic forecasts than professional economists,' she ruled.

Julius has chosen to remain an American citizen. Her salary at the Bank of England is £130,000. She has worked for a brutal espionage bureaucracy and two pariah corporations. Ken Livingstone was the only Labour MP to raise doubts about an appointment he described as 'incredible'. As soon as the leadership said it was going to pass the power to set interest rates to the Bank of England, he asked Brown if there would be consultation about the merits of candidates. Brown ducked the question, and the most powerful unelected jobs in British government were filled in secret. Livingstone asks what will happen when her loyalties clash and British and American economic interests conflict. Most Labour backbenchers have spent their time since the general election drooling over ministers. Is there a chance that MPs from industrial constituencies, for example, will start asking Brown hard questions?

Or can't they be bothered?

Observer October 1997

PS   One could. In June 1998 Brian Sedgemore, a left-wing Labour MP, embarrassed his colleagues by presuming to cross-examine Julius when she came before the Commons Treasury committee.

'I see from looking at your CV that in 1970–71 you worked for the CIA. Am I right in thinking once a member of the CIA, always a member of the CIA?'

'No, I'm afraid you are not.'

'The time you were there coincided with the undermining of Allende. Did you know about this?'

'No.'

'Did you subsequently feel any shame at working for an agency when it was undermining a democratic government?'

'I had nothing to be ashamed of.'

'You worked for Shell between 1989 and 1993 when the Nigerian government, allegedly with the collusion of Shell, was attacking the Ogoni people. Have you any worries about your occupation with Shell in relation to what you now know has happened in the Ogoni region?'

'None at all.'

'Between 1993 and 1997 you worked for British Airways when it was running its dirty tricks campaign against Virgin. Did you know about that?'

'No.'

'Would you describe yourself as an observant person . . .?'

You learn all you need to know about the Bank of England when you discover that the shameless Julius is considered a liberal softie. The other Brown appointees are far more extreme.

CHRISTIAN SOCIALISTS

No modern government has worshipped a supreme being as enthusiastically as the Blair administration. Its pious pols include St Tony himself, who prays with the mighty modern moralist and spanker Paul

Johnson; the Rev. Gordon Brown, who welcomes the moneylenders into the temple; His Eminence Cardinal Irvine, who battles daily with the sin of pride; and Jack Straw, the Pontius Pilate of penal reform. Chris Bryant, chairman of a Christian Socialist Movement many of us assumed died sometime between the Boer war and the arrival of women's suffrage, boasts that every department of state now has one of his members as a Cabinet or junior minister. 'The Scottish Office was a wasteland until Calum MacDonald was appointed,' he cried. Bryant did not seem to care that his disciple was able to fill the gap in the army of Christian soldiers only because he had done nothing to oppose the attack on single mothers, while his predecessor had resigned on principle.

When so many ministers have been born again, it is wise to find Jesus if you seek preferment. The movement is the fastest-growing society in the Labour Party. I don't wish to imply that Christian socialism is a road to office that opportunists can take without sacrifice. Converts suffer for their faith. The movement's pamphlets combine moral uplift and complacency in equal measure. The latest flaccid offering is *Party Games*, a discussion of what tactics the religious should adopt. It is worth ploughing through the dreary prose because gradually you learn the principles guiding British government and see the revealed gospel of the New Era.

For reasons that still escape me after several readings, Graeme Smith, the movement's publications officer, announces that the campaign Christian Socialists must study and emulate is the fight to persuade Major's government to build a new station in Stratford when the Channel Tunnel rail link was pushed through east London. The local authority was Labour and the district was desperately poor. Smith notes that councillors bit their tongues and refrained from attacking the Tories for fear of jeopardising a project they hoped would bring jobs. 'Was this justified?' he asks. 'Should Christian Socialists be prepared to restrict what they say in public because of the expediency of alliances? The answer is usually, but not always, "yes". For the sake of the alliances necessary to achieve certain goals, care should be taken with public speech. But there will be occasions when alliances should, and will, be broken because of the need for political protest. These occasions will however be rare.' So much for bearing witness. But will tactful silence produce greater victories than speaking in the tongues of angels? Smith thinks not and instructs Christian Socialists to recognise that they cannot change anything. He asks rhetorically how far they should go in cooperating with the 'dominant cultural norms' of a capitalist society. All the way, he replies. 'Should councillors have spent their time criticising the injustice caused by private enterprise and poverty which could have been addressed by increased public expenditure? The answer would be "yes" if dominant cultural norms could be changed quickly and easily. But they cannot.' Direct challenges to the system are 'often viewed as a form of extremism and consequently dismissed'. Far better to 'play the game of lobbyists, consultants, private enterprise and profitability'.

Smith should know that London & Continental Railways, the company allegedly running the channel railway, is a disaster. Extremist criticism of its private enterprise may therefore be in order when the game it is playing has been such a shabby failure. He does not mention the endless demands for public subsidy that led John Prescott to call for the heads of its executives. Nor does he worry about reports that the firm's plans for the line are such a shambles it may not even reach Stratford but stop outside London (if, that is, it is built at all). The innocent reader might be forgiven for thinking that the project was a triumph of free enterprise.

Whenever you attack New Labour for its capitulation to conservatism and mendacity, the party calls you cynical. Now we have Blair's spiritual advisers exalting the virtues of tactful silence and complicity with remarkably inept corporations. Cynics are saints in comparison.

Observer May 1998

MARTIN BELL

Discerning Mancunians once looked down their noses at Neil Hamilton's constituents in the north Cheshire gin-and-Jag belt. They held that his Tatton seat was dominated by golf-club bores, arrivistes and — how to put this delicately? — no-neck businessmen who had done well in the Moss Side commodities market. 'Alderley Edge for old money, Wilmslow for new money and Prestbury for funny money,' as a local saying had it. Although I'm a Cheshire man, I used to be able to see their point. I grew up in Bowdon, just outside Tatton's boundaries. I spent my teenage years locked in my bedroom, my soul racked with longing. I did not dream of girls, glory or being the next Paul Weller, but of how to get away from Cheshire, from the businessmen who boasted about fiddling their taxes, the grammar-school teachers who taught us that the Labour Party was communist, the neighbours who felt their annual change of fitted kitchen was a suitable topic for conversation, the men who got maudlin drunk and sobbed about the betrayal of their first wives, the men who got angry drunk and smacked you in the face if you argued with them about the death penalty, the orders for 'G and T, ice and a slice' that rang in every bar, and — above all — the long roar of excitement that greeted the opening of Safeway (the first supermarket we had seen) and took years to dim. North Cheshire in the Seventies was so wretched I moved to Birmingham and found it exciting.

Cheshire deserved Neil Hamilton. His defence against corruption allegations had an angry, self-pitying and definingly Thatcherite subtext. 'Come off it, I'm on the take, you're on the take, we're all on the take. Nobody thinks that making money is a crime any more apart from my envious and hypocritical left-wing enemies who are the worst of the lot.' I thought Hamilton embodied the prejudices of the chi-chi dormitory towns so perfectly he would easily see off Martin Bell. I was wrong.

Is it time to go home? Particularly as, with the wisdom of middle age, I can recognise Safeway's charms? I might if I could find it. But home has become a foreign country, a land outside politics where all disputation is silenced by persons of goodwill coming together and electing decent representatives. Bell stood and won as a 'non-political' candidate. He had no programme, no reason for getting into Parliament. When he presented himself to the voters and media on Knutsford Heath, he said he was a 'political amateur' without ambition. He was opposed to Hamilton, not conservatism. If the Tories abandoned their man and ran a clean Conservative in his place, he would be happy to stand down and let them retain one of their safest seats. Hamilton refused to give way and Bell was smeared by the Tory press. For a few weeks his cause seemed hopeless, but his simple sincerity, which had been displayed on the BBC whenever he risked his life to bring us the truth from Bosnia, won through. Bell was elected with a huge majority. Yet elected to do what? For whom?

His supporters had no coherent answers; the fact of his victory was enough to satisfy them. They gathered at the launch party for *Purple Homicide*, a raucous account of the Tatton campaign by my *Observer* colleague, John Sweeney. He decided to entertain the crowd of sympathisers with a pantomime. Sweeney and David Soul, who had befriended Bell when he moved from America, acted out the election as farce. For five minutes, the show was a disaster. Soul put on a wig and pretended to be Christine Hamilton. It got worse. He sang. The audience fixed the players with that iron English gaze which reduces the voluble to silence and makes public speaking in this country a cruel and unusual punishment. But in life, as in his book, Sweeney's admiration for Bell could not be contained. The crowd's resolve broke as it remembered the joy of election night and the worthiness of the victor. We began to shout, laugh, cheer, boo and down cheap wine without a thought for liver disease. The only person who looked uncomfortable was Bell. He stood at the back of the room, semi-detached from the throng. His smile was striking. It was the thin grin of a man who wants to be a good fellow – no one likes being called a party pooper – but I could see it vanishing in an instant if 'things went too far'. That's a politician's smile, I thought, as he made an early exit.

Bell became a politician in Tatton. Not an old-fashioned politician with an ideology that enables the voters to predict where he will stand and how he will cope with the unforeseeable opportunities and disasters that will arise in his time in office, but a non-political politician, a professional amateur who sells himself as a man who can be trusted with the covert aid of the most modern marketing techniques available. The great myth about the Tatton campaign was that Bell was an *ingénu* and underdog – the star of a modern Ealing comedy – who won against the odds with the help of a plucky band of volunteers. While the press focused on Soul and Bell's belles, the comely young women who rallied to his cause, Labour and the Liberal Democrats smuggled Bill Le Bretton and Alan Olive, flinty fixers from Labour and the Liberal Democrats, past the hacks. They were professionals, men who knew how to brand Bell and market him as a product to tempt Cheshire consumers. Alastair Campbell offered his services, and by polling day the Bell machine had proved itself to be far more effective than the dwindling band of Conservative supporters. Bell got six leaflets to every home in the constituency. Hamilton's team delivered just two. Once Hamilton was beaten, Le Bretton was free to reveal how he had won the game. He had worried that the candidate and his trade-mark white suits could have been seen in one of two ways: 'the clean-cut dependable amateur, trustworthy white-knight' (I'm afraid this is exactly how these people talk); or 'the eccentric, intruding theatrical Hampstead no-hoper. Our task was to give the people of Tatton the confidence that they could trust Martin.'

Trust was to be built by the messages of Bell's manifesto, 'Where I Stand'. Most of it discussed the laudable measures he wanted to be taken against corruption. Once the stables had been cleaned, however, it was hard to discover what Bell wanted moral politicians to do with power. He had no desire to change Conservative education policy, for example, but did promise to give 'every sixth-former in Tatton the opportunity to meet me within a year,' which was sweet of him. He did not say he wanted more resources for the NHS, but did promise to 'visit as many hospitals as possible,' and that, too, was nice. He was sceptical about Europe, but apart from a brief mention of the single currency there was no discussion of the great issues of tax-and-spend, inequality, foreign policy, constitutional reform or the downsizing culture. The document reached a bathetic climax when Bell bravely proclaimed: 'The idealism of the young should be matched by the idealism of the not-so-young.' (You can almost hear his minders shouting: 'Martin, *never* call old people old.') Since he was elected to the Commons, Bell has continued in this anodyne vein. 'I'm getting on well with most people here,' he said, 'and generally back the government.' To his credit, he condemned forcefully Tony Blair's dealings with Bernie Ecclestone. New Labour, which does not like its creations getting exaggerated ideas about their importance, retaliated by leaking his election expenses to courtier journalists. His admirers were surprised to find that they were rather high for such a plain man. And that's been about it. Lawrence Matheson, news editor of Bell's local paper, said he'd done nothing to upset the neighbours. 'He's very popular. He meets Help the Aged and all the sixth formers, everyone thinks he's great apart from a few die-hard Tories.' What about his politics? Matheson was stumped. Bell writes a column for the paper, but the newsdesk cannot actually remember the MP discussing politics. 'He's like a schoolboy describing a trip. Like this week it's about life in Westminster and his father, who invented the *Times* crossword. He may have written about education once, but I can't swear to it.'

Martin Bell, in short, beat the Conservatives by running on a Conservative ticket. His promises were tiny, and posed no threat to the Thatcherite status quo. All he told the electorate was that he was a decent man who could be trusted to deal with them honestly. He wasn't alone.

From the mid-Eighties, the British liberal-left put its energy into a great and necessary task: the destruction of a Conservative government that was turning the country into a one-party state. Labour (and to a lesser extent, the Liberal Democrats and nationalists) abandoned their principles, used stunts that could make a moron weep, passed power from MPs to propagandists, changed policies daily and conceded ground faster than a routed army. It looked, and was, opportunist. But true opportunists fool others, not themselves. By the time of the 1997 election, New Labour believed its compromises were right as well as convenient. It supporters, who deluded themselves that Tony Blair was dissembling to win power and would educate the public by introducing rational democratic socialist policies after the election, were shocked when they discovered they couldn't trust politicians to tell lies anymore. Blair, like Bell, wanted to be seen as a 'trustworthy white knight', a non-political politician who accepted large parts of the Conservative legacy. If you criticise him, you are denounced as a 'cynic', and it is pointless to reply – after a sharp intake of breath – that his rage is the rage of Caliban at seeing his face in the mirror. It is a little rich to hear 'cynic' fall from the lips of a man who has cynically abandoned pretty much everything he once stood by. Yet Blair not only sells sincerity but may be a success because he sincerely believes he is sincere himself. Although I'm wary of the babble of psycho-journalism, he does seem able to convince himself that he is a 'regular guy' and that anyone who believes what he believed five minutes earlier and criticises his turbo-powered apostasy must be warped. His Christianity is probably a great help here.

Like Bell, Blair surrounds himself with fixers – many of them bullies – while appearing pure himself. His characteristic speech is composed of staccato sentences. 'We said we'd do X, we've done it. We said we'll do Y, we're doing it. We're saying we'll do Z and, hey, we will.' At his first party conference as Labour leader he announced: 'Let us say what we mean, and mean what we say. Stop saying what we don't mean. And start saying what we do mean, what we stand by, what we stand for.' To modern ears able to tolerate the Prime Minister's atrocious syntax, such sentiments sound admirable, and we forget how odd it is for a politician to insist on the importance of keeping promises.

When Margaret Thatcher came to power she did not promise to crush the unions, impoverish a fifth of the population, privatise everything that wasn't nailed down and emasculate local government. It almost certainly had not occurred to her that she could. Yet after she had done all four, no one accused her of insincerity. She had an ideology from which her later policies flowed. Blair's promises are trivial on every issue except constitutional reform. They betray no ideology beyond the dominant norms of a conservative conventional wisdom he shares. In the past the cry: 'Why can't politicians stop arguing among themselves and just work together?' came from biddies in the *Question Time* audience; now it is government policy. Blair constantly talks of 'one nation,' 'inclusiveness' and 'community'. Like Bell, he gets on well with Tories and is happy to take the counsel of Thatcher and Rupert Murdoch. His real enemies are in his own party – the cynical sectarians who maintain that no amount of inclusiveness can reconcile the interests of the rich and the poor.

Explanations for the sincerity boom are inevitably tenuous. In *Cynicism and Postmodernism*, a study of the culture that produced Blair, the philosopher Timothy Bewes suggests that when the spirit of the age is deconstruction; when sexuality, grand narratives, great movements, great men and women, science and even the external world can be dismissed as suspect ideological constructs; politicians must put a premium on sincerity, even if all they are doing is sincerely promising to do little or nothing. Thus Bell, thus Blair, thus the triumph of feeling over thought, thus the gormless stars of daytime television revealing their every sexual and intestinal secret and proving that in a world of fakes they are genuine articles willing to discuss their very bowel movements if that will convince you that they are authentic. Even Neil and Christine Hamilton knew the postmodern score. They were not shamed into obscurity after their disgrace, but accepted every chat show invitation. They realised that they could be rehabilitated if enough viewers saw them sincerely showing their pain and protesting their innocence. They may well be right.

Unfortunately, the need for politics cannot be wished away. Wage inequality is now at its greatest since records began in the 1880s, the slums are spreading and the poor have found that burglary is a more effective mechanism for redistributing wealth than the Parliamentary Labour Party. If Blair does not change, then Hamilton will have the final victory.

He tried two attacks on Bell. First he called him a Labour stooge, then he said he was an innocent without an idea in his head. At the time, I thought his polemics were contradictory. Now I'm not so sure.

Modern Review November 1997

ERIC JOYCE

Time has at last done what all American magazines must do and produced its Cool Britannia special issue. Yet again we're told that London is swinging – it has very expensive restaurants and very strange fashion houses – and that the UK is hip – it has Oasis, *Trainspotting*, Damien Hirst and many modish cooks and decorators, all called Conran for some reason. The formula – developed at length in *Newsweek* and *Vanity Fair* – requires journalists to turn to the Prime Minister and hear him hail Labour's victory as a triumph of youth and hope. *Time* follows it doggedly. The May Day election was not a changing of the suits but represented something far more important, Blair explains. 'The victory is an expression of the fact that a new generation has come on that doesn't have the outdated attitudes of the past. There is a curious mixture of optimism about the future mixed with the realisation that the old British ways of getting things done are not going to be enough.'

No more outdated attitudes? Tell that to the marines – or, rather, the Army. Just after the election the Blairite Fabian Society showed the New Era's most attractive face when it published a pamphlet by Major Eric Joyce warning that class segregation in the forces was a threat to national security. He dissected the 'outmoded and distasteful' culture of a military high command 'saturated with institutionalised racism, sexism and obsession with social class'. The armed forces loved expensive technology but did not invest in the troops. 'We are suffering from a debilitating failure to attract young men and women, yet remain obsessed with the defence of the very social order and attitudes which repel them.' The chasm separating public-school generals and state-school soldiers (who find it all but impossible to join the officer class) was odious in principle and disastrous in practice. 'Few school-leavers today relish the idea of being a second-class citizen in an organisation which reserves the top places for a self-perpetuating elite.' The Army is 15,000 soldiers short as a result and has been forced to lower recruitment standards as it scrambles to fill the gaps.

I cannot think of a man who better embodies what New Labour propaganda says the party wants for Britain than the conscientious major. He worked out his ideas with the terribly modern Fabians, whom no man can call lefties (at a recent Young Fabian conference, bright wonks cheerfully discussed privatising the NHS). He is 37, clean-cut and engaging. His career is an inspiration to soldiers who want opportunity for all. After leaving his comprehensive, he joined the Army as a private. He took time off to study for a degree and returned as an officer. He is a patriot who has risked his career in an attempt to stop the country's defences being undermined by snobbery and cronyism.

Naturally, New Labour is trying to destroy him.

He expected 'to get a slapping' when the pamphlet was published. But the MoD went ballistic and decided Joyce should be sacked and, possibly, imprisoned. He could be court-martialled for engaging in 'conduct prejudicial to good order and discipline' and refusing to obey his superiors' orders to stop talking to the press. No decision has yet been taken by the Army Prosecuting Authority, but the MoD's anger makes a trial or an administrative dismissal inevitable. The Army has sent him to a Winchester base while his future is decided. 'I'm looking at Army language training,' he said. 'I'm hermetically sealed in an office at the end of a long corridor so I don't contaminate anyone.' Every time Joyce appears on television or is quoted in the newspapers he is interviewed by embarrassed members of the Special Investigations Unit of the Royal Military Police, whose masterly detective work consists of asking him to confirm whether he has indeed appeared on television or spoken to the newspapers.

Meanwhile, New Labour's commitment to the classless, optimistic world of the new generation seems to have shrunk to vanishing-point. John Reid, the Armed Forces minister, refuses to discuss Joyce when Labour colleagues tell him to take the major's arguments seriously. 'Reid and John Spellar [his deputy] tell us to "stop it" when we raise the case,' said one. 'They say it's an operational matter that's nothing to do with politicians.' The decision about the court-martial has been left in the hands of the high command that Joyce condemns. His political critique remains unanswered. The government will continue to dismiss homosexuals in the forces, even though the European Court of Human Rights is likely to declare the discrimination illegal. True, the Army is now trying to recruit black soldiers, but, as Joyce asks, how many can hope to be more than a non-commissioned officer? The Army has been Joyce's life and he will fight until the end. But I sense that if he and his cause fails, he won't be too sorry to be forced out. 'Unless the Army reforms,' he says, 'it'll decay in front of my eyes. I don't want to see that.'

Observer October 1997

DEMOS

The pace of James Hawes's London novel *A White Merc With Fins* slows for a moment so a blow can be struck which only the spinners and trimmers in metropolitan New Labour will feel. Hawes is introducing a former miner who adopts a new identity in the capital, when, apropos very little, he slips in a caveat. 'You must not go thinking that this shows he is a tosser who has changed his name by deed poll to sound more interesting, like someone I know who is really called Albert Scraggs but changed his name to Joey 8. Yes, 8. I award Mr Joey 8 the Nobel Prize for Sadness. I mean, who is so utterly boring at heart that they even have to try and make the name on their chequebook interesting?' The answer, as Hawes well knows, lies in the offices of the Blairite think-tank Demos, charged with supplying the ideas for what optimists hope will be the New Labour revolution. In the early Eighties an aspiring wonk called David Keith Ashworth announced that henceforth he wished to be known as Perri 6 – not Perri Six or Perri [sic] – but Perri 6. Yes, 6. Under his new identity he rose via the Greater London Council and the Independent to become Demos's research director.

The invention of Mr 6 – 'I am not a free man! I am a number!' – is not the only fat target Demos presents to its many critics. Right-wing newspapers have never warmed to its repetitions of the blindingly obvious fact that the breakdown of nuclear families is irreversible. When Helen Wilkinson, a Demos researcher, argued that today's young women rejected puritanism and authority, Telegraph reporters, who really should get out more, compared her to Kim Il Sung. The Sunday Times claimed that it was only in the Eighties that the left 'stumbled upon the novel concept that thinking was not necessarily an affront to the working classes' (so much for Marx, Morris and Tawney). Demos, it loftily decided, merely produced 'weightless, cost-free thinking, the undifferentiated babble of the postmodern Zeitgeist'. The sight of enemies who can still write 'Zeitgeist' without blushing makes the urge to defend Demos to the death close to irresistible. Close, but not close enough to make resistance useless. Many on the left agree with the Sunday Times. In this respect if no other, Demos has found what it seeks in so many other areas of discourse: the uniting of left and right in a new synthesis.

The think-tank is a strange mixture of the authoritarian and libertarian. It indulges in grand phrase-making but has yet to produce grand ideas. When Demos released its latest thoughts on feminism, the findings

were unexceptional but, to general bafflement, the report was illustrated with the fictional lives of five stereotypes – Networking Naomi,
Frustrated Fran, Back to Basics Barbara, Mannish Mel and New Age
Angela – that would make the most cocaine-raddled advertising man
hold his nose. There is a flightiness about Demos that is more magpie
than gadfly. This may sound familiar. It is meant to. Demos and New
Labour share the same contradictions and absurdities.

In 1993, Martin Jacques, former editor of *Marxism Today* – the theor-
etical journal of the by-then defunct Communist Party – decided he
wanted a new organisation for a new era, 'a think-tank which would
ignore the old boundaries'. And he got it in spades. Demos pronounces
death sentences like Judge Jeffreys with a migraine. In just four years,
it has declared 'the end of politics', 'the end of unemployment', 'the
end of social democracy', 'the end of 200 years of industrial society',
the end of 'traditional definitions of what it means to be a man or a
woman' and the end of 'class-based left–right politics'. As Angela Carter
put it: 'the *fin* is coming a little early this *siècle*.' The typical Demos
pamphlet begins: 'The old, tired struggle between left and right is dead,
destroyed by the Internet/fall of the Berlin Wall/global market/
Sainsbury's ready-to-eat Thai green curries (delete where applicable)
and in its place a new tough yet tender/firm yet fair/smart yet casual/
tasty yet low on carbohydrates (ditto) consensus is emerging that will
set the debate for the new century.'

Millennial windiness is tempered on occasion by Geoff Mulgan, the
Demos director. A neat, polite, public schoolboy (Westminster and
Balliol), he is frequently described as brilliant. Admittedly, anyone who
comes out of Balliol with a pulse, let alone a degree, is frequently
described as brilliant, but in Mulgan's case there may be substance
behind the back-slapping myth. Like many in New Labour, he is a former Trotskyist who has abandoned Marxism but retains a messianic
faith in the future and an impatience with boring, workerist Labourism.
He wants Demos to follow the example of socialist Fabians, who worked
against the grain for decades until the 1945 Labour government put

their ideas into practice. 'I hope to see our real influence coming in 30 years time,' he says. Rewards may come sooner. Mulgan is on a committee that advises Blair and helps him with speeches, along with that other noted intellectual, Peter Mandelson. Under Mulgan, Demos has grown from a tiny circle of wonks to a £600,000-a-year left-wing policy production line.

If, that is, you can describe Demos as left-wing. Because when the critics who ought to be friends start ranting about its glibness and arrogant tone, they seize on Demos's failure to develop radical, as distinct from gimmicky, ideas. 'If we were to be washed away tomorrow,' said one academic who works for Demos, 'I'd be struggling to think what ideas would be left behind.' Struggling? The criticism seems foolish. Demos is saturated with ideas. Its 1997 election manifesto, *The British Spring*, has social democracy – Demos wants to tackle privilege in the public schools, Oxbridge, the Army, judiciary and media conglomerates; conservatism – private corporations should run schools, dentists and surgeries; libertarianism – drugs and prostitution should be legalised; and nutty futurism – couples should have 'time-limited marriages' and the nation should be presented with a 'week of celebration of physical activity' each July in Manchester (don't ask me why). The tone is as optimistic as the title. Mulgan shares the Labour leader's love of promoting micro-policies with meta-rhetoric. He calls for 'a radically new way of governing', but on closer inspection his revolution will be achieved by parents signing contracts to help their children with homework, and businesses 'following the Dutch model' of agreed environmental targets. Blair was equally deflating at the 1996 party conference: 'A Labour Government will have a thousand days to prepare for a thousand years,' the Great Leader cried in Hitlerian tones, but the new world, apparently, would be brought about by 'sound finance and good housekeeping'.

We are in for bathetic times, but they may be hard times, too. The one Demos dogma New Labour has wrapped its arms around is communitarianism, the doctrine that you cannot have rights without responsibilities (a slogan originally deployed, incidentally, in the attacks on democracy by European fascists, monarchists and Catholics after the First World War). When Mulgan brought Amitai Etzioni, the American sociologist who revived the concept (while jettisoning, of course, the demand to overthrow elected governments) to Britain, critics said his communitarianism was nothing more than the banal recommendation to be kind to your children and neighbours. 'Pinning him down any further is like trying to nail custard to the wall,' muttered one. Only a few saw the dark side of communitarianism which, as a Demos pamphlet on crime (*The Self-Policing Society*) shows, can be very nasty indeed. The author, Charles Leadbeater, starts with Demos's usual banishment to the dustbin of history of all who might doubt him. 'We have left behind the old argument. The tired old ideological conflicts have been replaced by a new common sense.' And what does this common sense entail? A revival of shame, says Leadbeater. 'A radical and to some disquieting suggestion would be to return to some latter-day form of the stocks for burglars. The shame it would generate would make it a powerful form of punishment, although it would possibly foster even more violence.' It possibly would. In the eighteenth century, a sentence to the stocks could be a death sentence. The mob treated homosexuals particularly roughly. But like its political patrons, Demos seems to dislike studying a past that is so, y'know, old.

Demos and New Labour use the language of radical modernisation. But the evidence is that, constitutional reform aside, they don't want radical change. Blair's decision to accept the Tory tax-and-spending structure may mean that however you vote, old conservative policies will win, and recent Tory history may provide the best map of the future. If Blair sticks to his word, then talk of New Labour giving New Britain New Hope in the New Millennium will mean more of the same, and Demos's wonks will find themselves playing the debased part of courtier intellectuals who justify the opportunism of their champions.

Hawes ends his discussion of Joey 8 with a timely warning: 'This is a good principle in life: the more wacky the haircut or clothes or politics, the more boring the person is likely to be once you get used to them.'

Observer March 1997

PS   Mulgan joined the Downing Street Policy Unit after the election as an adviser to Tony Blair. Leadbeater helped Peter Mandelson draw up competition policy in the weeks before the minister's resignation and disgrace in December 1998. Demos inspired the new government to rebrand the United Kingdom and sell it to the world as 'Cool Britannia', the hippest most happening post-industrial, late capitalist, medium-sized nuclear client of the United States on the planet. After a period of mockery so intense it inspired several leading satirists to turn to religion so they could thank whatever gods there may be for allowing them to live in such joyously asinine times, Cool Britannia was abandoned and the Foreign Office instructed to carry on as before. True to Hawes's prediction, Demos decided in 1998 that the modern course was to advise the Conservative Party.

CHARLES HANDY

Charles Handy is, indisputably, a kind and concerned man. His benevolence is so obvious that attacking him feels the critical equivalent of pushing Michael Palin into an acid bath. His *Hungry Spirit* – which bears the bold subtitle of 'Beyond Capitalism, a Quest for Purpose in the Modern World' – makes all the right noises. The global market brings misery and instability, he says; money worship destroys the environment, and its fetishisation of efficiency and beatification of the wealthy produces societies, such as the United States, where the richest 1 per cent had a net worth in 1993 as great as the combined gross national products of India, Bangladesh, Nepal and Sri Lanka. Other and better red-green writers have covered this territory before and produced more compelling arguments. Still it's good to have Handy on board: why monster him?

Part of the answer can be found in Handy's record. In the Eighties he applauded downsizing and portfolio careers as roads to freedom in his *Age of Unreason*. He recanted in the Nineties and appeared on *Thought for the Day* offering simple morality tales and quasi-mystical words of comfort to the victims of casino capitalism. His performances alone should make his admirers pause. To be first a consultant spouting management-speak and then a radio preacher oozing the platitudes of the counselling culture shows that Handy is more than a plodder through the dry plains of intellectual fashion. He is a pioneer, a leader of wonks, who has managed to bag the twin peaks of modern triteness.

Then there is his use of imagery. For example, I'm certain I am not a geranium. I'm as confident as I can be that you are not a geranium either (if you were you would be dying back for the winter rather than reading the *New Statesman*). Handy is not so sure. His doubts about whether he's a pundit or a bedding plant occupy four pages of *The Hungry Spirit* and are puffed on the back cover as a highlight of the book. I'll try to summarise. Handy's existential crisis begins when he is on a terrace in Italy worrying about the future of the world. A friend tells him not to bother and observes that a nearby geranium has no similar concerns and takes life pretty much as it finds it. Handy replies with aplomb that he is not a geranium. His friend counters that Handy is really no different from a geranium and should lie back, enjoy the Tuscan sun and do what his instincts tell him. Handy (his self-assurance crumbling as he sees his opponent's point) exclaims: 'But if you were a geranium, wouldn't you want to be a better geranium?' Only if he were a geranium from a self-improving strain programmed to want to better itself, replies his tenacious companion. Some time and much effort is expended before the reader realises that Handy is trying to grapple with the genetic determinism of Richard Dawkins and E. O. Wilson (which few but Dawkins and Wilson take seriously). The fight must be called a draw because his intellectual agonising on the terrace ends with the guarded conclusion: 'You can believe, as I do, that humans are more than animated geraniums, that we have evolved into beings with a capacity for self-awareness.' Thank you, Charles, but I think we knew that.

Handy has a vicar's ability to produce maxims that sound very wise until you think about them. 'Cram your days too full and it's hard to find time to think'; 'we all dream dreams, but few of us do anything about them'; and, my favourite, 'life is a marathon, not a horse race.' How very true. On occasion he misses all available points. After his psychoanalyst compares him to Christ, Muhammad and Marx (now why did I suspect he was in therapy?), he decides, 'if you want to change the world you have to start with your own life'. I'm sorry, but if you want to change the world, you try to change the world, and your private life is, inevitably, neglected.

But, and this is why it is necessary to be stern with our confused author, it is far from clear that Handy wants to change the world. True, he can be interesting about small issues: how 'just in time' manufacturers cut the costs of warehousing by putting their stocks into polluting lorries on publicly funded roads, for example; and on how 'efficient' hospitals pass on the burden of caring to relatives by discharging patients early. Yet his policy recommendations are stuck in the Eighties. Government should get off people's backs, he says. There must be health and education vouchers and compulsory private pensions and insurance. If we still lived in a world of full employment then it would be feasible to require personal provision for unemployment and old age, but the insecurities produced by the modern flip-flop careers Handy once welcomed make compulsory private insurance a cruel joke for all but the comfortable. Any modern society that wants to reduce poverty and vulnerability must support larger, not smaller, state safety nets. Handy, a child of his time, recognises the mayhem caused by markets, but then recommends damp-eyed concern, anaemic spirituality, personal growth and right-wing economics as panaceas. The affinity between

his arguments and the cant of the dominant political culture is too
obvious to labour.

New Statesman March 1997

SIR OSWALD MOSLEY

Maybe the martyrdom of St Diana has made us sweeter people and
Tony is right to think one-nation Britain can envelop everyone in its
clammy embrace. Good fellowship is all around us. Only those who
condemn the contemptible face social exclusion. When asked for his
reaction to Enoch Powell's death, Blair missed an excellent opportunity to shrug and move to next business. Instead, he praised Powell's
sincerity and tenacity. Within days, poisonous policies were again examined in Channel 4's life of Oswald Mosley.

The writers, Maurice Gran and Laurence Marks (who gave us *Birds
of a Feather*) and many of the senior production staff were Jewish. Did
they denounce a man who terrorised the old Jewish East End of London;
who wanted to send socialists, Jews and trade unionists to concentration camps; and who told screaming crowds that the 'big Jew controls
the old parties, both Conservative and socialist, and the little Jew sweats
you in the sweatshop'? Well, they did and they didn't. They objected
persistently when I wrote a critical piece in the *Observer*, and I ran an
apology saying that they believed their work showed Mosley was a monster. I am happy to repeat that I do not see them as anti-Semites or
'traitors to their race', as they said in one letter. Gran's sister remembers running away from Blackshirts when she was young, and the authors
accurately portrayed Mosley as a Jew baiter and as a potential British
Hitler. But they also presented him as a flawed protagonist and formi-
dable adulterer whose passions were realised in the most exquisitely
decorated bedroom sets we have seen since we last visited Brideshead,
a fantastic speaker who hated the pallid old men who had slaughtered

much of his generation in the Great War and given the survivors a dismal peace. 'His heart was in the right place, though his brain was in the wrong place,' said Marks. The drama had vignettes of Mosley's decent side. Mosley stands up to Hitler and is disturbed when he sees an old woman being forced to scrub up a pool of Jewish blood in Germany. When he is interned at the outbreak of war, he shares a fag with a black musician and listens sympathetically to his story. The Friends of Oswald Mosley, the ageing remnants of his anti-Semitic British Union of Fascists from the Thirties and black-bashing Union Movement of the Fifties was pleasantly surprised. Its newsletter *Comrade* said on the front page that Marks and Gran had taken 'an independent and principled line' and had been the victims of an 'orchestrated campaign of disinformation and vilification' from the 'forces of opposition and coercion' as represented by TV critics and Jewish ex-servicemen.

You can't blame Marks and Gran for the tribute. They were following a revisionist line on British fascism which has been developed for 50 years and is almost orthodoxy. As soon as the Nazi death camps were relieved, Mosley began to rewrite his anti-Semitic past. Since the Seventies, new admirers have claimed that attacks on Jews were the fault of the victims; that one of England's ugliest aristocrats wasn't too bad; and that Mosley and his sympathisers wouldn't have imitated the cowardly Europeans and collaborated if Hitler had invaded. Victim-blaming, servility and national self-regard are thoroughly modern vices – as is turning a blind eye to violence against minorities. In these respects, Mosley remains a thoroughly modern figure.

Mosley's political career began in the Twenties when he was a dandy about town and, as Channel 4 made clear at tedious length, a great fornicator. He switched from being a Conservative MP to a Labour minister and was willing to think about Keynesian solutions to mass unemployment when the first Labour government was stuck in nineteenth-century orthodoxy. (So, too, Mosley's admirers forget, were the Liberals and left-wing Labour MPs – while Keynes himself expounded his theories to anyone who would listen.) Disillusioned with Labour's calamitous response to the 1929 crash, he formed the New Party, which was converted into the British Union of Fascists in 1932 because fascism was the 'modern movement'. (Yes, thank you, I know we're living with another New Party that drones on about modernity. I'll deal with it later.) Whether the Blackshirts would turn on the Jews was an open question. Anti-Semites including William Joyce (the future Lord Haw-Haw) were founder members of the BUF, but Mosley's first hero was Mussolini, not Hitler. There were a handful of Jews in the Blackshirts, and Mosley's plans for a fascist state – in which authority would be invested in Mosley, 'the new Caesar' – guaranteed 'religious and racial tolerance', as well as a life for women of 'motherhood and carrying on the race' and people's courts for criminals. Pogroms were not part of the programme.

By 1935 contemporaries, both fascist and anti-fascist, saw racism as Mosley's defining characteristic. A weary George Orwell left a BUF meeting in Barnsley in 1935 and reported that Mosley's speech 'was the usual claptrap. The blame for everything was put on mysterious gangs of Jews who are said to be financing, among other things, the British Labour Party and the Soviet Union.' The Blackshirts' name changed from the British Union of Fascists to the British Union of Fascists and National Socialists. SS-style insignia appeared on their uniforms. Mosley visited Hitler in Germany – and I can't find evidence that he was dismayed by the persecution of the Jews.

What had changed? The obvious answer was that Hitler had come to power and electrified the European right. Mosley decided to rebrand the Blackshirts because Mussolini was old hat and Nazism was the wave of the future. (If we are following the money, we also should note that Mussolini made himself unpopular in British fascist circles by stopping his subsidies to the BUF.) But such straightforward explanations are far too brutal for the revisionists. They take their lead from Lord Skidelsky, the conservative academic who now preaches in the House of Lords on the need to slash the welfare state. Skidelsky befriended the Mosley family when he was a student at Oxford in the Fifties. He got to know the fascist's son Max, the New Labour business supporter who helped disgrace the party in the Formula One scandal. (Later. *Later!*) Both encouraged the ageing Sir Oswald to talk to the Oxford Union. The relationship continued as Skidelsky built his academic career – dons at King's College, Cambridge, still recall with anger the occasion when he brought Mosley to high table.

In 1975 Skidelsky published a biography of Mosley that was acclaimed even though it contained the startling thesis that the BUF embraced the Nazis because Jews made them. British Fascists had 'genuine reasons' to be anti-Semitic, he said. Jews heckled Mosley and boycotted German goods in the Thirties. Mosley had to respond and Jews 'must take some of the blame for what happened'. Mosley turned to anti-Semitism more in sorrow than in anger, defensively responding to unjustified provocation. Skidelsky faintly echoes the Blackshirts' attempts to justify themselves. 'The Jew himself created anti-Semitism,' said Mosleyite magazine *Action*, 'created it as he has always done by letting people see him and his methods. Even Hitler was not an anti-Semite before he saw a Jew.' A more direct link runs between Skidelsky and Mosley's special pleading after 1945. He was not anti-Semitic, he said, but opposed only to 'some' Jews who were behind the 'drive to the Second World War'.

To agree with his Lordship, you have to believe that the attacks on Jews by the BUF in the Thirties were self-defence and ignore the advantages of anti-Semitism. It was not, and is not, simple racist hatred of exiles driving down wages and competing for jobs. Anti-Semitism allows the standard hatred of poor immigrants, be they black, Irish or Asian, but provides an additional explanation of power. Its multiple uses – 'the big Jew controls the parties . . . the little Jew sweats you' – enabled Mosley to appeal to working class voters opposed to immigration in the East End of London, the one area where the BUF had significant support, and still satisfy a wider audience. The Jew could be a scheming financier to left-wing fascists, a pornographer to moral fascists and a communist to conservative fascists. Jewish money and Jewish control of the press explained the otherwise inexplicable failure of the country to heed the BUF message and made sense of the miseries and frustration of fascists' lives. As the economic crisis of the Thirties faded and recruits declined, anti-Semitism held the core of the party together. Whether Mosley sincerely believed what he preached (his son, Nicholas, who advised Channel 4, suggests he did not) is beside the point. The sensible answer to the question 'would you rather be beaten up by a convinced bigot or an opportunist?' is that, on the whole, I'd rather not be beaten up at all. Nor can Skidelsky explain why Mosley, the reluctant racist, saw his chance when Caribbean immigration began, returned from exile in France in 1958 and went straight to Kensington to incite murderous race riots by demanding immediate repatriation and a ban on inter-racial marriages. Historians have yet to say that the blacks of west London must take 'some of the blame' – but give them time.

Mosley's Fifties' Union Movement failed as completely as the BUF of the Thirties. His career was dominated by failure. The only parties he could tolerate were the parties he created. The only party members who stood by him were courtiers. The adulation the 'New Caesar' demanded was too much even for convinced fascists. John Beckett, the father of the historian Francis, was Mosley's right-hand man, but walked out of the BUF. 'My father ended up thinking Mosley was a fruitcake,' Beckett said. 'Mosley was a true fascist. He believed in the absolute power of the great master. You couldn't contradict Mosley or make fun of him. He could only work with sycophants who would address him as "The Leader" at all times.' John Beckett and Mosley fell out during the abdication crisis. Mosley (quite rightly) believed Edward VIII would make an ideal monarch in a fascist state. He was convinced (quite madly) that Edward Windsor would ask him to save his kingdom by taking power. Beckett went to a secret meeting at the Adelphi Hotel in Liverpool and wrote in an unpublished memoir that he found Mosley was in a 'state of great excitement'. The Leader was talking on the telephone in a schoolboy code to a society drunk in London, who was telling him that the BUF's moment had come. 'I am sure that Mosley really believed he was on the threshold of great power,' wrote Beckett senior. 'Self-delusion had finally conquered his sanity.'

Quite so. And it is at this point that the revisionist project falls apart. By the late Thirties, even the *Daily Mail* – which, lest we forget, had shouted 'Hurrah for the Blackshirts' – had dropped its support for a movement that could not win a Parliamentary seat or control a council. A successful fascist is terrifying. A failed fascist is ridiculous. At least Caesar crossed the Rubicon and took Rome. Mosley couldn't cross the Thames and take Bethnal Green. P. G. Wodehouse recognised Mosley's absurdity and had Bertie Wooster confront Sir Roderick Spode, leader of the Blackshorts, in *The Code of the Woosters*. 'The trouble with you, Spode,' Bertie says, 'is that just because you have succeeded in inducing a handful of halfwits to disfigure the London scene by going about in black shorts, you think you're someone. You hear them shouting "Heil, Spode!" and you imagine it is the Voice of the People. That is where you make your bloomer. What the Voice of the People is saying is: "Look at that frightful ass Spode swanking about in footer bags! Did you ever in your puff see such a perfect perisher?"' Orwell, too, found Mosley ridiculous. 'When I speak of Fascism in England, I am not necessarily thinking of Mosley and his pimpled followers,' he wrote in *The Road to Wigan Pier*. 'English Fascism, when it arrives, is likely to be of a sedate and subtle kind (presumably, at any rate, it won't be called Fascism), and it is doubtful whether a Gilbert and Sullivan heavy dragoon of Mosley's stamp would ever be more than a joke to the majority of English.'

Orwell and, it goes without saying, Wodehouse were far more incisive political commentators than Skidelsky. He begins his biography by portraying Mosley as Britain's lost leader. 'Essentially, he wanted to find a place for heroic values in politics . . . He could not believe that the problems of a machine civilisation could be overcome by small men, small measures. There I think he was right.' He concludes with a breathless passage of speculation which, in all seriousness, asks whether the Britain of the Seventies may still decide that Mosley should be her saviour. The omens were looking good. He's been on television in both the UK and the US! He knows many influential people! A. J. P. Taylor has called him a 'superb political thinker'! Skidelsky finds the question 'will the people recall him?' so perplexing he leaves it hanging in the air at the end of the final chapter. His concluding line quotes Faust's dictum that 'whoever strives can be redeemed'.

Mosley's strivings were in vain. He died just after the biography was published.

Much of the sympathy for Sir Oswald flows from the appeal of class in Britain, even to those who believe they despise it. Lord Longford remembers seeing Michael Foot hurry across a London restaurant to greet Mosley. It is impossible to imagine the left-wing tribune chatting amiably with the slimy, petit-bourgeois leaders of the modern National Front. But Mosley was an aristocrat and, therefore, a fascinating man who needs to be treated with indulgence not only because of his birth but because the history of the BUF can spoil the myth of 1940 and Britain's Great Patriotic War. All revisionist accounts of Mosley emphasise that he would not have collaborated if the Nazis had invaded. Their strange insistence betrays the continuing appeal of British particularism based on a portrait of a united nation standing alone against a treacherous and dangerous continent, which bedevils British attitudes to Europe to this day. To wonder whether collaboration would have followed occupation in Britain, as elsewhere, is like throwing a bottle of black ink over a stirring picture of nobility and sacrifice. Even Thirties fascists must be painted as patriots at heart.

The New Party of the Nineties is New Labour, and a surprisingly large number of *Observer* readers have written in, pointing out the similarities between the Mosleyites and the Blairites. At one level the letters are bonkers. Tony Blair does not want to dress up in black leather and hold torch-lit parades through the East End. At another, the comparisons make a kind of sense. There is a strong strain of futurist humbug in Blair's harping on modernity and the new and, as with Mosley, a ludicrous gap between lofty rhetoric and banal reality. Blair's Third

Way is proclaimed to be an inspirational force inspiring Europe and the world, when in reality it is little more than tired Thatcherism with a smirk on its face.

Mosley's history undermines a critique of New Labour that has become a little too popular of late. The crassest attacks on Blair begin with supposedly worldly comments that New Labour doesn't believe in anything, as if politicians or any of us can live in an ideological vacuum. What Mosley and Blair show is that when you abandon your principles and proclaim the need to be modern, your empty head is filled with the dominant dogmas of the status quo and you hitch your wagon to the ideology of the moment. For many on the left and right in the Thirties, that ideology was dictatorship – with its attendant slaughters. Today, it is the global market with its attendant destruction of communities, welfare states, environments and living standards.

Jewish Quarterly and *Observer* 1996 and 1998

DIANA'S MOURNERS

With communism now history, the loyal, foreign-owned press has discovered an alternative threat to the nation. Republicanism was the danger conservatives spied behind the moist mourning for the Princess of Wales. In the week after her death Ferdinand Mount, Margaret Thatcher's former adviser, warned on the opinion pages of the *Sunday Times* that 'those who have despaired of bringing about a revolution have turned to what looks a softer target – getting rid of the Royal Family'. Republicans had formed a 'strange alliance' with the crowds in London. 'Who now dares be a republican?' blustered Peter Hitchens on the same day in the *Sunday Express*. All too many, he concluded, bathetically, a few paragraphs later. 'Sadly, for this country [the Queen has] qualities which have become alien and incomprehensible to many brought up in a softer, weaker age.'

Sad, but also confusing. Soft democrats conspiring with the mob to bring down a monarch whose traditional values and dysfunctional family are undermined by the weakness of our age? Here is a concept that cannot be contemplated without the aid of strong drink. An attempt to find clarity can be begun by recognising that British republicans are not soft – their minds have been toughened by reading mountains of tosh about the monarchy. The worst came not from what Ben Pimlott called, in the nutty atmosphere after the car crash, 'the royalist, fascist' crowd, but from refined writers at the high-rent end of the market. The *New Yorker* magazine is, according to a recent eulogy, 'the best British glossy we have'. It commissions the finest British writers to write their best pieces. In an emergency issue its readers were treated to a requiem for Diana by Clive James. His grief is genuine, his sincerity indisputable, but, well, see what you think.

He began with a scream and built to a climax. 'No. It was the first word of that cataclysmic Sunday morning: "no" pronounced through an ascending sob, the consonant left behind in the chest voice as the vowel climbed into the head voice, the pure wail of lament whereby anyone, no matter how tone-deaf, for one terrible moment becomes a singer.' His head and chest will be singing for a while yet, for he continued: 'But there was not one terrible moment. There were, still are, hundreds of them, joining up in a long aria of anguish interrupted only by exhaustion. Hundreds of millions of people who loved her but never met her must be crying like this. Those who did meet her, and knew her faults, should have some detachment. But somehow it works in reverse. The physics of this unprecedented metaphysical explosion, this starburst of regret, are counter-intuitive, like relativity.'

Or not, as the case may be. For once the grief kicks in, metaphors mix like the percussion of quantum particles exploding in the Chernobyl of our souls. Death is the only release: yours as well as hers.

'The more you know she was never perfect, the less you, who are not perfect either, are able to detach the loss of her from the loss of yourself, and so you have gone with her, down that Acherontic tunnel by the Pont de L'Alma and into the Halls of Dis, the inane regions, where loneliness is the only thing there is, and the lost are together but can never find each other, because it is like looking for a shadow in the dark.'

Before descending into the underworld, James pauses for a fleeting moment of reason and wonders why he was so upset by the death of someone he knew only slightly and saw as 'a fruitcake on the rampage' at times. The reflective mood does not last. 'No, you don't have to tell me,' he continued. 'I am appearing ridiculous now [since you mentioned it, Clive], but it is part of the ceremony, is it not? And what flowers have I to send her except my memories? They are less than a wreath, not much more than a nosegay: just a *deuil blanc* table napkin wrapping a few blooms of frangipani, the blossom of broken bread.'

The frangipani touch won James the award for the most hyperbolic lament of the interminable grieving process. The judges were particularly impressed by his politic decision not to allow his aching sorrow for the Princess to drive him into condemning the Prince. But a stunning article by Tina Brown, editor of the *New Yorker*, who is often regarded as Britain's most splendid export to America, provided stiff competition.

'When the news came of her death my first thoughts were of place and time,' she wrote, 'of the wrongness of any royal princess, even a divorced one, contriving to be in that place at that time. In late summer, the Paris of the rich and the titled simply closes down . . . Diana's English friends and sisters tramp the Scottish heather or rusticate in the Tuscan villa that Archie and Amanda lend them. Paris in August? Dinner at the Ritz, weeks before *la rentrée*? The fact that she was there at all was discordant, a poignant symbol of a season of panic and flight.'

So there you have it. The French police can drop their investigation. Diana Spencer was killed by a social error. Brown betrayed no hint of republicanism and no one commented on her gaudy argument. But imagine the ferocious reaction that would have followed a British republican claiming the death of the Princess – 'even a divorced one'

– was the result of a grotesque faux pas. Euan Ferguson, the *Observer*'s comment editor, attempted nothing so crass in a short, sceptical article that was one of the few notes of dissent allowed to appear in our balanced media in the week after the smash-up. He pointed out that he and millions of others were not overwhelmed with grief and resented the media mob telling them what they must feel. His modest statement of the obvious was intolerable. In *The Guardian*, Linda Grant, a columnist, was so angered by the publication of his 'left-wing' views that her prose slipped the constraints of sense.

Attempting to explain Diana's transformation from a dim Sloane into a modern saint, she wrote: 'It's true that Diana began like a fur coat, a beautiful but empty skin, but then she grew some insides. For some people it's the other way round. In the old revolutionary song about wanting not just bread but also roses, no doubt the women who sang it envisaged wearing the roses on their hats. And here is the important unavoidable truth about reality: that you can't have depths without surfaces.'

It is always hard to uncover a writer's influences. In the case of Grant I would venture a tentative guess that at some point in the Seventies she may have been inspired by the popular Saturday teatime series, *Kung Fu*. Middle-aged readers may remember that 'Grasshopper' (David Carradine) would spend most of each episode kicking the living daylights out of his enemies. The violence was interrupted by dreamlike flashbacks in which the 'Old One', a blind, bald, oriental master, was heard dispensing cod wisdom to the young Grasshopper. I can almost hear him saying: 'Remember, Grasshopper, empty coats can grow insides (and vice versa for that matter) because the sages know that you can't have depths without surfaces.'

Elsewhere the vulgarity of monarchism was on display in the *Mail*, which proclaimed that Prince Charles had wept 'bitter tears of guilt'. He was, it said, 'stalking the moors, asking: Why? Why? Why?' The article produced no evidence that the Prince felt guilty or that he was shouting 'Why? Why? Why?' in the Balmoral heather, but evidence is not demanded from these quarters and a monarchist newspaper is able to treat the Prince with far greater contempt than any republican. (Blair would have sacked, and the media would have crucified, a republican Labour minister who stood up and said: 'Charles Windsor is unfit to be our sovereign. He admits he killed his ex-wife. He is also a lunatic who wanders the fells shouting "Why? Why? Why" at Highland cattle.')

The peculiar consequence flowing from all this drivel is that republicans are about the only people left who worry about Prince William. They can look at him and ask with a clear conscience whether he would have a far better chance of a contented life if Britain were a republic and he were left in relative peace. The media and the public cannot, because they want a royal family to flatter and torture. Republicanism is not based on the failings of individuals but on monarchism's forceful tendency to promote servility, cruelty and, as the above shows, hysterical writing that no amount of frangipani can sweeten. Even when wrapped in *deuil blanc* table napkins.

Ever since the Nazis, intellectuals have been wary about demanding the destruction of books. Their self-restraint had the virtue of encouraging a culture which on occasion could go through the motions of reasoned debate. Civilised discourse hasn't lasted. It cracked under assaults from the worst species of malignant writer: the type who seeks to enrich themselves by deliberately provoking scandal for its own sake, who ignores religious sentiment and decent values, and then refuses to contribute to police costs when their thoughtlessness provokes understandable threats to their safety. I refer to the heretics who doubted that Di was a saint.

Beatrix Campbell, who was once seen as a left-wing feminist, sounded as if she was chanting from the Ayatollah Khomeini's mosque when she reviewed *Different for Girls*, a study by Joan Smith, who still is regarded as a left-wing feminist, on the pressures on women to conform. 'Did anyone at Chatto wonder whether they should pulp this book?' asked Campbell. 'It is a raggy and rageful anthology which begins audaciously with a lazy leftist pout about Princess Diana.' What may have infuriated Campbell was that Smith was not only pouting but prescient. Writing before the Paris martyrdom she said the Princess had swapped the role of 'spoiled and unstable' aristocrat for that of 'archetypal wronged woman'. All the talk about Diana representing a modern feminised Britain was blether. She was following the old model of *la dame aux camélias* and Anna Karenina; of doomed, hopeless heroines who 'all wind up young, beautiful and dead'. Smith concluded that, 'one day in the not too distant future, it may occur to her that the part she has embraced so enthusiastically since the breakdown of her marriage is leading nowhere except to more tears and loneliness. Her public likes her this way, no question, but is it a role she is prepared to die for?'

In the week the collection of essays was published, Di died. Instead of asking Smith, the Nostradamus of literary London, to predict the next lottery numbers, Campbell said her book should be banned. Smith had committed the greatest of late twentieth-century crimes. She 'lacked empathy'.

Campbell empathised at length in her own study – *Diana, Princess of Wales: How Sexual Politics Shook the Monarchy*. For Campbell 'there can never be enough books' about her heroine because she validated the suffering of millions of women who, apparently, needed a celebrity to make sense of their otherwise meaningless little lives. She assures us the Princess was a 'republican', even though the role of Queen of Hearts who will stop suffering with hugs is directly descended from the medieval monarchs who cured scrofula with divine touches. Campbell reaches a lachrymose climax when she greets that *Panorama* interview with the peroration: 'To the chagrin of the Establishment, the recovery of her self-respect was to be witnessed by millions. By telling her story, Diana joined the constituency of the rejected – the survivors of harm and horror, from the holocaust, from world war and pogroms, from Vietnam and the civil wars of South America and South Africa, from torture and child abuse.'

Let me see if I can get this right. Marrying into the admittedly unpleasant Windsor family is the equivalent of being napalmed in Vietnam. Having affairs with rich young men is the equivalent of being beaten in a Cape Town jail. Bulimia is torture. Diana and the survivors of Nazi death camps are identical, and those who write otherwise must have their books pulped.

Observer September 1997 and May 1998

CHAPTER TWO

ETHICS AND EFFICACY

HOWE TO WIN FRIENDS

Lord Howe's public image is as genial as that of a beloved uncle. His role in presiding over the destruction of a large chunk of manufacturing industry in the monetarist recession of the early Eighties is all but forgotten. Howe is now the 'dead sheep': dull, safe, maybe even a statesman. But as we are told that zero tolerance is a contemporary virtue, I feel it would be inconsistent to exempt him from the culture of condemnation – particularly when the former Foreign Secretary has been travelling the world looking for trouble. He has just been to Hong Kong to demoralise democrats and give comfort to the Chinese dictatorship. His speeches caused a scandal in Asia and America, but they failed to raise an eyebrow in London. You might say his disgrace is ours, to an extent.

On 30 June the British will follow the terms of a deal negotiated by Howe when he was Foreign Secretary and pull out of Hong Kong. The limited democracy that Chris Patten, the last Governor, granted very late in the day appears fragile. China has already named the puppets who will replace popular legislators. With elected government disappearing, what freedom the press has to expose arbitrary and corrupt power has become a critical zone of conflict. Anson Chan, Hong Kong's

Chief Secretary, has urged journalists to carry on writing without 'fear or favour' when the Chinese take charge. 'How well they do their job will decide how well our other freedoms will be protected,' she said. Patten told them to 'fight like hell every step of the way'. Qian Qichen, the Chinese Foreign Minister, responded by warning reporters that Beijing will not tolerate 'rumours or lies', 'personal attacks on Chinese leaders' or 'advocacy' of the rights of Tibetans. In other words, critical and investigative journalism, holding the Communist Party to account and the monitoring of human rights abuses will be beyond the pale.

Faced with a choice between siding with freedom or repression, Howe chose repression. In a speech to the Asian Newspaper Publishers' Convention he told Hong Kong editors to show 'sensible self-restraint'. The next day he warmed to his theme at a lunch organised by the British and Australian chambers of commerce. Andrew Higgins, the *Observer*'s man in Hong Kong, was sitting way below the salt in the magnificent ballroom of the Shangri-la Hotel as the defender of free markets and free societies rose to speak. Given the sumptuous surroundings and an audience drawn from the upper end of the business class, Higgins was surprised to hear Howe uphold the cause of the 'broad masses' and slip with ease into the pseudo-proletarian cant of the Communist elite. 'The huge mass of the people of Hong Kong want to see the transition succeed,' Howe told the hacks in the throng. 'I hope that those of you who report these events will take great care not to give disproportionate attention to the occasional hazard. You have a tremendous responsibility to see that the world understands the good side of what is going to happen to Hong Kong.' Asked about the Tiananmen Square massacre, he said that it was 'in a strange and perverse way, a shock to the leadership of China,' and intimated that we should feel pity for a gerontocracy that had suffered under the Cultural Revolution and may well have seen the peaceful protesters as the heirs of the Red Guards.

The pro-Chinese press, which routinely calls Patten 'fatty' and a 'whore' for supporting democracy, loved him. 'Howe's words wake up the people of Hong Kong: opposition is useless', cried a Dalek's headline in *Ta Kung Pao*. 'Howe is merely speaking the truth,' purred another. Democrats were furious. Emily Lau, a member of the legislature, said: 'It's crazy for him to have said this. Hong Kong journalists are already trembling, they're so scared.' In America, the *Wall Street Journal* described Howe as 'embarrassing to Britain' and correctly saw as the sub-text to his lectures a colonial assumption that rights and the rule of law were essential in the West but dispensable in the coolie East. He seems to think that 'Asians are somehow different from Englishmen in their basic aspirations,' the paper said.

The anger abroad has not been matched by interest at home. I have seen just one tiny article about Howe in the London papers. Although you don't expect the British media to worry about freedom of the press, their silence was puzzling none the less because Howe is a former Conservative minister, and it goes without saying you do not have to dig too deep to find intriguing financial interests. He is a special adviser to Cable & Wireless, which owns 57 per cent of Hong Kong Telecom – a company that must keep Beijing sweet if it is to retain its lucrative monopoly of international calls from the colony. He is also a non-executive director on the board of BICC, which owns Balfour Beatty – a construction company which again needs to cuddle close to China, in this case because it has a slice of the £13 billion construction contract for Hong Kong's new Chep Lap Kok airport. Other supporters of China are doing well. Sir Percy Craddock, Margaret Thatcher's former policy adviser and a ferocious critic of Patten, advises Standard Chartered Bank in Hong Kong. Henry Kissinger combines public backing for Beijing with business interests in China.

Simple and necessary cynicism may not, however, be enough to explain the Howe affair. Howe's Foreign Office ruled Hong Kong as a colony and was content to see the Chinese take up the white man's burden. From this perspective, Patten's reforms not only offended business patrons but were an affront to neo-imperial ideology. 'Howe has been entirely consistent – consistently bad from our point of view,' said Lau. 'He always subscribed to a policy of appeasement.' His consistency should be recognised and the truth faced that he would probably have attacked freedom of speech if a ministerial pension were his sole means of support.

Observer January 1997

PR FOR GENOCIDE

Mike Johnson is a middle-aged, mid-American public relations man. His days are filled with the depressingly easy chore of selling his clients to business journalists. Last Thursday the amiable executive had an exciting change of routine. He was put to work on the account of one of the world's premier dictatorships and told to convince the British press of its rectitude.

His firm, Burson-Marsteller, is a long-time servant of an Indonesian government now concerned that the award of the Nobel Peace Prize to the East Timorese opposition leaders Jose Ramos-Horta and Bishop Carlos Bel may, finally, draw the world's attention to the invasion of their island – one of the most neglected crimes of the twentieth century. The Jakarta government demanded that the agency prove it was earning its fees and Burson responded with a damage-limitation strategy. Reporters were to be invited to the Indonesian embassy in Mayfair and given everything necessary to make us feel mellow and positive: a lunch consisting of delicacies from the East; fine wines (a white Rioja and red Burgundy); and a little box of presents topped with an elegant bow. While we were eating, we were to hear a gentle lecture. 'We want to sort out all these demands for self-determination,' Christopher Hunter-Ward, an upper-class, English, Burson representative told me beforehand. 'It's all a little misguided.'

The sorting was to consist of the Indonesian ambassador and his colleagues stating that, contrary to received wisdom and all eye-witness accounts, Indonesia had not invaded and occupied East Timor with para-

troops and landing craft in 1975 when the Portuguese colonial authorities left. Nor had its soldiers killed between 100,000 and 200,000
people in what was proportionately one of the largest recorded acts
of genocide, and then presided over a ferocious suppression of dissent.
Indonesia had, Burson insisted, moved in as a 'humanitarian response'
to a request from the majority of the East Timorese people, killed virtually no one and earned the gratitude of all law-abiding citizens by
stopping the 'reign of terror' of the Fretilin resistance.

I very much regret to be obliged to report that the lunch did not
meet the high standards we elevated correspondents have a right to
expect as our due. We were surprised to be greeted at the embassy
door by a grubby band of peace activists denouncing in coarse language
the British government's sale of Hawk fighters for use in East Timor.
Horrified by their manners and appearance, we skulked with as much
dignity as we could muster to the servants' entrance at the back. We
were hustled in by embassy staff who could not contain their undiplo-
matic anger. Upstairs in the splendid dining room, we at last relaxed.
The chants were faint and all but merged with the buzz of the traffic
as we sat down to eat. They grew louder, however, when four demonstrators threw a rope over the embassy flagpole, hauled themselves up
to its Georgian balcony and bellowed 'Free East Timor' through the
windows. Police and security guards pounded past the aperitif-gulping
diners, almost knocking our satay off the table. They emerged from
the balcony, dragged the grinning protesters into the dining room and
bundled them down the stairs

For the usually suave Ambassador Habibie, this was a rare loss of
face. Indonesian propaganda is usually sophisticated enough to quell
what tiny doubts Western governments may have about trading with a
tiger tyranny. Smooth talk of mutual interests makes it seem the height
of bad taste to mention the dead. In his little speech, the ambassador
discussed the 'events' of 1965; none of us had the impertinence to
heckle that a million had died in that year of living dangerously and
'events' was, on the whole, an inadequate synonym for massacre. Jakarta

employs the best to keep the conversation euphemistic. Burson-Marsteller is not a tiny PR outfit run out of a grubby office with a few dying pot plants but a US multinational that makes $150 million (£95 million) a year. It disdains the vulgar term 'public relations' and prefers to use the grand, if meaningless, phrase 'perception management' to describe its propaganda. The firm recently gave itself a touch of tarnished royal class by renting Prince Michael of Kent to host its receptions. Pierre Salinger, John F. Kennedy's Press Secretary, worked on the Indonesian account in its Washington office. Camelot and the Windsor Court have been co-opted to Suharto's cause.

The Indonesian government knows that the West may go to war to defend Kuwait but will not endanger trade by enforcing UN resolutions against their occupation of East Timor. The nexus of members of the Suharto family and crony businessmen ensures they will continue to have a profitable life by oiling political machines. Bill Clinton's election campaign received hundreds of thousands of dollars from an Indonesian conglomerate. No one has yet been able to prove a link between the money and Clinton's decision to drop demands that Indonesia improve conditions for its workers but, well . . .

British secrecy prevents us knowing who donates to parties and what they get in return. But it may be worth noting that Britain has not only sold Hawks to Indonesia but, as the Public Accounts Committee showed, trained Indonesian police out of an aid budget that credulous voters might have supposed was meant to be spent on feeding the starving.

The Jakarta regime, while not accepting UN resolutions, is happy to play along with the world community's timid requests for change. It allowed a UN human rights investigator into East Timor and has set up its own human rights commission. Lucia Withers, from Amnesty International, said the gestures were trivial. Indonesia refuses to consider a referendum on self-determination and asserts that its few supporters represent the 'silent majority' on the island. It is foolish to believe that resistance leaders are always popular heroes, but the Indonesians have given the majority of East Timorese excellent reasons for holding their tongues. Arbitrary arrest, torture and extra-judicial executions 'continue to be routine' in East Timor, says Amnesty. Recently, the charity has issued urgent communiques about ten men who were arrested in the village of Waihulae and then, according to the police, 'escaped' and 'vanished'; about another two who disappeared after a peaceful pro-independence demonstration in East Timor's capital, Dili; and about five Timorese reported to have been tortured after the killing of an Indonesian soldier. There are hundreds of equally bloody cases in Amnesty's files. Going through them, one experiences severe 'perception management' difficulties.

As I got ready to leave the embassy, I wondered if I should pick up the ambassador's box of presents and donate it to the Amnesty Christmas raffle. But I suspected they would bin it, and left it on the table.

Observer December 1996

BENETTON ETHICS

When New Labour assumed office on 2 May 1997, supporters who had watched the party's rush to the right had already learned to put their faith in the God of Small Things. True, they sighed, Blair and the rest had accepted social authoritarianism, 'flexible' working practices, rampaging inequality and Conservative tax-and-spending programmes. Yet for all the compromises, there were still cheering contrasts between the old and new regimes. You often heard the thoughts of the leftish Australian writer, Richard Neville, quoted with approval. 'There is perhaps an inch of difference between an Australia governed by Labour and an Australia governed by the right,' he had said. 'But, believe me, it is an inch worth living in.' Or as Charlie Whelan, Gordon Brown's spin doctor, put it when I remarked a month after the new dawn broke that it was difficult to know whether there had been a change of government: 'Bollocks, Cohen. What about the landmines? *What about the landmines?*'

A few weeks earlier Robin Cook had announced the government's first leftward shift. Labour would abandon a Tory foreign policy whose futile cynicism had been dissected in the Arms-to-Iraq inquiry, and Britain's relations with the rest of the world would now have 'an ethical dimension'. Cook embraced the favourite cause of the then unmartyred Diana by promising to support a global ban on anti-personnel mines carefully designed to maim rather than kill. (Injury is preferred to death because the finest minds in the 'defence community' have realised that a soldier may fight all the more fiercely if he sees a dead friend, but be slowed and terrified by a screaming comrade demanding immediate help.) The success of the new approach would be monitored, the Foreign Secretary added. The government would 'publish an annual report on our work in promoting human rights abroad'. Journalists obsessed with reporting the landmine ban as a triumph for Di ('I don't think that lassie would have got very far if I hadn't been in power,' Cook complained to the few who would listen) barely noticed the promise. But human rights groups were delighted. They had been campaigning for a rights audit for years and Cook was holding out the hope that Britain would follow the example of the US, where the State Department produces comprehensive annual studies of state killings, torture, arbitrary arrests, show trials, censorship and restrictions on freedom of movement, assembly and association in every country in the world – except, of course, its own.

There are criticisms of Washington's approach – Cuba received harsher treatment than it deserved in the Cold War. But at least an East Timorese, for example, can take the latest State Department report on Indonesia and say that even the US, which authorised the Indonesian invasion of East Timor in 1975 and tolerated the subsequent deaths of between 100,000 and 200,000 people, concedes that there has been 'no significant progress in accounting for persons missing'; that troop levels have remained 'unjustifiably high'; and that there are 'no reports of military personnel who committed abuses in East Timor being punished'. And at least American citizens can receive an honest summary of the consequences of their expensive foreign policy. Foreign Office assessments of the regimes that Britain – the second biggest arms exporter in a booming global market – does business with might have provided evidence as useful as the State Department's. Human rights groups believed they could hold the department to account. They expected crystalline statements of policy which might be quoted at wonks and fixers whenever Whitehall wanted to cut the aid budget or arm an oil-rich dictator.

They have got a Benetton catalogue instead. Of the 50 or so glossy pages in the first Annual Report on Human Rights from the Foreign Office and Department for International Development, six are filled with full-page pictures. On the front cover is a shot of a pretty girl. She may be a Kurd, but maybe not, the report does not say. Then there is a white girl, who could be from anywhere between Moscow and San Francisco; a black boy, probably from Africa, possibly Birmingham; a Malay or Indonesian boy; another boy who I think is South American, but don't hold me to it, he could be a Palestinian; and a charming girl I can say with quiet assurance is one of a billion or so Chinese. All have jolly smiles. Their teeth and hair shine. None shows visible signs of torture or of having missed a meal since leaving the womb.

Much of the rest is filled with smaller photographs of Blair, Cook, Short, their junior ministers and Her Majesty The Queen looking grave and busy in various capitals. One shot stands out – a picture of Cook shaking hands with President Suharto, the dictator of Indonesia. They look what they are, two men of business making a mutually advanta-geous deal. Both have faint yet chummy smiles. Their grips are manly. Eye contact has been established and you could be forgiven for assuming that celebratory toasts will be exchanged shortly. The deal in question is an arms deal, although the reader would never guess it from the text.

The report so perfectly represents the feel-good mendacity of New Labour that it is hard to know where to begin. I think I will stay with Indonesia because the attempt to describe the archipelago with politic tact pushes the mandarin style to its limits.

When Jakarta went up in flames and Suharto – but not his regime – fell, the British press scrambled its journalists. Most news organisa tions did not have an informed reporter on the spot and packed off London-based firefighters whose specialist knowledge consisted of what they could cram from head office cuttings files on the flight out. A British angle is the line editors love the most. Yet no one mentioned the UK's active encouragement of the massacres of about one million when Suharto came to power in 1965. Reporters did not need to go to the Public Record Office to find evidence of Foreign Office compli- city with slaughter. Mark Curtis, author of *The Great Deception*, had done the legwork. The journalists did not even have to read his book: he had summarised his findings in a pointed (if regrettably hacked-back) article in the *Observer* in 1996. The results of Curtis's digging were news even by the self-referential standards of the gated media village. In 1990, Kathy Kadane, a lowly journalist with an American news agency, made her name when she revealed that CIA officers had passed death sentences on five thousand members of the Indonesian Communist Party, the PKI, by handing their names to the insurgent generals. Curtis provided evid- ence that Britain was no less active than the US in the 1965 coup against Achmad Sukarno, the nationalist leader who was willing to work with the PKI. Yet when the Indonesian dictatorship installed in the great game of the Cold War was threatened, Curtis's work was all but unknown.

On 5 October 1965, as the massacres began, Sir Andrew Gilchrist, Britain's ambassador in Jakarta, told the Foreign Office: 'I have never concealed from you my belief that a little shooting in Indonesia would be an essential preliminary to effective change,' Curtis reported. On the following day, the Foreign Office replied: 'The crucial question still remains whether the generals will pluck up enough courage to take decisive action against the PKI.' Gilchrist shared his superiors' worries that the generals were pussy liberals. Although the Army was 'full of good anti-Communist ideas,' he said, it was 'reluctant to take, or incap- able of taking, effective action in the political field'. His superiors resolved on a strategy. 'It seems pretty clear that the generals are going to need all the help they can get and accept without being tagged as hopelessly pro-Western, if they are going to be able gain ascendancy over the Communists. In the short run, and while the present confusion continues, we can hardly go wrong by tacitly backing the generals.' It is difficult to say how far British 'help' extended – although the fact that the relevant files will be kept secret until well into the next century is suggestive. Even the sanitised documents in the Record Office show Britain supported the coup with propaganda. 'We certainly do not exclude any unattributable propaganda or psy-war [psychological warfare] activities which would contribute to weakening the PKI permanently,' the Foreign Office said. More importantly, Britain agreed to give the Indonesian generals a free hand by privately promising not to take advantage of the civil war. British troops were facing the Indonesian Army in the disputed territory of Borneo. The Foreign Office said it 'did not want to distract the Indonesian Army by getting them engaged in fighting in Borneo and so discourage them from the attempts which they now seem to be making to deal with the PKI'. Michael Stewart, the Foreign Secretary, saw the imposition of a genocidal martial law on the Chinese minority as good for business. 'It is only the economic chaos of Indonesia which prevents that country from offering great potential opportunities to British exporters,' he wrote to Harold Wilson. 'If there is going to be a deal with Indonesia, as I hope one day there may be, I think we ought to take an active part and try to secure a slice of the cake ourselves.'

Not a word of this was discussed by broadcasters when journalists talked of 'mobs' on the streets and Suharto's fantastic wealth. It was as if the Western media had reported that the Berlin Wall had been felled by a mindless crowd revolted by the Baltic villas of the East German elite and forgotten to recall the crimes of Stalinism. But, then, Surharto was our criminal. When Gilchrist died in 1993, he was presented as a lovable British eccentric. His obituaries recounted how he ordered his attaché to subdue a protesting Indonesian crowd by marching through the embassy garden playing the bagpipes.

It is over-optimistic to expect the Foreign Office to acknowledge its role in Suharto's rise to power. You might think it would be bold enough to say that the Suharto dictatorship was, indeed, a dictatorship. The State Department does not treat Indonesia's wretched state as an official secret. The section on Indonesia runs to 38 tightly written pages of A4. It describes the rigged elections and the murdered journalists and how the ghastly anti-subversion laws (still in force) operate. The author of the 34 wide-spaced *lines* on Indonesia that fill half a sheet of A4 in the FO and International Development Department report finds a simple statement of the uncontested fact that Indonesia is a tyranny far too dangerous to record. We are told that Robin Cook went to Indonesia, offered support to human rights groups and urged 'dialogue' in East Timor. Ignorant readers are not given a clue why the initiatives may be necessary.

Nor are they told that Stewart's dream of securing a slice of the cake has been realised and Britain has become Indonesia's largest arms supplier. The weapons trade, apparently, has no bearing on human rights. It is discussed and dismissed in a few reassuring paragraphs that begin: 'We want arms transfers to be managed responsibly, to avoid the sale of weapons that might be used for internal repression or international aggression. In July we announced new criteria . . . and will not issue an export licence where there is a clearly identifiable risk that the arms might be used for internal repression.' The author – deliberately? – misses a loophole in the guidelines. The apparently cast-iron rules will not apply if the government believes weapons can be used for 'protection of members of the security forces'. Between 2 May 1997 and 6 March 1998, New Labour delivered 51 batches of arms to Indonesia through the gap in its ethical defences. In a blackly comic illustration of the naïvety of Realpolitik it appears we will be robbed of our thirty pieces of silver. The weapons sales were covered by £2 billion of outstanding government credits to Indonesia and you, dear taxpayer, not the arms companies, will pick up the bill when the bankrupt regime defaults. Cook dismissed fears that the shipments will be used to suppress Indonesians – even though murdering, terrifying and robbing civilians has long been the prime mission of Indonesia's valiant armed forces. Licences, Cook told the *Today* programme, 'have just been given for things like naval patrol boats, radar on the offshore oil rigs, offshore winches for the naval boats; those are not things that could conceivably be used in internal repression'. Surely he knows better. In Parliamentary answers Labour admits to agreeing to the export of small arms, machine-guns, riot control 'agents' (including tear gas), computerised surveillance equipment, body armour and toxological agents that will be used in internal repression.

As with Indonesia so with the rest of the globe. The bland paragraph on Algeria recognises 'widespread concern over appalling massacres,' but does not discuss evidence that some are perpetrated by the Algerian government. (The EU depends on Algerian gas, much of it pumped by British Petroleum.) There are no condemnations of the theocratic tyranny of the House of Saud: Britain and Saudi Arabia are partners in the biggest, murkiest and, possibly, most corrupt arms deal in history. Corporate thrusters anxious to penetrate the expanding Chinese market need have no fear that the FO will embarrass them by raising awkward questions about persecuted dissidents and trade unionists: 'dialogue and practical cooperation' is the best way forward, the report concludes. Only Iraq and Burma, where Britain has no substantial business interests, are roundly condemned.

Meanwhile, the human rights record at home is discussed with more than a touch of Pecksniffery. There is not a word on the imprisonment without trial of asylum-seekers, nor of the obstacles placed in the way of refugees trying to reach Heathrow – policies designed to deter the genuine victims of oppression from finding sanctuary. The anonymous author acknowledges that Central European Gypsies are persecuted but fails to add that when the same Gypsies tried to claim asylum in Dover, Jack Straw immediately, and without evidence, denounced them as bogus asylum-seekers, thereby inflaming an already ugly racial confrontation. In fairness, the Foreign Office can cite Labour's commitment to bring the European Convention on Human Rights into British law and Cook's support for a permanent UN criminal court for war criminals, which Russia, China and the US oppose, as evidence that the inch of difference exists. It is better to have Cook in the Foreign Office than Douglas Hurd. But so what? His elevation does not justify Britain remaining the dictators' quartermaster or a human rights report that pretends to be an audit, but is little more than a sham.

The brochure is more than an insult to the intelligence of readers, it is a sign of how Old Britain prospers despite all the promises of constitutional reform. Congress requires the State Department to provide comprehensive audits. The American legislature holds the executive to account and ensures that there is a tiny part of the imperial polity bound by law to examine the victims of the regimes the US supports. Even the severest critics of American foreign policy in Washington acknowledge that the results are generally honest. The Foreign Office audit is a sop from the Establishment, delivered from above to citizens who remain subjects and have no means of insisting that a full account is given and uncomfortable truths are recorded. The result is nothing more than government puffery.

The word is being put out, incidentally, that the shot of Cook bonding with Suharto was a mistake. Short spotted it when she saw a draft and said it must be cut. So, too, did Cook's office. But as the Sierra Leone fiasco showed, the Foreign Office does not take much notice of Labour ministers. Cook and Short are demanding to know how the picture appeared. It will be remembered whenever the words Labour, ethical and foreign policy are placed in the same sentence. In true New Labour fashion, what upsets them is bad PR, not bad policies.

London Review of Books July 1998

OPIUM AND THE PEOPLE

Ah yes, the War on Drugs. What news is there from the front? Well, Brian Harvey of East 17 has caused consternation – a rock star? *On Ecstasy??* – and been denounced by all our righteous newspapers and politicians. The Home Secretary Michael Howard (backed, as ever, by his faithful shadow, Jack Straw) has named druggies as the prime target of his campaign to turn Britain into Europe's largest prison. Fear of addiction has guaranteed that Howard's plans to give mandatory sentences to drug dealers and limit the wet, if ancient, practice of judges judging cases on their merits will be accepted by all parties.

Meanwhile in Brussels, the Eurocrats the government spends so much time condemning are doing their bit by seeking to remove the trade privileges of the Burmese military junta, which protects the world's largest suppliers of heroin and opium. The dictatorship – known by its pleasingly sinister title of the Slorc (State Law and Order Restoration Council) – also enslaves hundreds of thousands of forced labourers, allows unimaginable poverty and orders the mass detention of democrats. National interest and democratic principle are in agreement. Britain has the chance to fight the heroin trade and oppression simultaneously. You would assume that the Foreign Office would seize the opportunity to back the government's incessant anti-drugs rhetoric by supporting the European Union sanctions against manufactured goods from Burma. And you would be wrong.

When the Foreign Office is asked what Britain intends to do, it refuses to talk on or off the record. The Foreign Secretary Malcolm Rifkind has failed to reply to a Labour motion urging him not to oppose the withdrawal of trade privileges. Glenys Kinnock, who as a Labour MEP has been leading the fight to punish the Slorc for its use of child slave labour, is being told privately that Britain and France will sabotage the measure. It is easy to explain France's friendship with the generals: the French oil company Total is building a $1.2 billion gas pipeline across Burma. It has squared the military. Scores of accounts of the army forcing labourers to work on the pipeline and soldiers clearing villagers out of Total's way show that the junta's troops made excellent foremen. Britain has no significant interests in Burma. Why should the Foreign Office want to support France's shabby manoeuvres? Mrs Kinnock thinks Britain is determined not to offend the Chinese and Indonesian dictatorships, which hold that pressure for human rights in Asia is a Western, neo-colonial imposition – particularly when the citizens of East Timor and Hong Kong show their decadence by demanding freedom. She also suspects that the FO is anxious to begin doing serious business with the Slorc. In December 1995 the Department of Trade and Industry held a private seminar for business leaders with the go-getting title of 'Burma: The New Tiger Cub?' The meeting was infiltrated by democrats whose verbatim transcript of the proceedings shows businessmen and civil servants giving each other helpful advice on how to meet the exciting challenge of dealing with one of the world's worst governments. 'I recommend anyone who works in the country,' chirped an executive from the West Merchant Bank, 'to visit the Embassy Club – it's a superb place to make contacts.' (Well, you need a country club to avoid the sight of lice-covered children being herded into shanty towns so they don't disturb the tourists.) Robert Gordon, Britain's ambassador to Burma, told the audience not to be troubled by sentimental concerns about slavery and tyranny. There were 'pressure groups' and 'lobbyists' demanding sanctions, he said. But 'I wouldn't like you to over stress this at the moment. It isn't a weighty risk.'

Put this way, Whitehall sounds as if it has a brutal but hard-headed approach. I'm sure this is how ministers and civil servants see themselves. In reality they are Pollyannas. You cannot separate the heroin business from legitimate business in Burma. Even Robert S. Gelbard, the American Assistant Secretary of State for Narcotics, describes it as a narco-capitalist dictatorship where the Slorc's 'lawless and authoritarian rule not only harms dissidents, [but] results in the corruption and the criminalisation of the state'. The leaders of drug armies are photographed in Burma's lackey press shaking hands with Slorc officials. Eight Cabinet ministers attended the wedding of the son of the country's leading heroin exporter. The US embassy in Rangoon reports that the garment industry is owned in part by the heroin lords. Many of the hotels being built for Western tourists are financed by smack. 'Burma's most important drug traffickers are no longer holed up in the jungle,' concludes Gelbard. 'The drug trade is entrenched in Burma's economic life.'

We shall have to change the definition of warfare the next time Major, Howard or Rifkind declares war on drugs. Uniquely in the history of combat, the Conservatives have vowed to do battle in Fleet Street, Westminster, the music industry and their overcrowded prisons; everywhere, in fact, but on the battlefield.

Observer January 1997

ZEN AND THE ART OF RETAIL PRICE MAINTENANCE

When the book burners and assassins got to work on all associated with *The Satanic Verses*, blokes in pubs responded with a good black joke – well, good the first time you heard it, anyway.

'Heard what Salman Rushdie's next novel's gonna be called?'

'I'm sorry Mr Rushdie has yet to inform me of his plans.'

'*Buddha, You Big Fat Bastard . . .*'

The point was that only the most militant atheist could hate Buddhism and only a sick mind would want to offend the petit-celebrities who use the mysteries of the East as crutches to help them hobble through middle age. Boy George, Sandy Shaw, Annabel Heseltine, Billy Connolly, Annie Lennox and the deeply moral Lolicia Aitken agree that Buddhism is the best road to tolerance and peace. Dr Robin Skinner, who writes do-it-yourself psychiatry books with John Cleese, summed up the consensus when he said: 'In Buddhism you can come to your own conclusions. You don't have to stand to attention like being in the Brigade of Guards.'

I may have missed something, but although I have heard several of the above support the Dalai Lama, an obscurantist priest-king, in his struggle against China, I have yet to hear condemnations of the Burmese dictatorship which, according to the International Labour Organisation, runs the world's only Buddhist slave state. Reading the UN agency's findings can induce a trance-like state, but brings no inner peace. The ILO is painfully fair, its language is dry and modest, it bends over backwards to put both sides as it sets out its grotesque, irrefutable conclusions. Standing to attention is the smallest of the Burmese people's problems. Slavery is not an exception in Burma, but as essential to the junta's economy as it was to the Roman emperors. Forced labour was used by the army in battle and to keep the bribes flowing from the corrupt economy. Soldiers fighting the understandably large contingents of rebels press-ganged villagers. Men were pushed ahead of army columns to detonate mines and forced to act as human shields. If a mine exploded under them, the army took it as evidence of local complicity with guerrillas, and the survivors received additional punishments – the rape of women and children being a particular favourite. Slave porters who could no longer carry the military's loads 'were beaten to death, had their throats cuts or were thrown off mountains'.

Buddhism is central to the junta's justification for forced labour. After putting every obstacle they could in the way of the UN, the dictators' spokesmen dismissed claims of tyranny as fabrications from prejudiced outsiders who failed to understand the Buddhist cultural tradition. 'The contribution of labour is a noble deed and the merit that attained from it contributed to a better personal well-being,' they said. The UN notes that the junta's life-affirming philosophy fails to explain what nobility was gained by the Christian, animist and Muslim minorities when they were forced to spend four years building a Buddha museum in the capital of Rakine state.

By contrast with a military that has prospered on the profits of slavery and the heroin trade, Aung San Suu Kyi, the leader of the democratic opposition, fits the Western liberal ideal of a noble dissident so perfectly that a Dickie Attenborough biopic must, surely, be in production. Suu Kyi is not a communist. She is not a fundamentalist. She has neither resorted to violence nor incited ethnic and religious hatred. She speaks good English and looks impressive on television. She is the elected leader of Burma who has survived arrest and separation from a husband who happens to be – and again this helps – an Oxford don. The Nobel Peace Prize in 1991 and the higher honour of being shortlisted for the *Today* Personality of the Year in 1996 attest to her appeal. No one who is not irredeemably warped ignores her urgent request that Western businesses should boycott Burma.

The British have a special responsibility for the slave state because the laws used to justify forced labour are a product of Empire as well as Buddhism. Before the election one of the few discernible differences between John Major and Tony Blair was that New Labour was willing to back the opposition. At his 1996 party conference, a moist Blair broke off from his speech and said in his sad and – y'know – sincere voice that: 'For reasons everyone here will understand, Aung San Suu Kyi cannot be with us. Let me invite her to come next year, a free citizen and an example to democrats all over the world!' In opposition, Derek Fatchett, now a Foreign Office minister, promised unequivocally that Labour would draw up sanctions in office. The promise was well within spending limits. Only one British company, Premier Oil, which employs few British workers, has investments worth worrying about in Burma.

No real penalties followed Labour's victory, although the Foreign Office did persuade trusting newspapers to run stories saying Britain would try to do something about Burma after yet more opposition politicians were rounded up. The feeble threat not only fell a long way short of the pre-election promises but concealed the news that Britain and the rest of the European Union were taking proceedings at the World Trade Organisation in Geneva against the state government of

Massachusetts. The Americans are charged with refusing to hire firms that trade with the junta. In a second assault in the Boston courts, the EU will support US corporations that want to make an example of Massachusetts before the grassroots movement against Burma grows. Not only has New Labour failed to act, it is prosecuting those who stick to the principles it once held.

If the EU has its way, Americans and everyone else will be unable to vote for local politicians who challenge corporate immunity from democratic control. The penalties imposed on firms in the Eighties which dealt with South Africa would become illegal. Simon Billenness, from Boston's Franklin Research Development legal centre, says the gap between the rhetoric of the market and real choice is being exposed. 'The EU and the free-market companies who are pulling its strings are arguing that the public can have no freedom of choice in the market.' British civil servants at the Washington embassy and the Boston consulate have been active in the campaign to protect the generals and destroy the only worthwhile sanctions against the junta. A Burmese general, Khin Nyunt, testified to the effectiveness of the stance taken by Massachusetts and 17 other US states and cities by admitting they were creating an economic crisis.

The Foreign Office offered a curious explanation for Labour's apostasy. 'This is nothing to do with politics,' said a spokesman. 'We want to stop US states imposing their law on European companies. It is a point of principle.' As we listened to him burble, we thought that somewhere in Britain was a village that lost a first-class idiot when our man joined the diplomatic corps. What could be more unprincipled and nakedly political than aiding Burma's tyrants? After further inquiry, we discovered he wasn't a lunatic but a sober propagator of the government line. America punishes European companies that trade with Cuba, it goes, and if we let it do the same with importers to Burma, imperial Washington will be running our foreign policy.

The government will have to work hard to convince even the British press that the two cases are comparable. European firms who deal legally with Castro can have their US assets seized by exiles who lost their property in the revolution; they risk seeing their well-groomed executives arrested and charged in the American courts. But companies trading with Burma do not face the threat of jail or confiscation of property. They just lose orders from US legislatures who are choosing how to spend their own money. The EU is not defending Europe against American arrogance, as its alliance with US corporations shows. It is supporting a hubristic capitalist order that wants to make it illegal to decide not to buy its wares.

Burma, too, is making alliances. In 1998 the generals realised they had something of an image problem and hired two firms of management consultants (the Washington-based Bain and Jefferson Waterman) to lobby governments and rebrand their dictatorship. The records of one of New Labour's favourite London lobbying firms, GJW (which has Karl Milner, a former aide to Gordon Brown, as an influence-peddler), show that Premier Oil, the possessors of a pipeline running through an area where 25,000 were driven out of their homes to make way for oil industry infrastructure, was a client.

Western advisers told the junta it needed a makeover. Its name was changed from the resonant State Law and Order Restoration Council to the kinder, gentler State Peace and Development Council. The lobbyists can now boast that an unresisting Britain has been pushed from the moral high ground and put on message. Perhaps we shouldn't be surprised. *Today* dropped the Personality of the Year awards after 1996 because, in a pitiful example of gerrymandering, New Labour discredited the annual poll of listeners when its fixers were caught trying to rig the poll so Tony Blair would win and Suu Kyi lose.

Observer June 1998

PS   The partnership between European Union governments and American corporations was successful. A district court in Boston agreed with the Chambers of Commerce of the United States that it was unconstitutional for state legislatures to impose sanctions as they infringed on the sole right of the central government to conduct foreign policy. At the end of 1998, most armed resistance in Burma had been suppressed and peaceful pressure for change had become impossible. Britain's sole sanction – the banning of senior members of the Burmese government from entering the UK – was dropped.

CHAPTER THREE

RIGHTS AND
RESPONSIBILITIES

THOMAS HAMILTON

Once he was dead, everyone knew how to describe Thomas Hamilton. He was a lone madman in the Lee Harvey Oswald mould; an obsessive misfit who bottled up his paranoid resentment until he was ready to write himself into the national consciousness with other people's blood. The boys he ordered to strip and run around in swimming trunks laughed at him behind his back and called him 'Mr Creepy'. To their parents he was 'Spock'. Hamilton's podgy face and insinuating voice made their flesh crawl. Even if they had not heard the rumours about Hamilton and his boys' camps which had been whispered for 25 years, they felt uneasy in his presence. To his neighbours in Kent Road, Stirling, he stood out in the poor but friendly street as a man with little to say. George Smart said he had not got a word out of him in two years. He would see Hamilton dressed in the classic nerd's anorak, head down, hands shoved into pockets. Passers-by glanced through Hamilton's windows and were faintly disturbed to see pictures of semi-naked children covering the walls. Only one person dissented from the uneasy consensus: Cathleen Kerr, a pensioner who lived opposite the Hamilton home and was the nearest thing he had to a friend in the neighbourhood. He called round for coffee and always asked kindly about her sick husband. Mrs Kerr knew a different Hamilton, a 'quietly spoken, well dressed and placid' Hamilton. And as for the anorak her neighbours mocked, well, she said, he 'always wore a collar and tie underneath'.

As the investigations into Thomas Hamilton developed, it became possible to recognise the man that Mrs Kerr knew. Mr Creepy did not disappear, but he acquired an extra dimension. The psychopath who killed 16 children and their teacher in Dunblane Primary School – and who would have murdered two more teachers and 12 more children if his aim had been surer – was not a deranged drifter but a rooted man who had his collar-and-tie moments, his respectable moments, when he could be persuasive and deploy what charm he had to good effect.

He was 22 when he was given the grievance that festered inside him for the rest of his life: dismissal from the 4/6 Stirling District Scouts for being unfit to be a troop leader. Convinced from that moment that the world saw him as a pervert, Hamilton fought a running battle with officialdom for the next 21 years. And most of the time the misfit beat the police and council officers. Four Scottish police forces investigated Hamilton. Each time detectives failed to find a case that would stand up in court. The Central Regional Council tried to stop him holding his boys' club meetings in Dunblane High School in the early Eighties. He forced it to back down. Hamilton was not merely lucky, he was clever enough to organise support. The local government ombudsman for Scotland, gun-club managers, gun-shop owners, police officers who approved gun certificates, councillors and parents came to his aid. The whispers never went away, but Hamilton dared his accusers to come into the open. Convinced that 'sinister' Scout officials were spreading rumours, he hand-delivered a letter to Dunblane parents proclaiming his innocence. Hamilton may have been obsessed with real and imagined enemies, but he was not frightened of them. Many in central Scotland believed that he was the victim of unsubstantiated gossip.

Francis Saunders, a retired Stirling councillor who helped Hamilton when the local authority tried to kick his club out of Dunblane in 1983, cast a bleak backward glance after the murders. 'I saw him in the street about once a month for ten years and he was always complaining,' he said. 'I never got the impression that he was concealing misconduct. He did have an ingratiating, almost oily manner but I put that down to the buffetings he had received.' To Saunders and others Hamilton was innocent until proved guilty. When he was wearing his tie, Thomas Hamilton's enthusiasm for turning boys into disciplined athletes and his denials of guilt could be very convincing.

Hamilton's childhood was not the usual background of a white-collar man. Shame was the dominant emotion in his family. His supposed grandparents pretended to be his parents and his mother pretended to be his sister to avoid exposure of bastardy. His mother, Agnes, was born in 1931, the illegitimate daughter of a widow, Rachel Hamilton. To prevent a scandal, the baby was given away to childless relatives, James and Catherine Hamilton. When she was 19 she fell in love with Thomas Watt, a bus driver. They married in Bridge Church, Glasgow in 1950. On 10 May 1952 their son Thomas was born. Eighteen months later, the father ran off with another woman and a second scandal had to be hushed up. Agnes went back to her adoptive parents. James and Catherine adopted Thomas as their child. His mother became his older sister.

Agnes Hamilton is still alive. After the shootings she said: 'He seemed to get on with everyone I know of. He had pictures of boys when they were out camping and things like that but I never thought he was capable of anything like this.' Thomas Watt, his natural father, was anxious to deny responsibility for the child he abandoned. He said he didn't know whether his son was dead or alive until the killings. 'I didn't want to know, I had my new family to think about. People who know me know I'm a good man. I don't want to be associated with Thomas Hamilton in any way. I need counselling.' James, the 'grandfather', is now 88. He lived in the Kent Road flat with Thomas Hamilton until he walked out in 1992. Neighbours say Thomas regularly humiliated the old man; he urinated in his drinks, they claimed, and pushed him around. All he would say was that Thomas 'wanted everything his own way. I got fed up and left him to it.'

Some crimes are so pitiless they appear beyond comprehension. Yet Thomas Watt Hamilton made sure that everyone would know his reasons for massacring the children. His joyless family was not mentioned. With a calculation that suggests he carefully planned the slaughter, he posted copies of letters to the great and the good which explained his grievances to BBC Scotland, the *Scotsman* and the men he thought were calling him a pervert. Only then did he pick out four of the six guns that the police allowed him to own and set off for Dunblane. The 14 A4 pages of letters and circulars were dated from March 1992 to a few days before the crime. They were variously addressed to Dunblane parents, the Queen, council officials and Michael Forsyth, the Secretary of State for Scotland. They were well written and, in the words of David Vass, Assistant Scout Commissioner for Stirling, 'utterly bewildering'.

Dr Vass was on the murderer's mailing list because Hamilton's hatred of the Scouts was his insistent theme. Scout leaders in Dunblane were 'jealous' of the success of his clubs, Hamilton told the Queen. They were spreading rumours that he was a weirdo; the tittle-tattle had 'over the past 20 years of youth work caused me untold damage'. His enemies lied to councillors, social workers and the police. The last letter in the bundle was a copy of an original sent to Forsyth in March 1993. He told the minister that 'the horrific murder of James Bulger' by two boys made his Boys' Sports Club Committee's labours to instil 'good discipline' all the more important. It was outrageous that he was a victim of a 'sinister witch hunt' that was alarming parents and destroying his youth group. Dr Vass was perplexed because Hamilton was expelled from the Scouts in 1974 for an offence so trivial 99 people in 100 would make a joke of it in middle age. The Scottish Scout Association was adamant that there had never been a hint that its officials believed

Hamilton was molesting boys. Nothing was said that could somehow have infuriated a repressed homosexual. Nor was there public disgrace. Hamilton was asked to resign for incompetence quietly and without fuss. He had led two camping trips to the Highlands. Before the first, he told the parents of eight boys that there was a hostel for their sons. No hostel had been booked and the children spent an uncomfortable night in the back of a van. On the second expedition, boys got tired and cold when they were told to dig snow holes. Parents complained to Comrie Deuchars, then the Scout organiser in Stirling, and Hamilton was asked to leave. In the letters, the identity of the imagined persecutor changes. He told Buckingham Palace that it was Deuchars who made up the story that 'I was a pervert, which was passed to the public in an underhand manner'. Yet Hamilton wrote to Vass saying he was the villain and Deuchars was a friend.

Oddly, when Hamilton and his grandfather moved to Kent Road in 1983, they went into a flat underneath Deuchars's home. 'I must admit that when I saw him get out of the removal van my heart sank,' said Deuchars. 'I thought "Oh My God, what have I done to deserve this?" But he was always very civil to me. When I was cutting the lawn he'd bring me cups of coffee. I wonder now that if he somehow saw me as the cause of all of this, why didn't he take me out instead of the kiddies?' Hamilton did not take him out. Like a good neighbour, he collected a morning paper for the former Scout leader on the day of the killings and posted it through Deuchars's letterbox before travelling the seven miles to Dunblane Primary School.

In a twisted sense, Hamilton was right to worry about the Scouts. He seemed to ask for trouble by citing his former position whenever he applied to open a new club. He did not reveal that he had been thrown out.

In prosperous Dunblane, opinions are formed and characters are judged on the golf course and at parties, not in formal meetings. Dr Vass said he was always being asked why Hamilton had left the Scouts at 'wine and cheese social occasions'. He could never give the full answer because he did not know it – he moved to the town in 1978. That did not stop people asking and did not stop Hamilton marking him out as a gossip. One evening in December 1984 he arrived at Vass's house carrying a brown bag. 'He was very intense, he accused me of maligning him. After ten minutes I asked him to leave; what he was saying was just wrong. He reached into his bag and turned off a tape recorder. I've been asking myself if there was something more I could have done to warn people. But there was nothing. We did not know anything concrete until it was too late. All people here knew were rumours at the mutter level.'

Many disliked the chatter. Between 1981 and 1984 council officers moved to get Hamilton out of Dunblane schools. They were defeated by parents and by Eric Gillett, the then local government ombudsman for Scotland. Formally, the council said it wanted to ban the club for 70 nine- to 16-year-old boys because the education department had been deceived into thinking that Hamilton was still connected to the Scouts. The real reason, the ombudsman ruled, was that council officers had listened to whispered assertions about Hamilton that no one was prepared to make in public. An injustice was being done on the strength of rumours so 'vague' they should 'have been heavily discounted'. Hamilton's treatment was unfair and unjust and the council was told to let him back into its schools. Parents were just as angry on Hamilton's behalf. Seventy signed a petition in 1983 which said he was the 'victim of malicious back-stabbing'. Councillors did not like their officers' initiative. One told the *Scotsman* in 1983 that the affair 'left a nasty taste in the mouth. At the end of the day all we have had is rumour.' Faced with this coalition, the council surrendered. Hamilton was still unhappy. He said his kitchen-fitting business, which relied on orders from Dunblane, had been destroyed by the whiff of scandal. Many still understand why parents thought they could trust Hamilton. Penny King's son Michael was sent to the club when he was six. The Englishwoman had moved to Dunblane to escape the stresses of city life and was quickly told about 'Spock'. She went to the club to confront Hamilton, but was reassured. 'He told me that people had been talking behind his back for years. He left me feeling ashamed for believing tosh. My son was happy playing with his friends and in the end I didn't see why I should stop him.'

A child killer with pictures of semi-naked boys is generally assumed to be a paedophile – and many in Dunblane made that assumption in the days after the killings. Yet it is possible that Hamilton was not a child abuser; certainly, he was never convicted. Dave Norris, who knew Hamilton for ten years, said he struck him as harmless. 'It seemed to me he wanted to give boys the childhood he never had. I couldn't believe it when I heard what this articulate, educated man had done.'

To date there has been one accusation of abuse of a boy, from a mother in Aberdeen. All other parents and former members of the boys' clubs told merely of unsettling behaviour. George Robertson, the shadow Secretary of State for Scotland, who lives in Dunblane, sent his eldest son to Hamilton's club. He heard the rumours and went to the High School. 'I didn't like what I saw,' he said. 'There were lots of little boys there all stripped to the waist and Tom Hamilton and his cohorts all swaggering around. It was like something out of the Hitler Youth. I took Malcolm away.' Typically, instead of just accepting Robertson's decision, Hamilton came to his home and demanded to know if he was making accusations against him. Robertson also received calls from angry Hamilton supporters. Looking back, the MP used the word on most lips in Dunblane. He had no proof against Hamilton; he was just 'uneasy'. Colin Louden, now 30, remembers going to the club as a child and playing snooker and pool and learning how to fire pistols. Again, he had no direct experience of abuse. 'There were some boys he was very familiar with; his favourites if you like, who we'd call teacher's pet. They'd go off on camps with him and seemed to be sworn to secrecy when they got back.'

Hamilton must have convinced himself that he was behaving properly. Nothing he did suggests that he was a man who thought he had guilty secrets to hide. The pictures of bare-chested boys on his walls could be seen by anyone looking in his window; a woman neighbour was shown his videos of boys running around a camp at Loch Lomond as if they were the most natural thing in the world for a youth leader to collect. Hamilton explained, to anyone who questioned him, that he had a mission to instil old-fashioned respect for order and stop boys turning into 'thugs, scum and vandals'. He had an absolute confidence in his own virtue. Time and again he confronted those he suspected of traducing him. When he thought Scout leaders were spreading 'sinister' rumours, he sent a circular to parents. When the police investigated him, he complained to the Scottish Office about a witch hunt. When he heard teachers were warning pupils to have nothing to do with him, he demanded an apology from the council. Both Robertson and Vass got the impression that Hamilton was looking for a chance to sue them for slander. Neither had evidence that would convince a jury.

For all his bravado, Hamilton may have felt his enemies were closing in. One mother handed the police a dossier in 1988 and they followed it up by raiding the Loch Lomond camp. By the early Nineties, photography shops in Stirling were refusing to develop Hamilton's pictures of boys. They said they were obscene, but the police said they were not obscene enough to justify charges. In 1992 Fife Council, which borders Dunblane, banned Hamilton from its schools because it was worried about the films he shot of boys. Two more police inquiries were made in 1993 and Central Regional Council warned teachers to contact its legal department before dealing with Hamilton. In 1994, he was cautioned by police after being caught behaving indecently with a man in Edinburgh. In the months before the murders, a gun club refused to let Hamilton join. Two members said the club should have nothing to do with him.

Was it the mounting pressure that caused Hamilton to snap? Were the gossip and inquiries into a man acutely conscious of his position – in a part of Scotland where position and reputation matter greatly – getting to him? Even if they were, how can they begin to explain the massacre. All kinds of reasons from the psychological to the crassly political are being advanced to rationalise the killings. None impressed Canon Kenyon Wright, who was a minister in Dunblane for many years. He turned to a hopeless passage in Matthew ii, 18 after the shootings and read: 'A sound is heard in Rama, the sound of bitter crying and weeping; Rachel weeps for her children, she weeps and will not be comforted, because they are no more.' The Canon substituted Dunblane for Rama and asked: 'Why us?' No one can answer him.

Independent on Sunday March 1996

GRAVE ROBBING

The *Daily Mail*, the voice of lower-middle management, grows hoarse from screaming at refugees. They are bogus scroungers, sneaking into the country and stealing everything our security cameras and reinforced glass can't protect. Until, that is, the other week when the paper became quite nostalgic about the liberal British tradition of giving sanctuary to desperate strangers. The death of Stevan Popovich brought a wondrous transformation. Popovich, who fled Yugoslavia after the defeat of the Serb Chetniks by Tito's partisans, was 74 when he lost himself in the Chapeltown district of Leeds – a slum now euphemistically described as inner-city. He wound down his car window to ask for directions. A man dragged him out and robbed him. The thief made to take the car. Popovich died trying to stop him. 'Eastertide is a time of regeneration and of hope,' said the *Mail* as its harsh line on crime trumped its bigot prejudice about asylum. 'But today we should pause to ask what has become of the kinder and gentler Britain which gave refuge to him half a century ago.'

The question was rhetorical rather than real. The Sixties destroyed it. Social workers, moral relativism, sexual liberation, gay liberation, women's liberation, anyone's and everyone's liberation swept it away. Today no crime is too grotesque to be turned to political advantage and blamed on the Devil's decade. The bodies of the dead of Dunblane and the mutilated victims of Rosemary and Fred West have been snatched and used as ammunition in Britain's culture wars. Never mind that the children of the Sixties have turned out to be a big disappointment all round and are more likely to vote Conservative than succeeding generations or, indeed, that the party they have done so much to encourage has been in power for what feels like an age. We have to believe the permissive society unleashed monsters that 17 years of Tory policies have been unable to subdue. If we did not, the public could develop the uncomfortable idea that the government might carry a little responsibility for the state of the country.

Each crime is unique. To fit it into a wider social trend may, on occasion, be justified – if unemployment and burglaries rise together or if the children of divorcees show a predilection for delinquency, it is reasonable, although unpopular in many quarters, to look for links. But generalisation deprives the victim of individuality and the criminal of responsibility. Once, it was the left that was inclined to excuse individual shortcomings ('it's a fair cop, guv, and society is to blame'). Now the right has produced a flower power defence for suspects – 'Not guilty because, m'lud, my mind was deranged by Tamla Motown.'

Journalists and politicians have always been prone to shout about crime and the decline of the West, particularly after lunch. Their cries became noticeably fiercer after the murder of James Bulger in 1993 provoked a self-interested panic about punishment among the opinion-forming classes. Tony Blair, who was then Labour's home affairs spokesman, said it was 'a hammer-blow against the sleeping conscience of the country'. Most newspapers agreed and watched with approval as Blair employed a dead toddler to shift Labour to a hard line on law and order. They applauded all the more loudly when the Conservatives responded to the challenge and the parties began an arms race to see which could invent the sterner penalties.

However genuine the expressions of horror over James Bulger's murder, his death 'said' nothing more (and nothing less) than that a dreadful crime had taken place. It was neither a symptom nor a part of a horrendous trend. There was no wake-up call to a slumbering nation. Between 15 and 20 juveniles are convicted of murder or manslaughter each year. Nearly all are aged between 14 and 17. There has been no recent rise in their number. Pre-pubescent killers, such as the boys who killed James Bulger, are even rarer. They are oddities who appear on average once every two years without reason or pattern. Their existence tells you as much about the state of British society as the 1987 hurricane tells you about the state of the weather.

Criminologists protested in vain. However irrational it may have been, James Bulger's murder was manipulated to encourage genuine fears of crime, and no statistics were going to change popular perceptions. In the following years irrationality has been replaced with mendacity. The history of major crimes has been twisted to justify every convenient prejudice. The rapes and murders their and others' children committed by Rosemary and Fred West were processed into propaganda. When the trial of Rosemary West ended, the *Mail* knew where the guilt lay. The Wests and the majority of their victims came from dysfunctional families, it said. 'The sort which have become ever more common since the permissive 1960s when both Wests grew up.' Peter Hitchens, a noisy *Express* commentator, was convinced that Sixties children bore collective guilt. 'They wanted to be free,' he wrote from his London desk. 'They thought the family was tyranny.' His stunning glibness was too much for Duncan Campbell, *The Guardian*'s crime correspondent, who had, boring old hack that he was, taken the trouble to get on a train and listen to the court case before pontificating about it. 'Do these people read what they write?' he exploded. 'For every child murdered or living, a tyranny was exactly what the West family was.' The metropolitan Hitchens was unrepentant. He replied that along with the West horrors, he considered the Sixties responsible for drugs, social breakdown, permissiveness and Dr Richard Beeching's decision to cut 5,000 miles of railway track (a response that conjures up a terrifying picture of the doctor slashing the network during a bad acid trip).

The treatment of the Wests, however, was tame compared to the transmutation of Thomas Hamilton from mass murderer into victim of modern relativism. Another columnist who did not feel the need to pick up his pen and notebook and leave his desk, decided on the basis of unidentified evidence that the permissive society allowed Hamilton to kill. 'We have started to go to the most insane lengths not to judge anyone at all,' Simon Heffer wrote in the *Mail*. 'Thirty years ago a man like Hamilton would have been run out of every town in which he attempted to practise his bizarre habits. But now all manner of undesirable conduct is tolerated.' His newspaper agreed. In a leading article it said the Dunblane massacre was a sign of a world in which 'social workers and the politically correct' say we cannot be judgmental about other people's lifestyle choices. Heffer and his editor did not know or care that Hamilton came from a society all-too willing to judge. His mother was put out to adoption when she was a baby to hide the shameful secret that she was born out of wedlock. His father ran away when Hamilton was a child. To avoid a second scandal, his mother's adoptive parents adopted Hamilton as well. So successful was the deception that he grew up thinking his mother was his sister. Hamilton himself was obsessed by real and imagined fears that Dunblane gossips would judge him to be a homosexual with an unhealthy interest in the boys who came to his club. He did not sound like a prophet of permissiveness in the bizarre protestations of innocence he sent to the Queen and politicians. On the contrary, his views would not have been out of place in a *Mail* leader. He only wanted to discipline boys, he said, so they would not turn out to be thugs like James Bulger's killers. And what of the 'politically correct' social workers? The Central Regional Council and social services authority tried to ban Hamilton's boys' club from Dunblane schools. Opposition from parents – and criticism from the local government ombudsman – ensured its defeat.

In America, too, the right has taken to grave-robbing. Susan Smith, a single mother in the white, religious town of Union, Georgia, drowned her two children. She had been sexually abused as a girl and claimed she was disturbed because no one would marry her. Newt Gingrich said the case 'reminds every American how sick the society is getting and how much we need to change things. The only way to get change is to vote Republican.' He did not bother to inquire into Smith's background. If he had, he would have found that Smith came from a staunchly Republican family.

Many are in despair about a polity that honours the meanest nonsense as common sense. But the failure of conservatives in all parties to make even the most cursory attempts to check their facts before turning suffering to their political advantage suggests an intellectual bankruptcy that can never deal with a messy reality they have no interest in understanding.

Independent on Sunday April 1996

THE CRACKS IN *CRACKER*

The case against Colin Stagg will go down in English legal history as the first in which the central line of inquiry was, in the words of the prosecution counsel, 'controlled and interpreted at each stage not by the police but by a psychologist'. The first and, if the authorities can surprise us by developing an elementary capacity to learn from disaster, the last. The result of letting the psychologist play 'puppet master', as Mr Justice Ognall put it, was a police operation that was 'misconceived', 'wholly reprehensible' and a blatant attempt to incriminate a suspect by 'deceptive conduct of the grossest kind'. With these and many other damning words, the judge ruled that it was unsafe to allow Stagg to face trial by jury.

The shock was felt throughout the legal establishment. Once again, the judgment of Barbara Mills, the Director of Public Prosecutions, has been questioned. So, too, has the role of two senior government lawyers and the Chief Crown Prosecutor for London, who supported the decision to take Stagg to court. The Crown Prosecution Service and Metropolitan Police bickered in public about how closely lawyers had supervised the police operation. They were joined in argument by the country's leading psychologists, who criticised Paul Britton, the inspiration for *Cracker*, for concluding that Stagg was the killer after orchestrating a psychodrama that came close to mental torture. As for Colin Stagg, he spent 13 months in prison awaiting trial. Ever since his release he has been hounded by the press and police, who flirt with the laws of libel by hinting that he is really guilty. The family of Rachel Nickell, meanwhile, has had its hopes of seeing a conviction raised and then dashed. 'Where's the justice?' asked Andrew Nickell, Rachel's father, as he left court. 'When my daughter was murdered I believed the law was even-handed. I am afraid the last two-and-a-quarter years have been a period of disillusionment.'

How could the prosecution of Colin Stagg – the conclusion of one of the biggest murder hunts in modern times – end in such a fiasco? The answers lie in the pressures on the police to get a conviction and in the use (or, rather, misuse) of the supposed science of psychological profiling.

When Stagg was first arrested in September 1992 the press was told he was 'the prime suspect'. Four out of scores of callers said he looked like a photofit shown on the BBC's *Crimewatch*. He lived off the A3 road by Wimbledon Common in south London. Inside his flat police found an altar, some books on the occult, a sheath knife, and gloves. But that was it. There was nothing to link him with the murder, and he was released. While in custody, he was charged with indecent exposure on Wimbledon Common and fined £200 for sunbathing in the nude. By the time they ruled out Stagg the police were running out of options. They had examined and rejected 547 suspects and still had no idea who was responsible for a terrible murder which, as the newspapers were telling them, cried out for retribution.

At about 10 am on 15 July 1992, Ms Nickell, a 23-year-old former model, was walking across the common with her two-year-old son and labrador when she was attacked, stabbed 49 times and sexually abused. The child saw it all and was found clinging to his mother's bloodstained body an hour later, crying: 'Get up mummy. Get up mummy.' There were, however, no semen stains, clothing fibres, blood that did not match the victim's group, or weapons that could be used as forensic evidence. Detectives were stuck until Julie Pines phoned the incident room. The factory worker had exchanged letters with Stagg after he replied to a lonely hearts advert. His third note disgusted her and she broke off the correspondence. Detectives took another look at Stagg and tried to break him by letting Britton build an elaborate psychological trap. He was given the assistance of an undercover police woman who was to be known to the public only by her codename of Lizzie James. She wrote to Stagg saying she was a friend of Pines who had been intrigued by his letters and wanted to get to know him. He replied and Britton began examining the correspondence and tapes of the couple's calls. Each time contact was made he told James how to respond. Their conversations became more and more explicit as Lizzie promised the 31-year-old more and more favours. She urged him to say anything 'because my fantasies hold no bounds and my imagination runs riot'.

Months of undercover work produced nothing. In what the defence called 'an act of desperation' Lizzie James (and Britton) increased the pressure. She pretended she had taken part in a satanic murder of a young mother and child – whose fictional death bore carefully crafted similarities to the murder of Rachel Nickell. She could, she said, only make love to someone who had done the same. Stagg responded by 'confessing' to a murder in the New Forest. He was lying to please his strange girlfriend. The controllers checked the records. There had been no killing, they told James. In an attempt to turn the conversation to Rachel Nickell, the policewoman said: 'I don't believe the New Forest story . . . If only you had done the Wimbledon Common murder; if only you had killed her it would be all right.' 'I'm terribly sorry but I haven't,' Stagg replied.

And this shamefaced admission was all the police and Britton got. A sad and lonely man was manipulated, enticed and entrapped, promised an affair with a beautiful woman if only he would confess – and the conclusion was a mumbled apology. Justifying themselves later, the police said that under questioning from Lizzie James, Stagg revealed three things about Ms Nickell's body which only the murderer could know. The defence argued that the police had shown him photographs of the body and that he had also got many facts about the murder wrong.

But these were secondary points. John Nutting, the prosecutor, told the judge that the aim of the undercover operation was not to trick Stagg into a confession – that would be unlawful – rather, it was to show that his sexual fantasies, including one in which he, Lizzie and a man with a knife met on the common, fitted the psychological profile of the killer. Britton had ruled that the fantasies he shared with Lizzie James showed a 'sexual dysfunction' that was 'indistinguishable' from the sexual dysfunction of the murderer. Stagg was facing trial for a shocking crime with a life sentence in a prison where he would have to be isolated for the rest of his days from inmates who would kick the living daylights out of him if they got the chance, not because he had confessed under caution or been seen by witnesses or caught by forensic scientists, but because he fitted Britton's picture of the killer. A great deal rested on Britton's reputation as a very clever psychologist containing more than a germ of truth.

The head of Trent Regional Psychology Service has impressed detectives and crime correspondents. He has been involved in 70 police investigations, including the murders of James Bulger and Julie Dart and the abduction of Abbie Humphries. He offers his services gratis to any police force that wants him. He used to get on well with the government, which treated him as the king of his trade. The Home Office asked him in 1990 to evaluate the attempts of academic psychologists to create a national profiling system. They are still waiting for the results. He fell out with Whitehall when in a Central TV programme he interviewed Dennis Nilsen, the mass killer, about his sexual fantasies. Ministers tried and failed to get the programme stopped and MPs claimed it turned murderers into celebrities. Many of his colleagues did not rate him. Even before the collapse of the Stagg case, he was treated with a hint of disdain and perhaps envy. 'He has never published any significant academic work,' sniffed one. 'His name is known because of media coverage.' The misgivings of his peers did not, however, stop Britton being asked to provide a profile of the murderer of Rachel Nickell.

It was drawn up before Stagg was questioned by the police and was specific. The killer was a sadist and power over the victim and her degradation were important to him, Britton decided. His use of the knife meant he was excited by his victim's fear, submissiveness and acquiescence. These strands would be a recognisable theme in his sexual fantasies, which could also include a 'deviant interest in buggery'. Britton 'masterminded' what Lizzie James wrote to see if Stagg's behaviour fitted his profile of the murderer. He predicted, somewhat hazily, that it would take between two and 16 weeks to get an admission of guilt. In fact the operation lasted 28 weeks, and Stagg always denied killing Ms Nickell. For all the confident detail, there was a glaring flaw in the profile that inspired the prosecution. The judge spotted it on the first day of the legal arguments. Were not, he asked, most of the characteristics Britton noted in his profile of the killer shared by 'a very large number of sexual psychopaths?' 'Apparently not,' said Nutting. 'The deviancy of that particular kind, when you add in the sadistic element of the knife, is very rare indeed.'

It had to be. If the profile was not 'very rare indeed', then the prosecution's attempts to claim that Stagg's conversations with James and the fantasies they shared were evidence that he was the murderer would be wasted breath. Hundreds of real or potential sex criminals would fit Britton's description. The prosecution could allege that Stagg may have been one of them, but the resemblance would not have meant he killed Rachel Nickell unless it could be proved that the odds against two such criminal types being near the common at the same time were fantastically high.

The defence went further. Not only was the profile too general to be useful, but it was evidently doltish. The leading figure behind the assault on Britton was David Canter, Professor of Psychology at Liverpool University, who has criticised him in the past. Professor Canter is the author of *Criminal Shadows*, the first authoritative account of psychological profiling in the UK. He has worked on 100 cases, most notably the hunt for John Duffy, the 'railway killer' who committed three murders and a dozen rapes around London between 1982 and 1986. Canter's method is to look at what the attacks say about the criminal and what can be deduced about the 'inner narratives' the killer tells himself to justify his crimes. He provided the defence with a 35-page attack on Britton that asked whether the crime did show that the murderer was a 'very rare' sexual deviant rather than a vicious and violent man who, perhaps, went wild when he met resistance. 'The most significant aspect about this brutal assault was that it happened in broad daylight in a public park in front of a two-year-old child,' he said. 'But the presence of the child was hardly mentioned [by Britton] and the case for the murderer being a rare sexual deviant is far from clear.' Canter condemned Britton for not keeping notes of his work and for becoming far too cosy with the police investigation. The first rule graduates on his investigative psychology course are taught is 'keep your distance'. The need for detachment is basic. Otherwise the psychologist finds his or her conclusions being shaped by the inquiry and bias entering the research.

Armed with his critique, the defence tore into the case against Stagg. According to Britton, the killer was meant to be interested in anal sex. But the letters to Lizzie showed Stagg was not. He was meant to be dominant and have wild and uninhibited deviant fantasies. But far from being dominant, Stagg showed a deference to James which bordered on the pathetic. At one point he apologised for being a 'right prat' and added: 'I'll understand if you do not want to know any more.' James told him how she and a former boyfriend enjoyed hurting others. He replied: 'Please explain as I live a quiet life. If I have disappointed you please don't dump me. Nothing like this has happened to me before. I need you, Lizzie. Please, please tell me what you want in every detail.'

After going through the 700 pages of letters and transcripts on the relationship between Stagg and the policewoman, William Clegg, the defence counsel, said it was obvious who was dominant. 'She is at the forefront and leading the relationship. She is driving it.' Mr Justice Ognall was scathing when he threw out the case. The idea of presenting the argument to a jury that Stagg should be jailed for life because he matched the psychological profile of the killer was 'redolent with danger'.

The release of Stagg ends a decade of favourable publicity for psychological profiling. In the United States, the FBI has taken the method to its heart. Mind-hunters have a computerised profiling centre in Virginia that receives 300 inquiries a year. The results have been mixed. In the Sixties, a committee of psychiatrists and psychologists decided that the Boston Strangler was not one man but two men, likely to be schoolteachers, who lived alone. One was homosexual, they added with confident precision. When the strangler was caught, he was one man, a construction worker who lived with his wife and children and was aggressively heterosexual. There have been successes. In 1974, psychologists cut down 3,500 suspects for a series of killings to 100. On their list was Ted Bundy, who was convicted of killing 40 women.

No psychologist will admit that human behaviour cannot be studied like a science – the research grants would dry up instantly – but Professor Canter presents sceptics with a distinction. There is nothing new about trying to guess the features of a criminal, he says, and quotes Shakespeare's Julius Caesar who accurately profiled his assassin when he said: 'Yond' Cassius has a lean and hungry look; / Such men are dangerous.'

Studies of crime can produce models showing, for example, that most serial killers stay close to their homes when they murder. The value of the research is, however, limited. Psychologists are there to help the police, not to run operations. 'We are not trained in the legal implications of collecting evidence. We are not a substitute for police work.' Canter's *Criminal Shadows* concludes with a warning. If the police developed a belief that they understood what happened in people's heads, the use of behavioural science could mean more innocent people being set up by detectives convinced by their psychological sophistication of a suspect's guilt. 'I think we have come very close to seeing that happen,' he added.

Independent on Sunday September 1994

BARBARIC PRACTICES

Hard times are good for hard men, and few judges are harder than Ian Gillespie, Wolverhampton's stipendiary magistrate. He is so tough it is impossible to understand why Tony Blair has failed to recruit him to advise New Labour on its Old Testament morality. While politicians and the press proclaim that Britain – the country with the highest prison population in Europe – is being stabbed in the back by a soft liberal judiciary, Gillespie shows what a good, old-fashioned judge, uncontaminated by the Sixties, can achieve.

He was saluted by lawyers defending the poorest suspects in the system. They maintained that in 1996 Gillespie and his Wolverhampton bench jailed one quarter of all the women imprisoned in England and Wales for failing to pay court fines. This is impressive, a feat that could enter any forthcoming Guinness Book of Legal Records. Can it be true? Richard Wise, a Staffordshire lawyer who conducted the survey, is sure his figures are right. Gillespie's office dismisses the allegation and says only a tiny proportion of the male and female fine defaulters he sees are jailed. Unfortunately, it is impossible to adjudicate because most women and men who cannot, or will not, meet demands to buy a television licence, or pay poll-tax arrears, do not have determined lawyers such as Wise in their corner. They are often not represented at all and just disappear into the prisons without anyone knowing much about them.

We can, none the less, get a flavour of life in Gillespie's court. He judges the underclass so often condemned for its swinish refusal to understand that they cannot enjoy Britain's generous rights without accepting responsibilities. The specific responsibility Kevin Perks failed to meet was the demand that he pay arrears dating from the poll-tax disaster. Gillespie told him that if he did not cough up he would go to prison for 30 days. The problem was that the 38-year-old Perks was in no condition to understand the lecture. He was suffering from what carers euphemistically call 'severe learning difficulties'. Put bluntly, he was left brain-damaged by childhood meningitis. A shunt – a kind of medical tap – was fitted into his skull to draw surplus fluid from his brain. He could not read or write and was incontinent. As you would expect, he was all but penniless. When appeal judges got the hapless Perks out of prison, Gillespie told them he had not noticed anything wrong with the man when he locked him up.

The reprimand from the High Court in the Perks case was not an isolated rebuff. Gillespie has been censured for stopping a defendant bringing a friend to court to help him fight imprisonment for failing to pay the poll tax. Seltana Kiffin, a 35-year-old single mother, was freed on appeal from a month's sentence imposed by one of Gillespie's colleagues. The High Court heard her four children were taken into care when their mother was incarcerated. Then there was the case of Geri Andrews who was snatched by the police with her two crying children because she had not paid fines for an outstanding parking ticket and driving with an out-of-date tax disc. Andrews told the officers she would soon have the money they wanted – her insurance company was about to deliver compensation for the wrecking of her flat by vandals and burglars. Her protests did her no good. She too was jailed and released only on appeal.

The hard-headed may be left unmoved by these stories. Magistrates do not create poverty, after all. They just have to cope with the mess. What are they meant to do when fines for tax arrears, prostitution or TV licence-dodging are left unpaid? There has to be a deterrent. But be careful before you nod in agreement and endorse Jack Straw's and Michael Howard's hard way to law and order. It is a road with many blind bends.

Wolverhampton crime made the news spectacularly in 1995 when Horrett Campbell went wild with a machete in St Luke's school. A brave teacher who risked her life to save the children became a national heroine. Eight months earlier, Campbell had been up before Gillespie for affray and minor motoring offences. Social workers and probation officers looked into his past. They reported that he was hearing voices whispering instructions. He had painted his car with emulsion and set fire to it. In the wet way of the liberal professions, they worried about him and decided he needed psychiatric help. Their report was brushed aside. Gillespie refused to adjourn the case for psychiatric assessment. He sent Campbell instead for a short, sharp stay in Birmingham's Winson Green Prison – a stinking jail described by the Prison Inspectorate as 'depressing' and infested with 'cockroaches, rats, feral cats and pigeons'. When he got out, he was a danger to himself and everyone he met and ready to storm a primary school.

Thankfully, there is hope for Gillespie. In the same month as the St Luke's assaults, he sentenced three men found guilty of organising a cockfight and inadvertently found the right words. 'I find it quite incredible,' he said, 'that on the eve of the twenty-first century I should be dealing with such barbaric practices.' Me too.

Observer November 1996

RACIAL BIOLOGY

The British prison population is at its highest level since the war, and climbing even though crime is falling. The chances of blacks being jailed are ten times those of whites. You are more likely to be locked up if you are a British black than if you are a Texan living in the most vicious state of the most punitive country in the developed world. Without the wit or will to deal with the causes of crime, an inclusive government is tackling 'social exclusion' by incarcerating the excluded. Yet when the Blairites are asked to let the public examine their packed cells, the keenest jailers in Europe become strangely coy. Journalists are banned from interviewing inmates. Official inspection reports are sat on for months. As the inquest into the violent death of Alton Manning showed, official shyness is now threatening the justice system.

The jury decided Manning had been unlawfully killed by officers working for a company controlled by the Corrections Corporation of America (CCA). He was asphyxiated in the Blakenhurst private prison, near Redditch. The pathologist found his windpipe had been crushed 'due to pressure on the neck'. Bruises on his neck, blood spots in the eyes and on the neck and face, dried blood in his ears and mouth, pointed to the same conclusion: a prison manager had grabbed Manning and locked him in a fatal neck hold. There was an embarrassment of evidence to support the verdict, along with strong reasons for believing an inept cover-up had been attempted. Before the election, New Labour would have seized on the case. The party had promised that penal capitalists would not profit from the jailing of British citizens. In power Labour recanted and pushed ahead with privatising the jails. What has not been reported is how it nearly succeeded in using legal bullying to protect its new friends in the liberty-deprivation racket.

The inquest into Manning's death was almost wrecked when the coroner told government and CCA lawyers he would allow the jury to consider unlawful killing as a verdict. The barristers, appalled by the possibility of a ruling which would be bad for business, ran to the High

Court for a gagging order to silence him. They threatened the coroner, Victor Round, with an injunction if he did not suspend the inquest while they tried to persuade a judge that the verdict was illegal. Facing the possibility of imprisonment for contempt of court if he continued to hear a case frozen under injunction, the coroner complied. The legal stratagem was cunning and novel. Inquest juries are a democratic check on official violence. Authoritarian governments have always hated them and have gradually stripped them of their powers to issue statements and recommendations on, say, the behaviour of the police in a riot. The Manning injunction took jury nobbling to a new level. Freedom-loving New Labour was trying to prevent an inquest jury doing its last remaining job: listening to the evidence and reaching an honest conclusion.

Manning died after being stripped in a drugs search. He cooperated at first even though, as tests later showed, he had not taken drugs or alcohol, but protested when he was ordered to squat so officers could gawp at his anus and genitals. One warder claimed anal and genital inspections were 'standard procedure' at Blakenhurst. If they were, CCA was breaking prison rules with abandon. The officers painted a terrifying picture of what happened next. Manning attacked them. He was 'like a wild beast' and was 'snorting like a bull'. (You may have guessed by now that he was black.) But while the prisoner's body was bloody and battered, only one of the eight officers involved had a scratch on him. As Manning was dragged from his cell, he passed two security cameras. Police collected the tapes later. They found that, although every other camera in the jail was working, the two crucial monitors had recorded nothing. A prison officer told the detectives that he didn't know why the videos had failed. When it was put to him during the inquest that the tapes had been wiped, he admitted making 'a false statement to the police'. He later found work – with the police.

Only a moron in a hurry could have missed the suspicious glint in the jurors' eyes. CCA and Home Office lawyers, whose fees ultimately come from the public, read the mood and decided to act. An unlawful killing verdict, they told the coroner, was out of the question, absolutely impermissible. If it was returned, the jury would have treated evidence from criminal inmates in Blakenhurst as if it was on a par with the sworn testimony of law-abiding warders. Yet the prisoners who described watching Manning being hauled through Blakenhurst with one officer's arm over his throat and a hand at the back of his neck weren't friends who would lie to avenge his death. None knew him. Several were frightened about the consequences of speaking out. The Manning family had to issue subpoenas to force them into the witness-box. In any case, there was the medical evidence, the missing tapes and the unconvincing performances of the guards for the jury to weigh. The inquest was stopped, nevertheless.

When the Home Office and CCA got before a High Court judge, he dismissed their arguments and ordered the hearing into Manning's death to continue and the jurors to be freed to reach whatever conclusion they wanted. If the judge had agreed to censor the coroner and jury by restricting possible verdicts, the Home Office would have hit gold. All coroners would have got the message that they shouldn't mess with Whitehall and its wealthy allies.

Downsized newspapers no longer send reporters to sit through every day of a trial. Journalism is caught in a classic free-market trap. Although it is in the general interest that one hack hears all the evidence and alerts the public and the rest of the media when, as in this case, tricks are being pulled, it is never in the particular interest of a single news organisation to tie up an expensive reporter for weeks in the hope that a story will break. No one reported the legal feints, and the death of Manning did not become news until Richard Tilt, director general of the Prison Service, gave a perfect demonstration of the prejudice in his department when he brushed aside questions about Manning by saying that blacks were genetically more likely to be suffocated and killed in custody than whites. He did not seem to understand that blacks are grotesquely over-represented in his jails and that Manning was not killed by faulty DNA but by the brutal and unlawful treatment of private warders.

His championing of racial biology should be seen in the light of the preceding attempts to stop the inquest. It was not an isolated gaffe but part of a campaign to protect penal capitalists which shows that Labour has not only accepted private prisons but abandoned the residual role of regulator. Rather than holding CCA to account for its failure to meet minimum standards, the Home Office and the conglomerate worked together and behaved as if the public and commercial interests were one. Far from being alarmed by the fatal actions of officers of a corporation that makes its money by locking up citizens, government lawyers fought alongside CCA to silence the coroner and jury. When the ploy failed, Tilt maintained that a mysterious creator had given blacks a design fault which meant that, when their windpipes are crushed, they die. Sad, but there you are. You can't expect a good Christian like Jack Straw to defy God's will.

Observer March 1998

BUSINESS SCHOOL JUSTICE

The last riot in mainland Britain was in December 1995. Like most riots before it, the looting and percussion of gunshots in the background were provoked by accusations of police violence against blacks – in this case, alleged violence against Wayne Douglas, a homeless black man, who died in Brixton police station. The aftermath was as predictable. It must be part of the constitution that a disturbance has to be followed by feverish diversionary shouts from the police, politicians and the press. Someone – anyone but the police will do! – must take the blame. First, the Brixton riot was all the fault of Rudy Narayan, a black lawyer, who reportedly incited a demonstration outside the station by crying: 'The Brixton police are killers.' Sir Paul Condon, the Metropolitan Police Commissioner, added that 'dangerously irresponsible' black newspapers 'fuelled discontent'. Other theorists were scarier still. They claimed, without producing anything resembling proof, that agitators from the Black Panthers and Socialist Workers' Party were behind the trouble.

It might be worth dragging up what happened in Brixton now that Jack Straw's promotion of zero-tolerance policing and the Bank of England's mismanagement of the economy are providing the ideal conditions for mayhem to return to the slums. Still, I would have held my tongue if the Court of Appeal had not delivered a telling verdict to the Douglas family, which has spent three years trying to get behind the establishment ravings and discover the truth.

Among the agreed facts, dragged out in three court hearings, was that the impoverished Douglas was a criminal. He had a record, and on the night of his death broke into the home of Katherine and Justin Short. The couple awoke at 2.30 am to find him waving their kitchen knife in their faces. He ran off with money and cashpoint cards into the streets of Brixton. The police were on his tail in minutes. He was cornered in a schoolyard. Officers said they smacked his arms to make him drop the knife. Civilian witnesses said he dropped it of his own accord before he was hit. The evidence is contradictory, but it was the follow-up to the arrest that turned his family's stomachs. Time and again, Douglas experienced what lawyers and policemen call 'posturally asphyxiating restraint'. You are posturally asphyxiated when you are shoved face down to the ground with your hands cuffed behind your back. Douglas's first taste of asphyxia was when he was carried to the police van. Jane Stokes saw him 'handcuffed', with his 'head slumped forward'. He was doing 'nothing aggressive', she said. When he got to the station he was 'a model prisoner', according to one officer; 'not violent or aggressive', agreed another. A third constable said Douglas could barely walk. He was taken out of the van 'shuffling and muttering' and stripped to his underpants. There was 'nasal mucus' (snot) on his face. Douglas, who was struggling for breath, was given the 'cell relocation technique' a baroque variant of 'posturally asphyxiating restraint' in which the prisoner is pinned face first on the floor by officers who then spring off his back and run away, slamming the cell door behind them.

The family's lawyers and the civil rights group, Inquest, said the obviously weak Douglas presented no threat and should have been allowed to sit or, at the very least, lie on his back. The failure to treat Douglas humanely amounted to 'unreasonable and excessive force'. They went through the evidence at an inquest into his death in front of a London coroner, Sir Montague Levine. No one criticises the hearing – Sir Montague, one of the best coroners around, allowed every fact to be discussed. But he got into a terrible muddle when he tried to advise the jury on what verdict it could reach. The Douglas lawyers claimed he confused two entirely separate grounds for finding that a man has been unlawfully killed. The first is that the dead man was the victim of a violent assault; the second that he was the victim of gross negligence. The coroner mixed up the two concepts and the befuddled jury unsurprisingly decided that Douglas's death was not unlawful. Douglas's lawyers are the noted lefties Louise Christian and Patrick O'Connor, and there is a hackneyed line of attack against their kind. They are Spartists, bleeding hearts, do-gooders, limousine liberals who probably live in Hampstead and care more about criminals than their victims. The sneers against them might have carried force if the conservative Court of Appeal had not decided that Christian and O'Connor were absolutely right. Sir Montague's 'exposition of the law was unclear and to that extent unsatisfactory,' the judges said. 'The coroner was wrong . . . there was just sufficient evidence to leave unlawful manslaughter to the jury.'

Having conceded victory to the family, the court ignored its claim for a fair hearing. The judges blithely failed to combat the occasionally riot-inducing suspicion that blacks cannot get justice. There was no need for a rerun of the inquiry, they said, because 'little more can be achieved by subjecting all concerned to the considerable expense and stress of a further inquest'. The pursuit of truth must be judged against the principles of business schools. Honest investigation of a man's death can be struck down by a cost-benefit analysis.

The case is a sign of a new mood in English justice which will affect tens of thousands of lives, in part because Lord Justice Hobhouse, one of the judges in the Douglas case, is on the verge of being promoted to the House of Lords where he will become one of the custodians of the new bill of rights; and in part because it ties in with a commercial assault on freedom.

Now, I am often accused of being too horrid about New Labour, but as a Labour-movement child, I have always believed that it retained a residual respect for liberty. For all my dislike of the man, I never expected to see Jack Straw propose the abolition of the right to trial by jury for about 22,000 citizens each year because it is too expensive to let juries reach verdicts. But the abolition of many juries is being discussed with grave seriousness by men who count themselves progressive. The way things are going I think all of us should learn to keep our heads down. In the future, if you get into trouble do not expect the criminal justice system to help. Politicians and a senior judiciary, composed of wealthy commercial lawyers with neither interest in nor understanding of human rights, will tell you that resources do not permit it.

Observer August 1998

MARY BELL

Oceans of sweat and ink flowed from pundits struggling to describe the Labour government on the occasion of its first birthday. Is it an administration, asked the thumb-suckers, of good-hearted reformers and cool modernisers? Or Tory opportunists and Uriah Heeps? No one, least of all a Prime Minister who aimlessly rambles down third ways, knew the answer. By the end of the week of national celebration the indecision was resolved. It was clear that New Labour was a mob. An elite mob, to be sure, filled with ministers in grey suits and pastel ties and portly newspaper editors grateful for official sanction to push the law to its limits, but a mob none the less. Jack Straw took the novel view that it is the job of the Home Secretary to incite the press to riot. He let journalists know that Gitta Sereny's payments to Mary Bell for co-operating with her psychobiography made the Bell family fair game. The authorities would not worry about a technical obligation to obey the law.

If hacks broke injunctions against revealing the identity of the now middle-aged Bell and the fact that she killed when she was 11, so be it. 'It's certainly the case that Mary Bell by bringing herself into the public arena in such a dramatic way has compromised her own claim for her own privacy,' Straw said. The pious 'her owns' revealed Straw's cynicism. As he and every journalist knows, the injunctions are not there to protect the privacy of Mary Bell but the privacy of her 14-year-old daughter.

The order preventing the girl's identity being revealed is so famous in legal and newspaper circles that all subsequent injunctions to guard the anonymity of children are nicknamed Mary Bell orders. The original Bell ruling is draconian, but it did not stop reporters surrounding the girl's home and making a laughing stock of the law by letting the neighbours know precisely who Bell once was. It did not stop them driving mother and child to seek sanctuary in a police cell. It did not stop the Prime Minister and Home Secretary tub-thumping on every medium from the *Sun* to the Internet. And it could do nothing to help when Bell, faced by the book burners and cheap politicians, had to explain the mayhem to her bewildered and ignorant daughter by telling her about her secret criminal record.

What happens to a teenager when she hears over the noise of wailing sirens and howling hacks her mother confess to being a child killer? Whatever it is, it will keep on happening. Once the press has found Mary Bell, we'll never let her go. We were, in truth, getting a little tired of running the disturbingly attractive picture of the young, blonde Myra Hindley. Now we have a new witch complete with fine photos from when she looked sultry and menacing. Bell will be news until she dies. Nice one, Jack. Well done, Gitta. Great work, Fleet Street. A girl's life is ruined, but everyone else is making money.

The government's law officers treated the scrum with insouciance. The office of Peter Harris, the Official Solicitor, said he was 'concerned', of course, but he did not bring contempt-of-court actions and waited until the story had died down before warning newspapers to be careful. His indulgence was surprising because Harris has persecuted women who break orders against publicising their children's plight. Sarah Keays has been forced to go to court repeatedly to fight a Mary Bell order imposed by Cecil Parkinson, which prohibits all mention of their child. I'm not meant to tell you that the girl's name is Flora, but what the hell: everyone else is ignoring the judges. Parkinson and the Official Solicitor have hounded Keays for years. The gag's only real effect is to stop Flora embarrassing the Conservative Party Chairman, who has never seen her. Keays has been forced to spend a small fortune on legal fees and is now broke. Flora has been severely ill, and the injunction has got in the way of her mother finding a special school and treatment. When Keays last spoke publicly about Flora, Harris seemed to claim she was not acting in the girl's best interests in a letter that was hard not to interpret as a threat to take the child from her mother and put her in care. What particularly annoys Keays is that Flora is not under the protection of the judiciary as a ward of court. Keays has to look after her while fighting Parkinson and Harris. No one doubts she is a loving mother. Her only fault was to have an affair with Parkinson, but a girl's allowed one mistake.

The children of Fred and Rosemary West, by contrast, are protected by a court order, but the Official Solicitor has sanctioned a biography and documentary film about their parents. In Cambridge, a man with a chronically ill daughter first had a court order to keep her identity secret and then persuaded the judges to lift the injunction when he wanted to publicise her story. A baby-sitter who blinded and brain damaged a child was protected from publicity because she had twins who could be harmed if the neighbours found out what their mother had done.

So according to Blair, Straw and the Official Solicitor, it is perfectly acceptable to out Mary Bell's daughter. But you cannot discomfort Cecil Parkinson. You can hear the story of Fred and Rosemary West, but not of Flora Keays. One minute a dying baby needs protection, the next she is public property. But we cannot expect consistency. All we can look forward to is the blackly comic day when someone – a paedophile? the next Mary Bell? – is killed by a crowd, and the nation hears the grave condemnations of mob justice from Downing Street and Fleet Street.

Observer May 1998

TORTURE ENGLISH STYLE

Officially, the most dangerous man in Britain is not the Yorkshire Ripper or even Tony Blair, but one George Sansom, a 45-year-old florist from Dulwich, south London. Don't feel a fool if his name means nothing to you. The newspapers have to tag him with the windy epithet 'cousin of the former Arsenal and England star, Kenny' to remind readers of his slight connection to fading fame. His obscurity failed to impress the authorities who have treated Sansom and his accomplice, Coleman Mulkerrins, as monsters.

They sit in the Special Secure Unit of Whitemoor jail, a modern Alcatraz for 'exceptional risks', and the most tightly guarded block in England's ever-expanding prison system. Surveillance is so pervasive that government medical advisers instruct psychiatrists to visit inmates every few months to check they haven't gone mad. Amnesty International says the security, imposed after IRA men almost escaped from Whitemoor, registers on the international oppression scale and should be recognised as a cruel, inhumane and degrading punishment. The IRA is long gone: its men got out in the deals leading to the Good Friday agreement rather than by nipping over the wall. The block built to deal with Ulster terrorists survives. As with so many other laws and institutions thrown up in an emergency, the unit continues to function when the danger that justified 'exceptional measures' has passed.

Sansom and Mulkerrins have virtually no one to talk to. Somewhere in its sterile corridors, which look more like a hospital than a prison, are an American contract killer and a Colombian drug dealer. No one sees them. Sansom wonders if they grassed and need to be hidden for their own safety. He has plenty of time to speculate. Other prisoners pass through Whitemoor, but Sansom and Mulkerrins have been in the jail within a jail since 1995. Contact with 'ordinary' villains is prohibited. They see visitors from behind toughened glass screens. Touching is forbidden. Daylight, education and exercise are scarce. They endure regular strip searches and anal examinations. These Napoleons of crime are considered so menacing their jailers veto rudimentary compassion on security grounds. When Mulkerrins's wife died of cancer, the 56-year-old was not allowed to go to her funeral.

Neither man is violent. They haven't tried to escape, never threatened a warder or fellow prisoner. When Mulkerrins was arrested, the magistrate allowed him to wait at home for his trial on bail. Sansom spent a few weeks in prison after he was collared, then was also judged to be harmless and bailed. Dean Sargeant, Sansom's solicitor, admits his client comes from a rough family who have kept him in work for many years, but says George is a 'kind and good man'. At their trial, the judge said the pair had 'no relevant convictions' the jury need worry about. Their criminal records were petty. Why on earth are they being treated as if they are worse than the Krays? The answer lies in the second biggest cocaine seizure in British history, a policing triumph that became a disaster.

In November 1992 South American drug dealers dropped 795 kilos of cocaine off the coast of Venezuela. It was picked up by *Foxtrot V,*

an oil-rig support craft bought from a Louisiana breaker's yard for
$200,000. The ship chugged across the Atlantic and docked in the
Thames. Police, Customs and the Navy's Special Boat Squadron knew
all about the smugglers. For 12 months they had been running 'Operation
Emerge' and were waiting to wrap it up when the drugs arrived. There
were a few hitches. An SBS boat tailing *Foxtrot V* capsized in the Channel
and the elite commandos had to cope with the indignity of calling on
common coastguards to rescue them. When the ship and its £125 million cargo came to port, the police were on hand to follow the drugs
to a lock-up and make simple arrests. For all the advance warning, the
three-month, £2 million trial of the *Foxtrot V* suspects was a catastrophe
for the prosecutors. Five members of the crew said they had no idea
drugs had been pulled from the water. A man who took the cocaine
to a warehouse claimed he had been forced to do so at gunpoint by
the real criminals, who were still free. All six were acquitted.

Sansom and Mulkerrins were the next to be charged, but, as we
have seen, magistrates did not see them as serious criminals. Sansom
was accused of being the cocaine distributor at the British end, Mulkerrins
of buying the boat. Both were meant to have run away when *Foxtrot V*
was taken. Their first trial was abandoned after the prosecution claimed
a jury member had received 'unwelcome approaches'. The retrial was
held in Norwich, where jurors were bused to the court. One ducked
out of the hearing when he complained that the intensive police protection 'clouded his views' and made it impossible for him to be impartial. The pair were found guilty and got 30 years – far longer than IRA
bombers or murderers. For these middle-aged men the life sentences
really will mean life. Both protest their innocence and say the policing
in Norwich prejudiced the jury. Sargeant, who has known Sansom for
years, cannot believe he's guilty. 'He was a bit of a wheeler-dealer in
flowers and cheap clothes. You only had to look at his very ordinary
lifestyle to know the prosecution claim that he was a rich, powerful
criminal able to punt massive amounts of cocaine round the country
was rubbish.' You'd expect his lawyer to defend him. We can be far

harsher and assume Sansom and his friend are guilty. But even if we do, they are still not premier league gangsters. The trial judge accepted that Sansom and Mulkerrins were not the masterminds – the 'principals', as the police say – behind the crime, but hangers-on. There are far, far worse people in the jails. But they are not trying to hold on to their sanity in Whitemoor's isolation cells.

The prison service won't say why they are there, but hints that intelligence suggests that they have powerful friends on the outside who can break them out of jail. I hope this is right. Because Sergeant and Stephen Shaw, the level-headed director of the Prison Reform Trust, have an ugly suspicion. Operation Emerge ended in failure. The big fish escaped. Sansom and Mulkerrins may be being kept in barbarous conditions in the expectation that relentless punishment will break their spirits and make them tell the police about the gang members still at large – information the luckless men say they do not possess. The vulgar word for this practice is torture, a crime our ethical government condemns in foreign dictatorships.

Observer August 1998

PS   Sansom and Mulkerrins were released from the unit and sent to an ordinary prison after this article appeared.

ACQUIRED IMMUNITY SYNDROME

If this newspaper's many criminal readers want a quiet life, we recommend you apply at once for jobs at Europol, the new European police force. Last week, almost unnoticed, Parliament gave monarchical privileges to its coppers and placed the upholders of Euro-law and order above the law. Right-wing Conservatives have always looked on the agency as a European FBI that will become the coercive arm of the super-state they fear will destroy Margaret Thatcher's magnificent legacy, and automatically opposed the extension of its powers. Still, just because the most embarrassing, boring and repellent people in Britain are Eurosceptic, it doesn't follow that they are necessarily wrong all the time about everything. (I hope you realise just how hard it was to write that sentence.) In any case, politicians who don't appear to be completely unhinged are also worried about Europol. The Liberal Democrats and Kenneth Clarke voted against granting it privileges that made its officers the successors of the medieval clergy, and miserable Labour MPs muttered impotently while they sat on their hands.

The government ignored them all. Derek Fatchett, a Foreign Office minister, shepherded in the order giving agency staff 'immunity from legal process in respect of words spoken or written, and of acts performed by them in the exercise of their duties'. It was standard for diplomats and others in international organisations to be given immunity from prosecution, he harrumphed. Europol officers deserved the same privileges because they wouldn't be real policemen with 'operational powers', but mere law enforcement librarians, analysing information and passing it on. Fatchett's soothing words were disingenuous, to use the mildest available word. As he ought to know, Europol was given wide 'operative powers' by EU ministers. The fight against mafias required Europol to 'facilitate and support the preparation, coordination and carrying out of specific investigations,' they said at the Amsterdam summit. It will engage in 'operational actions' alongside national forces and be allowed to demand that national forces undertake specific inquiries. Tony Bunyan, from the civil liberties monitoring group Statewatch, noted that Europol officers will not only be free from irksome legal action, but will be under no obligation to have their characters and methods tested under cross-examination by appearing in a witness box when a suspect is charged.

Secrecy is so ubiquitous that judges will not even be able to ask the European Court of Justice to stop Europol if it exceeds its powers. The only person who can waive immunity for Europol officers is the director of Europol – who can hardly be regarded as independent.

In other words, an officer can be held to account for his actions in an operation against drugs in Moss Side if he is employed by the Greater Manchester Police, but not if he behaves in the same way in the same place when he is working for Europol. So what? The power and fortunes being amassed by gangsters made rich by the prohibition of drugs are terrifying. Surely a little latitude is permissible? But like many secret policemen before them, Europol doesn't not know where to stop. Their definition of 'organised crime' is so broad it covers minor offences carrying a six-month prison sentence. Hubris is already pushing them into some very strange areas. The annual report of the Europol Drugs Unit, the only part of the agency up and running, showed it had protected informants by allowing 33 'controlled deliveries' of drugs in 1996. No more information was given, but controlled deliveries often lead to uncontrolled disaster. The Dutch police, for example, are still recovering from the scandalous handling of controlled deliveries in which bent detectives allowed organised crime to run amok. Supposed informants were given immunity from prosecution (those words again) and allowed to sell their drugs and keep the profits. In all, 400 tonnes of cannabis and 10,000 kilos of cocaine arrived under police control – and then disappeared. Drugs worth £1.5 billion flooded Western Europe. At one point, Dutch detectives had to explain to bemused British Customs officers that they were responsible for 1.5 million Ecstasy tablets found at Sheerness. The grand result of this enormous enterprise was the prosecution of one criminal.

A Dutch parliamentary inquiry concluded that officers were bribed and that it was very hard to tell if they 'were fighting organised crime or a part of organised crime'. At least there was an inquiry in Holland, which eventually brought the facts out. It is impossible to see how the courts or anyone else will be able to investigate Europol's controlled deliveries.

The government showed no desire to be open when Europol was discussed in the Commons. David Heath, a Liberal Democrat, quoted Robin Cook, the Foreign Secretary, promising on 4 November that he 'would certainly resist any immunity being granted to Europol beyond anything that might be available to the national police'. Now that Cook has broken his promise, Heath said, there were 'grave concerns about civil liberties'. Faced with a serious inquiry, Fatchett came back with an asinine answer that wouldn't pass muster in a Surrey saloon bar. By daring to raise questions the Lib Dems were proving that they were – wait for it – 'on the side of the criminal'. Isn't it fantastic to know that our rights and security are in the hands of intelligent, far-sighted statesmen such as this?

Observer November 1997

LIGHTS, CAMERA, CRIMINALS

This notebook hopes to be fair as well as firm and would love to cover the government's achievements in fighting inequality and taming big business. For reasons beyond our control, there have been no successes to report. Never mind, we are determined to get with the programme or die in the attempt, and today – at last! – we have found a 24-carat nugget of helpful news. One election promise is about to be honoured: New Labour is to revive the British film industry. It will, unfortunately, be an ugly renaissance, complementing Hollywood's obsession with violence. All the stories will be made-for-TV crime movies. Strangeways and Bristol prisons will be turned into studios so cons can share their shameful yet fascinating lives with an audience of judges, lawyers and channel-hoppers in courtroom public galleries.

Jack Straw, the Michael Winner of Whitehall, will be auteur and impresario. I don't know if the concept, as we show-business reporters call it, was developed over lunch but suspect that if it was, alcohol was taken. It grew, like so many great works of fiction, out of the resolution of a terrible struggle. Rather than be tough on the causes of crime, a policy that would necessarily involve the redistribution of wealth,

New Labour is jailing more citizens than any government in modern history. The buzz of the surveillance camera and snarl of the dead-eyed judge are the sounds of swinging Britain. The costs of the new authoritarianism – all those warders, all those trials – are high, but Labour doesn't want to raise taxes. This is what used to be called a dilemma, which required politicians to commit to one principle or another. Fortunately, utopian faith in technology has dissolved the need for hard choices, which is where the movies come in. One of the most irksome features of the punishment boom is that millions have to be spent on moving prisoners from jails to courts. Secure cars are expensive, and guards and, in the case of dangerous prisoners, marksmen demand recompense for their labours. The solution, explains Mary Wilkinson, a member of the Civil Service's security group, is L!ve TV from prisons. There is no need to go to the trouble of putting defendants in front of magistrates. Cameras can beam images of inmates facing remand, bail and mode-of-trial applications into courts. Pilots will be made in Manchester and Bristol in the autumn and the show will go national next year.

The critics are already carping. Lawyers and probation officers ask how a suspect will pass confidential instructions to his lawyer when everyone can watch his supposedly secret talks to camera. The courts are already overwhelmed with the human consequences of New Labour and Old Conservative policies. Hearings are delayed for hours while ushers struggle to coordinate papers, witnesses and lawyers. It is commonplace for a hearing set for 11 am to be delayed until 3 pm, so prisoners would have to spend hours waiting in the jail studio to perform. The Law Society can see jams building up as inmates compete to be on camera at the precise moment when the judiciary is ready to give them their 15 minutes of fame. Dozens of cameras may be needed in an inner-city remand jail that would have wings resembling mini-Pinewoods. In any case, isn't there something sick about a system that can't look a man in the eye when it takes away his liberty?

Like a true artist, Straw is not deterred by sniping moaners. His next step will be to put video boxes in courts. The 200,000 or so people who struggle to find the money to meet judges' fines each year will be invited to key in their details and receive news on how they can pay by credit card. The thought that the only credit cards the poor have are stolen does not seem to have troubled him. Meanwhile, in Kent, the newest of technologies will be tested by the Home Office. Defendants will have to carry 'voice-track' pagers so they can be monitored as they move around the county. A sample of the criminal's voice will be taken and held in a central computer, says Dick Whitfield, Kent's chief probation officer. Offenders will be given BT pagers that bleep when officers want to find out where they are. They will then phone a freephone number and talk for the 30 seconds needed for the computer to establish the identity and location of the caller. I think even the most reactionary readers will agree that it is a cruel and unusual punishment to treat decent criminals as if they were members of the Parliamentary Labour Party.

In the Thirties, naive left-wingers gazed on Stalin's Soviet Union and cried: 'I have seen the future and it works!' In the Nineties, their equally gormless grandchildren gaze on Bill Gates's Microsoft and chant: 'I have seen the future and it's cheap!'

Observer June 1998

THE PUNISHMENT BOOM

On the plane that took Tony and Cherie to schmooze with Bill and Hillary were two tame wonks from the Downing Street Policy Unit. Geoff Mulgan and David Miliband were preparing to network with the president's aides and develop the theory that Blair and Clinton were following a Third Way, a new way for progressive politics, a way that leads to the old conflicts between left and right vanishing like rabbits in a magician's hat.

To the suspicious, their discourse was so much wasted breath: a risible attempt to intellectualise their masters' abasement before corporate power. And as if to prove the point, Jack Straw was on the flight. The Home Secretary had decided, quite brilliantly, that he must look for ideas on law and order in the United States, the most violent and repressive country in the West. While the Blairs were fêted in the White House, Straw was packed off to see crime prevention schemes in Baltimore. A Fleet Street hack was told to skip the Washington parties and accompany the Home Secretary. He grabbed me on his return and demanded a life-threateningly large whisky, without water. Straw didn't get it, he said. As they were driving back to Washington, the Home Secretary had turned to him and cooed: 'Do you know, people are safer walking the streets of American cities than they are in Britain.'

Really, Jack? How did you work that one out? Since Clinton came to power in 1992, the number of Americans in jail has risen from 1,200,000 to 1,800,000. Six million lives are administered by the police in the land of the free – that is, they're in prison, on probation or awaiting trial. Included in there somewhere are 40 per cent of young black men in Washington DC, Clinton's capital. The figures are so large, sober criminologists talk of an 'American gulag' where three new prisons open each week and $100 billion (£63 billion) a year is spent on private and public law enforcement. The number of prisoners is three times higher than in 1980, but, to the astonishment of criminologists, warehousing suspects has had little – according to some, no – effect on the cyclical rises and falls in crime. Most of those in jail have hurt no one. They get angry and violent, riot, take drugs, come out and commit further crimes and . . . well, you know the tired story.

A cluster of statistics from California remains fresh, however. At the end of the Second World War, the state had one of the best public education systems in the world. Unsurprisingly, its economy boomed. The realistic American political class who cause New Labour to thump the table in admiration is now diverting billions of dollars into the prisons budget. The money had to come from somewhere, and California now spends more on jails than higher education. By 2002, 18 per cent of the state's budget will be poured into law enforcement. The salaries of public servants reveal the priorities of the state government. Warders earn $55,000 (£34,500); teachers $43,000. Prison officers' unions and penal corporations have become a well-funded penal-industrial lobby that finances politicians willing to boost trade by passing yet more draconian laws to cower the unruly poor, which in turn create more prisoners and more prison officers willing to fund politicians willing to pass more laws.

Wide-eyed commentators assure us California is the laboratory of the future and the capital of modernity, and don't question the citizens of the former Soviet Union on the consequences for a country's prosperity of preferring incarceration to education. We're used to hearing them say that what happens in America will happen in Britain in five years. The parroted prediction was little more than an *Any Questions?* platitude – American particularism and religious fundamentalism were never for export. But New Labour politicians have turned a space filler in mediocre think-tank reports into a self-fulfilling prophecy. Their campaign strategies come from Little Rock, their welfare policies from Wisconsin, their economic policies from Chicago and their prison policies from California.

The punishment boom fostered by 'progressive' administrations from Blair's and Clinton's oxymoronic radical centre is the most striking feature of American leadership in Third Way politics and, therefore, the least discussed. Never before in British and American history have so many been in jail and have so many liberties been destroyed. Blair and Straw have presided over a rise in the prison population to 65,000, the highest on record and in Western Europe (and most of Eastern Europe now that even Bulgaria has become more liberal than us). In 1998 Britain needed a new prison every fortnight. The right to silence, a protection against torture that has existed since the English Civil War, has gone. Labour and Conservative politicians responded to the Birmingham Six, Guildford Four and Maguire scandals by making it harder for suspects to find if the police are hiding evidence that may clear them. The loss of freedom is on such a scale that French politicians can respond to lectures from Clinton on how his low-pay, low-welfare flexible country keeps unemployment down, by saying that if France were to jail a significant chunk of the poor her jobless figures would look much better. The Californian sociologist Mike Davis records a Los Angeles where gated estates, shopping and art centres and bankers' tower blocks have been designed to be as impregnable as an army barracks. The de facto and often de jure apartheid that separates white suburbs with their armed response units from the black and Latino ghettos deprived of every public service except a repressive police force, have turned Los Angeles into a city where public space and the mixing of classes are faded memories. Class segregation has produced 'counter-urbanisation' in which the ideal of a unified city has been abandoned. A militarised police and mass imprisonment have led to a level of repression that treats the poor as insurgents in a civil war. Davis is impatient with futurists who find inspiration in his home town. 'Most current giddy discussions of the "postmodern" scene in Los Angeles neglect entirely these overbearing aspects of counter-urbanisation and counter-insurgency,' he writes in *City of Quartz*. 'A triumphal gloss – "urban renaissance", "city of the future" and so on – is laid over the brutalisation of inner-city neighbourhoods and the increasing South Africanisation of its spatial relations. Even as the walls have come down in Eastern Europe, they are being erected all over Los Angeles.'

Mainstream Anglo-Saxon liberals miss the strong whiff of class war and lazily ascribe the progressives' love of jail to simple electoral pragmatism. Regrettably, they say, their patrons must be brutal to appeal to the mob and the mob's media. The choice is between idealism and power. If they're not elected how can they implement all the desirable policies which, we're sure you'll agree, every decent person feels the country needs. If the audience persists with rough questions, however, a harsher tone is heard. Crime is destructive, murderously so. The people want punishment and only arrogant elitists think of thwarting their wishes. Live in the real world.

But no amount of progressive bombast can explain why the radical centre's crime policies are more right wing than their conservative

predecessors. The connection between punishment and the willed collapse in faith in social democracy is rarely made. If you neither want nor
believe in the redistribution of wealth, social justice and restraints on
the rich, what else can you do with the lower orders but jail them when
they become uppity? The ostentatious piety of Blair and Clinton helps.
The humbug preacher is a stock character of satire from Chaucer onwards
for good reason. Self-righteousness gives him the capacity to believe his
lies as he tells them and to justify his opportunism without qualms.

Doubters who cling on to the belief that Blair and Straw are civilised
men should ask when either has adopted a hard line with reluctance as
a sad political necessity. Third-wayers do not embrace punishment like
a virgin sado-masochist shyly picking up the whip for the first time,
but with the energetic lust of an experienced spanker. Their policies
fail, inspire corruption and misery, but they do not care. British real-
ists cannot be touched by American reality, as the histories of mandatory sentences and prison corporations show.

In California, 20,000 are in jail under the 'three strikes and you are
out for life' programme. Many are drug users and petty criminals. In
one celebrated case the courts were forced to jail a man for 25 years
for stealing a slice of pizza because the filched carry-out was a third
strike. Crime has not fallen as a result (US states without a three strikes
policy are safer) but Californian politicians can adopt menacing postures and mug the electorate's intelligence. Three strikes has helped
turn the Los Angeles county jail into the West's largest lock-up. Twenty
thousand convicted and unconvicted inmates are jammed into cells built
for 12,000, and the authorities haven't a clue how to deal with the
resulting violence. Californian courts are gummed up with defendants
fighting with a well-motivated tenacity to prevent a third conviction.
With the legal system at the end of its tether, prison governors quietly release inmates who are not serving the mandatory three-strikes sentences so places are freed for the convicts they must keep in. California
puts potentially dangerous men on the streets while arbitrarily jailing
criminals who may be harmless but can never be let out.

The absurdity has not struck Clinton. In his 1996 presidential campaign he produced an advert featuring the father of Polly Klass, a 12-year-old who was kidnapped and murdered by a criminal on parole. Marc Klass, her father, praised Clinton's support for three strikes. The shroud was waved so vigorously it allowed the unthinkable, and Californians were treated to the spectacle of Bob Dole attacking Clinton from the moral high ground. Clinton 'was trying to exploit the savage murder of a little girl,' said a Dole spokeswoman, with a 'cynicism that borders on the extreme'. I cannot say and do not particularly care whether Straw and Blair are cynical (to use the word accurately for once) or deluded. All I can do is note that they are introducing three-strike laws to Britain.

In all likelihood the judges, instructed to abandon the search for sentences that match crimes, will shovel the convicts into private jails. Before the election Jack Straw was adamant that there would be no place for 'morally repugnant' private prisons in the New Britain. Penal capitalists who made money out of depriving defendants of their liberty undermined a democratic state by privatising one of its most basic functions: control of the liberty of the citizen. In government, the need to incarcerate brought a pragmatic shift. Straw told the Prison Officers' Association that he had learned to love corporations and their punishments because they were cheap. Private jails were 'between 8 and 15 per cent less costly than their counterparts in the public sector,' he said. 'They had lower staff ratios, lower staff costs, fewer staff holidays and, in many cases, a longer working week.' A Labour Home Secretary was gloating about the exploitation of workers and fantasising about a world where microchips and private initiative might free him from the contradictions of populism.

The party believes interactive technology can replace old-fashioned and expensive teachers, and computer polling on the issues of the day and citizens' juries can replace old-fashioned representative democracy – which was pronounced dead by Peter Mandelson. Techno-utopianism also offers an escape from the problems of running a country with low taxes and large prisons. We do not need to tax, even to build the new jails our populist conservatism has made necessary, because innovation will save us from hard choices.

Given the love of gadgets and the pervasive gee-whizzery, the Home Office was a soft touch in 1997 when Securicor came to sell the low-cost, hi-tech prison of the future. Parc jail in south Wales was to be like a kitchen at the Ideal Home Exhibition filled with labour-saving devices and computer chips that eliminated the need for work and thought. Just one underpaid officer at a desk could control 75 prisoners, the firm enthused. An intercom would allow him to talk to each inmate in his cell. Expensive security patrols would be unnecessary: doors would be automatically locked from a central control system. Smart cards would let the lags buy goods from the shop. Parc would tick over with a minimum of human intervention.

The first suicide was within two weeks of the prison opening. David Jenkins was known to be a risk to himself. He tried to slash his wrists at the magistrates court when he was sentenced but Parc's tiny band of officers could not stop him taking his life. Dallas Lee, a 27-year-old, was the next to go. He was found hanging from a strap in his cell. By then, his fellow convicts had had it with Securicor. They mutinied and refused to obey the company's orders until a long list of grievances was addressed. The much-vaunted computer system crashed repeatedly. Despised state prison officers were called in to contain violence. Jim Heyes (the jail's head of programmes), Bernard Higgins (its first director) and Tony French (its second governor) all left for 'personal reasons'. Staff, most of whom had no previous experience of working with prisoners, described how drug-taking and racial tension were tearing the jail apart. One said: 'There's no respect for officers. Prisoners know there is no control.' The Prison Governors Association told the story of two building contractors who were walking through the jail with a ladder. They stopped by the gate and leant the ladder on a wall while they waited to be let out. Officers, assuming they had a breakout on their hands, stripped them and threw them into the isolation block.

To be fair, Securicor has invested in essentials. It hired one of the most expensive PR companies in the country, Bell Pottinger Good Relations, to salvage its reputation. David Hill, a new director, has muttered the words 'teething troubles' and 'minor difficulties' in journalists' ears. He was a senior Labour spin doctor who worked for the party when it opposed private prisons. The firm pays him a six-figure sum, which he earns by networking with his former friends and colleagues.

I'm sure he will have no problems with a government that has encouraged the penal-industrial complex by making Britain the fastest-growing private prison market in the world. The Corrections Corporation of America (CCA), which runs Blakenhurst Prison, near Worcester, is one of the firms Straw has in mind when he boasts about the savings free enterprise can bring. In 1996 the American General Accounting Office reported that a CCA prison in Tennessee cost only one per cent less to operate than comparable state jails. Saving public money was not necessarily the issue of choice for the businessmen and politicians carving up the prison system. The first CCA contract in Tennessee was renewed by state commissioners whose number included one who had been given a pest control contract by CCA, a second who received work landscaping its grounds, a third who ran the removal firm that settled the warden into his new home, and a fourth whose son was on the CCA payroll. To get the profits that make it the darling of Wall Street, CCA cuts back on staff and care for prisoners. 'We give them the bare minimum,' said a CCA warder. 'We're always short [of staff],' added a colleague. 'That's how we keep costs down.' Attacks on inmates and guards in one Tennessee jail it manages are 50 per cent higher than in public prisons.

The scandals have no effect on the demand for CCA jails. The Third Way not only abdicates democratic control of law and order but does not presume to act as a mere regulator. CCA has flourished in the moral and political vacuum. Its value grew from $50 million in 1986 to $3.5 billion in 1996 – a record that has drawn admiring purrs of 'crime pays' from financial analysts. CCA's philosophy was neatly expressed by Thomas Beasley, a co-founder of the company, who sees no reason to fear that progressive governments will threaten his profits. You can sell the idea of private prisons, he said, 'like you were selling cars or real estate or hamburgers'.

What is the Third Way? It is the road that takes us further to the right than we have ever been before.

Observer 1997–8

CHAPTER FOUR

THE NEWS IS WHAT WE SAY IT IS

THE DEATH OF NEWS

Just after the 1997 general election, Peter Horrocks, the editor of *Newsnight*, told his staff that the days of digging up facts that might disconcert the powerful had passed. 'Labour has a huge mandate,' he wrote. 'Our job should not be to quarrel with the purpose of policy but question its implementation. Ennui is over for now.' In the unlikely event of his minions mistaking his meaning, Horrocks deployed the English establishment's most condescending put-down to get them on message. 'Clever-clever' questioning of the warm, new consensus was inappropriate. *Newsnight*'s tradition of sceptical inquiry was mere 'tricksiness and world-weariness'. What the show needed was a 'lighter feel'. And, by God, it quickly got it. Sian Kevill, his successor, was equally confident that the times required fluffier hacks. At a conference in 1998, she ruled that the old class and ideological conflicts that generated news were history – and the world was a better place for it. Her only difficulty with modernity was logistical. New Labour's spin doctors controlled their party tightly and she could not always shepherd into the studio the ministers she wanted to grill (presumably lightly). Short of consulting Mystic Meg or reading *The Times*, an on-the-record interview

123

with a media-literate politician is the worst possible way of eliciting information the government would prefer to keep hidden (all you can do is make them sound shifty, as exasperated *Today* programme listeners know). Kevill might have considered hiring clever journalists instead and sending them into the world to investigate and report, but the notion did not seem to have occurred to her.

The love of lightness at a BBC current affairs programme whose name is flourished as a trump card at those who wonder if the network is hurtling into crassness, makes evident a crisis in liberal news. Kevill and Horrocks are authentic representatives of a media management class that has turned the coverage of issues of public importance – regardless of whether the public wants to know about them, by reporters who make a stab at getting it right – into an insecure vocation. Wherever you look, practitioners of investigative reporting are nervous and unloved. Downsizing capitalism has shrunk newsrooms. The questioning by the dominant intellectual fashion of postmodernism of the possibility and desirability of accurate reporting has sapped self-confidence.

In the Fifties the most revered newspaper journalists were reporters: crime and foreign correspondents. Some, such as James Cameron and Martha Gellhorn, became household names, but a list of the great and the dead misses the ethos of a time when the *Sheffield Morning Telegraph* earned enormous kudos for becoming the first paper to expose police brutality. Most journalism was rarely brilliant and often feeble; London crime correspondents, for example, failed to cover the wanton corruption in Scotland Yard in the 1960s. But reporting – the best way of getting under the skin of a society if you wish to be radical, or of finding something more interesting to write about than yourself and your favourite restaurants if you do not – produced a grubby, semi-skilled, but proud sub-culture in which almost all journalists spent their lives and earned what prestige the despised trade offered.

Today, if you want to get ahead, get a column, preferably with a blurred picture of your puffy face at the head. During the last of the *Independent*'s innumerable crises, its rivals decided to weaken the competition by capturing its stars. Offers were made to Polly Toynbee, Andrew Marr and Suzanne Moore, all columnists. To my knowledge no one bid for Robert Fisk, the brilliant Middle East correspondent. There are, I would guess, only a handful of newspaper reporters left whose names produce a flicker of recognition. TV journalists are stopped in the street, but they are known for their moist eyes and gym-toned bodies, not their work, and might as well be actors. Locally and nationally in broadsheets, tabloids, radio and television, news is dying.

With their customary insight, expert opiners have decided we are living in an information age; a time when we can learn all we want to know and much, much more from CNN, Sky, BBC 24-hour news, weekend papers the size of paving stones, Radio 5 and a *Today* programme that drones on for half the morning. But faith in the abundance of information vaporises when you examine how rolling news channels repeat unreflective reports again and again – with intermittent breaks for smiling experts who compete to see who can fit the most platitudes into one sentence. Those who believe in the information revolution should measure the space in newspapers filled with consumer and show-business journalism, trite features and opinion from the same pundits who – the best fat can be chewed for ever – will be back on television later in the day to read out their columns. Why is it that local papers cannot thrill you with pleasing tales of how the magistrate punished your neighbours' petty crimes? Or national papers say what actually happened in the Commons or Middle East as opposed to what commentators think happened or would like to have happened?

Ian Jack, one of the many former editors of the *Independent on Sunday*, described Britain as having 'a singular sort of media culture which places a high premium on excitement, controversy and sentimentality and where information takes second place to the opinion it arouses'. He was being far too optimistic. Real controversy necessarily allows polarisation. Yet in the days following the death of Diana Spencer, the most intensively reported week of the decade, ITV apologised for interviewing an academic who dared to balance Didolatry by doubting the

Princess was a saint, and BBC Radio 4 pulled *Feedback*, a programme that is meant to give listeners the chance to complain, because it did not want to broadcast a selection from the hundreds of letters protesting about its dopey coverage. Grief was permitted, practically required, grievance was stifled. Choice in journalism, as in so many other areas, is a choice between hundreds of outlets packed with the same stock.

Shallow uniformity is not an accident but a consequence of what Marxists optimistically call late capitalism. Anglo-Saxon economies put short-term gains for transient shareholders above the long-term future of organisations. In the media, news is the first casualty because it is time-consuming to collect and, when a tip-off involves investigation, managers cannot guarantee that there will be a story they can run when the hacks finish their investigations. By contrast, lifestyle pieces, opinion polls, interviews, ruminations on 'Aren't husbands horrid?' 'Is the New Lad dead?' or 'Does Tony Blair hate Gordon Brown?' are cheap and certain. The staff count of national newspapers has not changed since the Sixties but the size of newspapers has doubled: the same number of people are doing twice the work. Thirty years ago, one-third of journalists were based outside London – either in the regions or on foreign postings. Their job was to report the world beyond head office. Now no national newspaper has a staff reporter in Wales, which may as well not exist as far as Fleet Street is concerned, and 90 per cent of national journalists work in London. Most are penned in the compounds of Canary Wharf and Wapping, where barbed wire, private security patrols, CCTV cameras and card swipers on every door emphasise their isolation from the country they are meant to cover. News comes via agencies or on the telephone or from one of the few businesses to survive the combined onslaughts of Margaret Thatcher and Gordon Brown – the PR industry. David Michie, a City public relations consultant, calculates that the number of PR companies and departments grew from 766 in 1967 to 9,200 in 1997. The business is worth £2.3 billion a year and appears to be recession-proof. There are now 25,000 PRs in Britain and 50,000 journalists – one persuader for every two mediators. Admittedly, the UK has yet to catch up with America where PRs outnumber journalists and can engage in man-to-man marking, but the trend is unmistakable and parity is merely a matter of time. Michie's colleague, Quentin Bell, estimated that 80 per cent of business news and 40 per cent of general news comes straight from the mouths of PRs. It is worth considering at this point the stories that weren't printed while ready-cooked pap was spooned into papers; the leads that were ignored, the articles that were spiked because reporters did not want to alienate essential contacts who provide the stream of 'news' cost-cutting managers need to fill space. Many journalists affect to despise PRs. 'Everything that ever has been said, is being said and will be said by a PR is, by definition a lie,' reads one rule in a spoof set of instructions for leftie hacks *Observer* reporters give new recruits. Yet we rarely insult them to their face. Drowning men do not curse lifeboats.

From television, Martin Bell warns that modern technology is bringing an age of tosh rather than information. Reporters covering a war can no longer disappear for a few days with their crew, talk to people, smell the air and generally get a vague idea of what, if anything, is going on. Satellite communication allows constant contact with a price-conscious head office, grateful that it can always put an often clueless reporter in a khaki suit and spotless flak jacket on air within minutes of the flight touching down. Even the best journalists are suffering. Jean Seaton, a media academic, invited civil servants and reporters to a conference on freedom of information. Britain being the way it is, the meeting was held in secret. The mandarins said they were desperate to get information out and would be delighted if reporters examined official documents because specialists might spot problems the Civil Service had missed. (Yes I know, I don't believe it either. I'm just reporting what was said.) Nicholas Timmins, the ferociously learned social services correspondent of the *Financial Times* and author of the standard history of the welfare state, looked at them glumly. It was simply impossible in the modern newspaper industry to spend time reading voluminous files, he said, even if there was every likelihood he would find an interesting nugget or two. There wasn't the time.

In my darker moments, I wonder where the next Timmins will come from. He belongs to a generation of reporters who were required, thanks to union agreements, to spend three years in the regions before they worked on a national newspaper. By the time you arrived in London, you had a basic knowledge of law and government. You also noticed as you plodded the streets of Bristol or Sheffield that the vast majority of people in Britain shared few of your interests. I was hired by the *Independent* in 1987, after working in Birmingham. I had a secure contract, a salary of £21,000 and was surrounded by trained journalists with a craft pride in their job and a condescension which, on the frequent occasions drink was taken, bordered on contempt for colleagues who were not hard enough to file hard news. By the time I left in 1996, reporters were impotent and sober. What little industrial power they had disappeared when the print unions were crushed by Rupert Murdoch at Wapping, although most journalists were too snobbish to realise that their fate was tied to that of rude mechanicals at the time. Solemn agreements had been torn up and untrained newsroom fodder without contacts or discernible knowledge was being recruited straight from college to a national paper for £10,000 a head. They were, like many others in Fleet Street and television, on casual contracts that encouraged docility.

It is doubtless Spartist to mention the other, more obvious, pressure to conform. But boring though it may be to dwell on the subject, the fact remains that 90 per cent of national newspaper circulations are controlled by five men: Rupert Murdoch, Conrad Black, David Montgomery and My Lords Hollick and Rothermere. Two are foreigners. All are rich and anti-union – a combination that notoriously restricts the range of events they allow to be covered. All, with the exception of Rothermere, have squeezed news and used their papers as cash cows. Freedom of the press means the freedom for these gentlemen to do what they want. They, and their counterparts in television, have changed journalism from a trade that encouraged reporters to develop specialist knowledge to a kind of feudal system with a few over-paid managers, columnists and newscasters at the top and a mass of casual, pressured and often ignorant serfs underneath.

In place of wide-ranging coverage the papers are filled with the temporary enthusiasms of media managers whose members can be divided between those who think north London is the centre of the world and those who think north London is the world. Their seclusion explains the media's otherwise inexplicable susceptibility to metropolitan crazes and self-reference; a mentality that can assume the nation is obsessed by the failure of Rupert Murdoch's marriage one week and Hanif Kureishi's the next.

Although it is easy and necessary to mock them, the dynamic behind what is dumbly called dumbing down is the result of an economic revolution rather than the witlessness of managers. The great change in Anglo-Saxon capitalism since the Seventies has been the rise in power of shareholders who have the most fleeting interest in the long-term health of businesses. You do not hear now from the economists who once maintained that investors were all but irrelevant. J. K. Galbraith accurately described a post-war world where influence lay with professional managers who could cut profits to allow the long-term growth of a business. Shareholders could not stop them, because they did not know how to run complex corporations and develop alternative strategies. The managers themselves were constrained by the regulations of Keynesian societies that emphasised stability, security and growth – as well as profitability – were legitimate goals. Obviously, a disastrously managed company would suffer a flight of capital, but managers with elementary levels of competence, who could keep up with innovation in their industry, faced few pressures and received protection from government. They were not, as Galbraith repeatedly emphasised, the risk-taking buccaneers of capitalist myth, but administrators who were not very different from the state bureaucrats who had such a large say in the running of their businesses.

Shareholders, encouraged by deregulatory governments, have broken out of the social democratic prison by becoming footloose. If a corporation does not produce short-term profits, they sell and the company faces takeover or closure. Meanwhile the invention of share options has given managers the most basic of reasons to keep share prices high, regardless of the often lamentable consequences for their companies. Galbraith's conflicts of interest between managers and share-holders no longer exist. The two groups have merged, a union seen at its most striking in the British media in the gilded but calamitous career of David Montgomery.

The Fool Monty, as his employees call him without affection, had great power. For several years he controlled five of the 20 national newspapers – the *Mirror*, *Sunday Mirror*, *People*, *Independent* and *Independent on Sunday* as well as the *Scottish Daily Record*, *Birmingham Post & Mail*, *Sporting Life* and L!VE TV. By any rational standard, his record was appalling. Every paper he ran saw sales fall. The *Mirror* went from 2.8 million in 1993 to 2.3 million in January 1998. The *Independent* and *Independent on Sunday* all but closed. The *Sporting Life* did close. Wave after wave of journalists walked out or were made redundant. They were replaced, when they were replaced, with cheap staff on casual con-tracts. Young reporters were offered salaries of £0.0 on L!VE TV and told they were privileged to be gaining invaluable experience by work-ing for nothing. The average editor was lucky to last long enough to enjoy 15 minutes of fame. Yet investors did not mind. Far from being a failure, Montgomery was a brilliant success. He cut costs faster than he lost readers and produced quick profits. He was both shareholder and manager. Between 1996 and 1998 he made £2.4 million from share options. He will go, eventually, I'm sure. As the sackings multiplied, the City started to notice that the hollowed-out empire was in trouble and to whisper that perhaps Monty wasn't the right man after all. But this, too, is part of the process: the moment when the short-term hits the long-term and horrified fund managers look at the wreckage and deny all responsibility for the drunk driver they put behind the wheel.

The vitriol Montgomery attracts makes him seem uniquely awful, but there is nothing exceptional about him. In 1998 American readers of the usually staid *Columbia Journalism Review* were presented with a special issue on the asset-stripping of the media which a swivel-eyed revolutionary might have found excessive. 'If a story needs a real investment we don't do it anymore,' said a reporter from a Mid-West daily. 'Instead of racing out of the newsroom with a camera crew when an important story breaks, we're more likely to stay at our desks and work the phones,' agreed a network television reporter. Editors described continual pressures to cut margins to unsustainably low levels and the collapse of reporting. 'A new era has dawned in American journalism,' the review concluded, 'with a massively increased sensitivity to all things financial. As print and TV news outlets purvey more "life-style" stories, trivia, scandal, celebrity gossip, sensational crime, sex in high places, and tabloidism at the expense of serious news; as editors collude ever more willingly with marketers, promotion "experts," and advertisers, thus ceding a portion of their sacred editorial trust; as editors shrink from tough coverage of major advertisers lest they jeopardise revenue; as news executives cut muscle and sinew from budgets to satisfy their corporate overseers' demands for higher profit margins each year; as top managers fail to reinvest profits in staff training, investigative reports, salaries, plant, and equipment – then the broadly-felt consequence is a diminished and deracinated journalism of a sort that hasn't been seen in this country until now and which, if it persists, will be a fatal erosion of the ancient bond between journalists and the public.'

Quite so. But the casino capitalism that the review laments does not operate in an intellectual vacuum. It was the fate of the luckless hack that the drying up of the money to cover news coincided with an intellectual shift that undermined the will to report. This is not the place for a discussion of the crypto-conservative philosophy of postmodernism (nowhere is), but the subjectivity of our age has subverted the belief that there are events of importance that can – indeed, must – be reported. You do not have to strain too hard to grasp the connection between Baudrillard's claim that the Gulf War did not happen and Murdoch's boast that it did not matter that the Hitler Diaries were fake because newspapers were in the 'entertainment business'.

It may seem unnecessarily lofty to claim that something as self-consciously obscurantist as postmodern philosophy can affect a trade as prosaic as journalism. But all times have their dominant ideologies that influence popular attitudes. When great writers, causes, texts, genders and nature are dismissed as false constructs, the confessional and the solipsistic can seem the last refuge of authenticity. People who blurt out their most intimate secrets on television and in personal columns appear to be truthful in a world where everything is suspect, even though the emotionally honest are often the biggest liars of all.

The economic and the ideological biases against journalism have produced a fatalism on Fleet Street which takes the decline in news as a given; where anyone interested in finding out about the world is 'boring' or a 'miserabilist' if they write badly, and a 'ranter' if they write well. As I am banging out this piece, a copy of the London *Evening Standard* lands on my desk, and it seems perfectly natural that the front page should puff articles on 'Why blond men have more fun', 'Where the big girls boogie' and 'The rise of the PR girl'. It takes an effort to ask: who on earth wants to read this? Or, as pertinently: who on earth wants to write it? You do not find a great deal of self-doubt in media boardrooms. People in power are generally able to intellectualise financial necessity, and newspapers editors do not as a rule wring their hands and say that they would love to hire more reporters if only they could. On the rare occasions editorial priorities are questioned, doubters are told television has taken the place of papers in breaking news. Yet broadcasters have never been able to match the depth and scope of a serious newspaper. In any case, quality television journalism was the product of the tightly regulated BBC-ITV duopoly. Now that dozens of new channels are opening, not only *Newsnight* but *Panorama*, *World in Action*, *News at Ten*, *Channel 4 News*, *The World Tonight*, *Dispatches*, the *Today* programme and the World Service have been cretinised or are under threat. Resistance is tame because at the back of liberal journalists' minds is the nagging suspicion that the public do not want to be informed. (And in truth, it is difficult to sustain a belief in the intelligence of your fellow citizens when the *Sun* is the biggest-selling newspaper.) As audiences dwindle – newspapers have been in continuous decline for a quarter of a century – hysteria follows. 'How can we get more readers/viewers?' cry managers. 'Let's redesign, hire management consultants, move upmarket – no, downmarket – appeal to single women worried about their bottoms, middle-aged men worried about their potency, fire everyone and hire A. A. Gill, do something, do anything except concentrate on the business of collecting and presenting news.'

From this standpoint, the rise of trash appears inevitable, but there is nothing preordained about it. Bad journalism is a consequence of an unregulated market in which would-be monopolists are free to treat the channels of democratic debate as their private property. Jean Seaton is the co-author with James Curran of *Power Without Responsibility*, the best guide to the British media. It ends with a series of modest proposals. The independence of the BBC should be strengthened and all broadcasters should be made to follow public service standards. There should be free channels open to civic groups and small programme-makers. Journalists should have a legal right to refuse to break their code of conduct. The media oligopoly should be broken.

These are mild and achievable democratic socialist policies that a determined administration might implement within months. Unfortunately it is hard to imagine reform while we have a Prime Minister who cannot control his tongue when Rupert Murdoch's posterior passes by. The invariably foolish and occasionally depraved world of British journalism seems likely to continue its raucous decline into irrelevance.

New Statesman June 1998

PS   Montgomery was compelled to leave the Mirror Group in January 1999, a dismissal made less traumatic by the receipt of £2 million in compensation. None of the conceivable new owners of the group has a strategy to release it from the spiral of downsized decline. The world of British documentary making was briefly shaken when Carlton television was found to have broadcast a film about drug-smuggling from South America which was a fraud. Carlton did not lose its licence.

BEYOND THE FRINGE

Tom Lehrer abandoned his piano and stifled the urge to write satirical songs in 1973 when Henry Kissinger received the Nobel Peace Prize. Lehrer reasonably concluded that if the man who had paved the way for Pol Pot by bombing neutral Cambodia 'back to the Stone Age' was to be blessed as a peacemaker, 'political satire had become obsolete'. What then would be the reasonable response to the following full-page advertisement in *Variety* – 'The International Entertainment Weekly'? Under the headline 'Leading the way to a Better World', the United Jewish Appeal Federation proudly informs readers that at the Waldorf-Astoria, New York City, on 29 May its Humanitarian of the Year Award will be bestowed by Dr Henry A. Kissinger on Rupert Murdoch, in recognition of his 'global philanthropic efforts'.

A sick joke? Not at all. A call to Norman Eisenberg, the federation's director of corporate affairs, reveals that Murdoch and Kissinger will be fêted with solemn sincerity. Murdoch is to be acclaimed for supporting Israel and upholding human rights, particularly the rights of persecuted Jews in the former Soviet Union. Kissinger had been 'a controversial figure' after the massacre of millions in south-east Asia, Eisenberg conceded. But the controversy had died after 'a couple of years' and he was now a valued member of New York society. The federation is not a home for the crazies of the Jewish right. Although much of the $700 million it raises each year goes to help Jews settle in Israel, no money is spent in the occupied territories. Palestinians may wonder on whose land the immigrants will eventually find a home, but by American standards federation members are moderates. Tickets are $1,000 a head, and Eisenberg's colleagues are confident 1,000 guests (mainly from the film industry) will pay to watch the rare spectacle in the hotel's grand ballroom.

These people are, in short, serious. And we must be, too. First there is a parochial matter, which may interest the federation, of the support the born-again Christian Murdoch gave to the television evangelist Pat Robertson when he ran for the US presidency in 1988. As well as claiming to have the power to cure cancer victims and turn away hurricanes with his prayers, Robertson thought he had found a 'conspiracy of European bankers' against America in which the Jewish Rothschild family provided the 'missing link between the occult and the world of high finance'. I don't know about you, but I'm sure I have heard about this conspiracy before. In his biography, *Full Disclosure*, Andrew Neil, ex-editor of the *Sunday Times*, describes his former employer as 'much more right wing than is generally thought'. He buys the Moral Majority's combination of free markets, tough laws, superstition and the policing of other people's bodies as a job lot and told Neil in 1988: 'You can say what you like, but he [Robertson] is right on all the issues.'

On the wider stage, both Kissinger and Murdoch have been busily displaying their humanitarianism in the Nineties. Kissinger has been handicapped by being out of power since 1976. His last acts of statesmanship were to cut off American aid to the revolting Kurds of Iraq, leaving them to the mercy of Saddam Hussein, and to sanction Indonesia's genocidal invasion of East Timor. Yet, despite his disabilities, he has still been able to bow his head to brute force. He was hired by US companies to lobby the Chinese dictatorship, which remembers him as the architect of Richard Nixon's detente with China. After the Tiananmen Square massacre he excused the killing and argued against sanctions. He is always on hand to deliver sermons against the West 'imposing' its human rights standards on Asia. Last year in Washington the Richard Nixon Centre for Peace and Freedom – I swear I'm not making this up, international directory inquiries will give you the number – honoured Lee Kuan Yew, the capo of Singapore, as an 'Architect of the New Century'. Even former Nixon officials found the grovelling too much to bear. But Kissinger was happy. 'I enthusiastically endorse his coming,' he said. 'He's a great man.'

Murdoch has been equally eager to serve the Chinese. He threw BBC World Service TV off his Star Asian satellite because the BBC's straight reporting on China was annoying Beijing. Murdoch's Harper-Collins has published a Robert Maxwell-style hagiography of the late Deng Xiaoping, and the political chief of the *People's Daily*, the regime's mouthpiece, was invited to London by Murdoch's *Times*. Neil believes he lost his job because he threatened Murdoch's potential to expand in the Far East. The authoritarian Malaysian Prime Minister, Mahathir Mohamed, did not like *Sunday Times* stories of how kickbacks had been used and the British aid budget abused to build the Pergau dam in return for Malaysia punting an arms contract Britain's way. Neil quotes a British diplomat saying that Mahathir 'made it clear that Murdoch would never do business in his country again as long as Andrew Neil was editor'. While dictators are cosseted, wet democrats are treated with contempt. Kissinger started the paranoid fear of leaks which led to the Watergate scandal and Nixon's resignation. For good measure, he helped to overthrow the democratic government of Chile. Murdoch and his newspapers loved Margaret Thatcher, but despised her weak successor. He has every right to be scornful. Thatcher (the last Prime Minister), John Major (the current Prime Minister) and Tony Blair (the next Prime Minister) debased themselves – and us – by begging Murdoch to support them in the run-up to the election.

What would Lehrer make of a world where Kissinger, a man stained with everyone's blood but his own, and Murdoch, the dictators' facilitator, are the guests of honour at a humanitarian dinner? I hadn't the faintest idea, so I phoned him. His admirers will be pleased to learn that despite the provocation given by events since 1973, he has not fled to join a Paraguayan monastic order or locked himself in his piano and refused to come out. He is teaching maths at the University of California in Santa Cruz and sounded very chirpy until I told him about Kissinger and Murdoch. 'Oh dear,' he said. 'I suppose it's like Mother Teresa winning Woman of the Year from the Planned Parenthood Federation. It's mind-boggling.'

Observer March 1997

PS   The Murdoch organisation was integrated into the New Labour establishment as employees of both shifted between the two. Murdoch enjoyed many meetings with the new Prime Minister and his influence helped dilute the party's commitments to the European single currency and trade union rights. Kissinger was also welcomed into the Prime Minister's office. A Downing Street spokesman said Blair saw him as a friend whose advice on statesmanship he respected. After the judges ruled that Augusto Pinochet and other murderous statesmen might have to answer for their actions, however, a few hoped he would find pressing reasons not to return to London.

MODIFIED NEWS

Sweet and reasonable corporate voices have been muttering in all the best ears. Editors have been squared in private meetings and politicians lobbied in the Palace of Westminster. Advertising agencies followed up the charming of opinion-formers with a £1 million campaign to convince the nation that genetically engineered food presented no threat whatsoever to public health.

The persuaders from the American bio-technology conglomerate, Monsanto, appeared to have an unenviable task. Monsanto seeds are designed to maximise its profits. They have had genes spliced in their

DNA, which allows crops to tolerate expensive herbicides made, naturally (or, rather, unnaturally), by Monsanto. The tinkering with plants' genetic code will allow farmers to spray poisons on their fields with abandon and without risking the destruction of their crops. Sober scientists warn of the danger that genes will jump from the crops into weeds, creating new species of super weeds with a resistance to herbicides. Their more alarmist colleagues talk of genetically manipulated organisms running amok in ecosystems that cannot handle them, like mink in the Norfolk Broads, and worry about how crops injected with the genes of bacteria, viruses, fish and insects will affect the 8 per cent of children who cannot keep their dinners down because they are allergic to industrial food. Yet apart from a heated meeting at *The Guardian* ('Do you guys have something against American multi-nationals?' bellowed an angry man from Monsanto. 'Er, yes, actually we do.'), the company met little resistance. *The Economist* reinforced its reputation as the tired voice of conventional wisdom when it made a defence of the gene manipulators its lead item: those who opposed agribusiness were Luddites, it thundered. And, in truth, environmentalists were made to look ungracious by Monsanto's advertisements, which presented the company as an exceptionally fair-minded conglomerate. The firm promised to supply readers with the addresses of vocal critics of the food industry. It was rare for a company to give free publicity to its opponents, Monsanto boasted, 'but we believe that food is so fundamentally important, everyone should know all they want to about it'.

The claim that here was an open company willing to take on its critics in free debate raised hollow laughs on the other side of the Atlantic. The American press is beginning to notice a scandal at a Florida TV station owned by Rupert Murdoch. Two of the station's reporters investigated Monsanto and allege they were bullied, censored and then fired for their presumption. Their case raises the question whether media owned by multi-nationals can honestly investigate corporate power. The answer, as far as Jane Akre and Steve Wilson are concerned, is clear enough. The husband and wife team joined Tampa's WTVT station, a subsidiary of Murdoch's Fox TV, in November 1996. They were reporters with decades of experience rather than radical, young hotheads out to make trouble. Their job was to break news, and Akre found what looked like a scoop. Florida's milk was coming from cows fed with an artificial Monsanto hormone called BGH. The hormone is legal in the United States but was banned in many European countries after suggestions from medical researchers that it may lead to cancer of the human colon. Florida supermarkets admitted that they had quietly broken a promise not to buy milk from farms that used the hormone and were supplying it to their unsuspecting customers. Wilson said: 'We found farmers who said the company wasn't properly reporting the drug's adverse effects on animals, a charge Monsanto eventually acknowledged. We also documented how Monsanto was using its legal and political muscle to oppose labelling efforts that would have helped consumers make a choice.'

WTVT thought it had a great story and booked radio ads to promote the investigation. Just before the reports were due to be aired, Monsanto's lawyers contacted executives at Fox TV's head office and complained that the documentaries were inaccurate. WTVT went through the reports and told Fox managers they could not fault their journalists' work. Fox disagreed, the programme was pulled and Wilson and Akre were sentenced to a Sisyphean punishment. They were ordered to write and rewrite the script 70 times. Each time they presented a fresh draft it was rejected. They could not understand what was happening and told David Boylan, a Murdoch manager sent by Fox to Florida, that valid, well-sourced research was being stifled. Boylan's reply broke with all the traditions of media management. In a moment of insane candour, he told an unvarnished truth that should be framed and stuck on the top of every television set. 'We paid $3 billion for these television stations,' he snapped. 'We'll decide what the news is. News is what we say it is.'

According to documents supporting a court case the journalists are bringing against Fox, Murdoch's people insisted the reporters accept that 'the public can be confident that milk from BGH-treated cows is safe'. Monsanto told Fox that it had studies to support the assertion. Wilson and Akre said the studies were of cows, not humans. They claim the management replied with: 'That's what Monsanto want, put it in.' The couple refused, saying they would not broadcast false reports. At one point the station offered them 'large cash settlements' on condition they never talked about the hormone or how Fox handled news. They refused to be bought off and were ordered to carry on changing their script despite being locked out of their offices at one point. After a year of fighting Fox, they were fired in December 1997. Their report was never aired. Fox accuses its journalists of having 'delusions of grandeur' and being 'advocates' for consumers. The hacks say the management could not point to a single factual error in their documentaries.

Murdoch owns, among many, many other companies, Actmedia, a PR firm that counts Monsanto as one of its clients. But Akre and Wilson do not believe they were silenced to avoid upsetting one of the old brute's customers. They see censorship as the natural consequence of the domination of communications by businesses whose owners have more in common with the perpetrators of scandals than with their audiences.

'We set out to tell the truth about a giant chemical company,' said Wilson. 'That used to be something reporters won awards for. As we've learnt the hard way, it's something you can be fired for these days.'

Observer July 1998

RUPERT THE BLAIR

Only the mad, drunk or drug-dependent could have imagined denunciations of 'cronyism' and 'protectionism' falling from the lips of Rupert Murdoch. But there the angry old man was at the European Audio-Visual conference in Birmingham cursing . . . Who? What? His new crony, Tony Blair, who will shortly force Labour MPs to endorse the elderly monopolist's drive to eliminate his business rivals? A tractable government that offers him access and privileges in return for 'helpful' coverage? Tycoons do not as a rule commit suicide in public, regrettably. An unblushing Rupert was on his hind legs to traduce the BBC for daring to compete with BSkyB by establishing a 24-hour news channel.

The few journalists present whose careers did not depend on him eagerly scanned the audience of mediacrats and Euro-pols. Robin Cook was in the throng, listening carefully to a man who owns nearly all of the Australian, much of the American and a slice of the Chinese media; as well as, in his British outpost, the *Sun*, *The Times*, *News of the World*, *Sunday Times*, BSkyB and a chit for the soul of the Prime Minister. Reporters who had followed and admired the Foreign Secretary over the years thought they knew he rejected everything Murdoch represents and looked forward to a scrap. They had seen Cook and the Culture Secretary, Chris Smith, greet Murdoch warmly. He sat at their table. The ministers smiled when Murdoch smiled; were grave when he was troubled. Yet the hacks knew that the necessary insincerities of political small-talk would soon be over. They had scanned advance copies of Cook's speech and highlighted pointed passages intended, surely, to send the defiantly democratic message to Murdoch that the government would defend British culture from the crushing power of the global entertainment conglomerates.

Murdoch seemed to play into Cook's hands as he gave a speech of breath-catching speciousness. Public service television stations – the BBC, ITV and Channel 4 – were feather-bedded recipients of special favours, he ranted, while the plucky swashbuckling little Murdoch fought bravely in the bracing air of competitive capitalism. 'We are about change and progress, not about protectionism through legislation and cronyism. We are about vigorous competition, not about whingeing or distorting the market,' he whinged. The BBC's 24-hour news channel was singled out for special contempt. It was in breach of its charter and therefore,

I suppose, illegal. With his entrance prepared by the patsy, Cook, the man who savaged the Conservatives Murdoch devoted so much time and wasted ink to supporting, took the stage – beard neatly trimmed, voice purposeful and persuasive – and said . . . absolutely nothing. The paragraphs that might have challenged Murdoch were dropped from his speech at the last minute. Why? asked the non-Murdoch correspondents afterwards. Why does the Foreign Secretary have to prostrate himself before trash like that? Cook's lip curled. The deletions had been made 'completely because of pressure of time', he exploded. There was nothing sinister. No tricks. 'You think there's a conspiracy? You people see conspiracies everywhere.'

I can understand that a minister with the affairs of the world and secret marriages to arrange may be forced to speed read. I have also heard politicians complain that jumped-up modern reporters are far more interested in punditry and scandal-mongering than the lowly but wholesome task of reporting political speeches accurately and without interpretation. So here, in the interests of making the first draft of history as reliable as possible, are the sections of his talk the busy Cook cut – with a few notes under each which only the maddest of paranoid conspiracy theorists will find relevant.

'The European audiovisual industry needs to be geared to the European citizen,' Cook was going to proclaim, but in the end did not. (*NB conspiracy theorists: Murdoch is neither a British nor European citizen. He was an Australian citizen and his father was a famous Australian patriot. But he has taken American citizenship because it allows him to buy US companies.*)

'That means nurturing and reflecting European cultural identities as well as meeting consumer demands,' the Foreign Secretary had planned to continue. 'Yours is one industry where success works on many levels enriching, entertaining and moulding our societies at the same time.' (*NB: in what may be termed an act of cronyism or at least favouritism, Tony Blair lobbied the Italian government on Murdoch's behalf and tried to persuade it not to stand in the way of the tycoon's ambitions in the Mediterranean.*)

Labour spin doctors explained, after a cover-up had failed, that it was perfectly reasonable for the Prime Minister to bat for a 'British company' that enriches this country. They initially side-stepped the minor point that not only is Rupert Murdoch not British but his British company, News International, refuses to enrich Britain. Between 1985 and 1995 News International paid a £11.74 million tax on profits of almost £1 billion — a rate of 1.2p in the pound. Taxpayers without Cayman Island bankers to help them duck demands are indirectly funding Murdoch's predatory pricing.)

Cook had then meant to ask, before the pressure of time undid him: 'How can we produce high-quality content that is both internationally competitive and sustains the cultural traditions of Europe?' (*NB: after hearing mocking laughter, Blair's aides 'accepted' that Murdoch was neither British nor European and changed their story. The PM's aim was to draw him into the European cultural tradition and persuade him to drop his opposition to the single currency. The Prime Minister was not, on this account, at all worried about one man controlling much of the press. He would welcome the suppression of competing voices as long as Murdoch gave him total support on Europe in the run-up to the next election. What mattered was Blair and Murdoch reaching an understanding, not pluralism and the integrity of public discourse.*)

'A lot of the answer has to do with how much we invest in production. In the UK the BBC and ITV both invest around £900 million, and Channel 4 close on £300 million each year,' came the undelivered reply to a rhetorical question that was never posed. 'Public-service broadcasters set standards, provide reliable and impartial news, and offer educational opportunities.' (*NB: despite investment by British broadcasters, we have a £224 million television trade deficit with the US because of the cheap American shows dumped on the airwaves of BSkyB. For some reason, Chris Smith refuses to impose on Sky a European law that would force it to produce home-grown programmes.*)

And there the self-censorship stopped and Cook carried on with the rest of a speech that could offend only those who had higher hopes of him. By their nature, conspiracies are difficult to detect. Unravelling them takes a fair degree of intelligence and much painstaking work.

Cook must have been right, after all. There is no conspiracy. How can there be when the most bewildered beggar on the street can understand New Labour's dealings with Murdoch in a moment?

Observer April 1998

ACCREDITED CORRESPONDENTS

Journalists are the world's worst bores: never get stuck with us at parties. Civilised accountants, say, stop wallowing in the office gossip of Price Waterhouse when an outsider joins their table. Hacks think we fascinate the nation. Nothing can deter us from droning on about ourselves – hence the media sections and the confessional columns about our spellbinding private lives. Occasionally, however, the idle chatter of Fleet Street has a wider resonance, as it had last week when the state made it embarrassingly obvious that New Labour can decide which trusties should be allowed to cover its administration in the pages of Britain's brave, free press.

On 24 April 1998 Paul Routledge of the *Independent on Sunday* accepted the post of political editor of the *Express*. Routledge was delighted. His salary would double when he left the failing Sunday for a mass circulation tabloid. Money aside, he was looking forward to working with his old friend Rosie Boycott. Routledge had been political correspondent for Boycott when she edited the *Independent on Sunday* and they had got on tremendously well. After a more-than-usually insane game of newspaper musical chairs stopped with Boycott's bottom in the *Express* editor's seat, one of her first decisions was to offer Routledge a job. Nobody doubts this sequence of events. At an *Observer* debate on government and the media a few days later, Jon Craig, an *Express* political correspondent, said Routledge was his new boss. Routledge's many friends (among whom I number myself) were happy to see him prosper. He is liked not only because he stands his round and enjoys his lunch but because he is an old-fashioned left-wing reporter. He takes trade union leaders seriously because he is a trade unionist himself, who lost his job on *The Times* when he refused to cross the picket line and work behind the barbed wire of Rupert Murdoch's Wapping camp. Charlie Whelan, Gordon Brown's spinner, is often at Routledge's side. So comradely is New Labour that a friend of Whelan is an enemy of Peter Mandelson and Alastair Campbell, the Prime Minister's propagandist. Perhaps they have good cause for their enmity. Routledge's semi-authorised biography of the Chancellor revealed the tensions between the Brown and Blair camps. Mandelson has not spoken to him for years. Their relationship is unlikely to improve when Routledge publishes *Peter Mandelson: The Unauthorised Biography*.

The hatred in Blairite circles would not have damaged Routledge if the *Express* was not, apparently, run by the government. Clive Hollick, the paper's chairman, is a super-rich Labour peer and consultant to Margaret Beckett. Philip Gould advises Hollick and has an office in the *Express* building. Gould's public obscurity hides the influence of one of the most powerful men in the land. He tests focus group reactions to New Labour and tells the Prime Minister what to do when the findings conflict with government policy. When the editorship of the *Express* fell vacant, Hollick told Gould he wanted to give it to Campbell. Gould said Campbell would never desert Tone and recommended Boycott, a friend of his wife's, should be favoured instead. Labour London is a small world.

You can probably guess what happened next. Routledge was called by a flustered *Express* executive who told him that Boycott was terribly sorry but she was not allowed to employ him. The political editorship was to go to the *Independent*'s Anthony Bevins. In better days, Bevins was an inspiration. He fought Margaret Thatcher's attempts to control political journalism. In the Nineties, his awkward phase passed. Alastair Campbell is an admirer. 'I think Tony Bevins is great,' he said in 1997. The *Express* made no effort to deny that Routledge had been blacklisted. I put the charge three times to assorted spokespersons. A PR finally came back and said Boycott still considered Routledge a friend and that he would make a lot of money from his Mandelson biography. I thanked her for sharing the information with me, but wondered if she had quite answered the question.

If the Routledge affair had happened under Thatcher, metropolitan liberals would have made a great noise about censorship and creeping fascism. Now their friends are in office, they are silent. Boycott will still appear on *Start the Week* with New Labour's Lord Bragg and be treated as a respectable intellectual. Routledge now knows that the Blairites will try to stop him getting another job if the *Independent* goes under or dispenses with his services. The rest of us can wonder how united the administration is when Blairites are ecstatic because they have knifed a Brown man.

The case would matter less if it were an isolated incident. But complicity with suppression is commonplace in swinging London. I know several journalists New Labour has tried to get fired. The party does not come out and say 'you can't hire X because he's not in our pocket,' or 'we want Y out because she thinks we're Tory hypocrites'. Editors are gently told that X and Y get it wrong constantly and 'no one takes them seriously'. I have also spoken to penal reform groups and Church of England family charities which have been warned that their grants may well be cut if they continue to question the wisdom of ministers. They won't go public because they know they will have to cope with a decade of Labour power. Even when incontrovertible evidence of the political manipulation of cultural life is produced, it is ignored. *The Guardian* columnist Francis Wheen ran a letter from Trevor Nunn, director of the National Theatre, to Howard Brenton and Tariq Ali. Nunn rejected the dramatists' proposed satire of New Labour in part because it would upset 'influential members of the government'. Nunn is meant to be a public servant, not a partisan censor, but no paper took up the story and demanded his resignation.

The glossy magazine *Vanity Fair* got into enormous trouble recently when it was caught allowing Hollywood stars to vet what it printed about them. The practice is called copy approval. Actors agree to talk only if they can edit an article and sanction pictures. There was a noisy debate in America and Britain. Media pundits agonised at length on the morality of it all and *Vanity Fair* received strong lectures on the need to maintain journalistic independence. Last week everyone in Westminster knew the government had 'reporter approval' and no one thought it was worth making a fuss.

Observer May 1998

A FIVE-MINUTE GUIDE TO THE POLITICAL CLASS

In the United States it is common to say that politicians from both parties, media tycoons, corporations and lobbyists form a single 'political class', whose members promote each other's interests. You do not mark yourself out as a Trotskyist or a hopeless cynic by using the term. Even in the best society it is accepted that a permanent government rules the country. The British, clinging to the quaint belief that elections can actually change conservative policies, may find the concept difficult to grasp. Perhaps the following story will help confused readers.

Last weekend Kevin Maguire, political editor of the *Mirror*, noted that Bill Clinton was in Britain for the G7 summit just days before the referendum on the Irish settlement. He decided to ask Clinton to urge the people of Ulster to vote 'Yes' to what peace was on offer. Maguire phoned Alastair Campbell, Tony Blair's spokesman and Britain's unelected Minister of Information. Campbell thought a plea for reconciliation from the most powerful man on Earth would be possible. But there was a snag. Clinton was far too busy to rush out 600 words for a British tabloid, so Maguire would have to write it himself. Undeterred, the reporter from South Shields, Tyne and Wear, tried to put himself into the mind of the President from Hope, Arkansas. It took some doing as Maguire is a decent fellow with the odd principle left. He finally hit the right low note, however, and sugary prose in the Clinton style flowed from his pen. Maguire sent his work to Campbell who passed it on to Clinton's spin doctor, Mike McCurry. The Americans made amendments on Monday and the *Mirror* was given permission to publish. Clinton – or, rather, Maguire – sentimentally recalled visiting Ulster in 1995. 'My trip was one of the high-points of my Presidency and my life,' he/they sighed. 'Most of all, I remembered the faces of the school children. I hope all of those voting on Friday will have the children of Northern Ireland in mind when they choose . . . What dreams will those children realise if you seize the chance for peace and vote "Yes"?'

The 'Clinton' address to the Irish was set on Tuesday night for the *Mirror* of Wednesday morning. At about 10 pm the first edition of the *Sun* arrived. Its front-page lead was labelled 'exclusive'. The headline read: 'US President writes for the *Sun*. Say YES to peace.' Underneath was the appeal from 'Clinton', which had not, in fact, been written exclusively by Clinton for the *Sun*, but by Maguire for the *Mirror*.

Piers Morgan, editor of the *Mirror*, exploded. Campbell called him to explain what had happened and was bawled out. At first, the PM's PR denied giving the copy to the *Sun*. Morgan refused to believe him. He pointed out that Rupert Murdoch was in London and, once again, Tony Blair had been checking that the rootless tycoon approved of his governance of Britain. Campbell's defence became more and more wretched until he finally admitted his treachery with a self-serving bleat of: 'But, Piers, I did it for Peace!' Peace with Murdoch, spat the *Mirror* hacks as they threw out the Clinton appeal on the grounds that it was, on reflection, deathly dull.

That very night the news broke that Lucille McLauchlan and Deborah Parry were being freed from their Saudi jail. All the papers changed their front pages to bring the hot news of the release of two nurses tied into a captivating tale of murder, medieval justice and lesbianism in the Arabian desert. Every paper, that is, except the *Sun*, which lost the chance of putting on sales by leaving its 'exclusive' call for reconciliation by 'Clinton' undisturbed. It didn't want to offend Campbell. It didn't want to offend its proprietor's new friend Tony Blair.

Here's a basic test for you. Is Tony Blair the servant of Rupert Murdoch? Or is Rupert Murdoch the servant of Tony Blair? If you'd say the answer to both questions is, without contradiction, yes, you would display a complete understanding of the nature of a political class.

Observer May 1998

THE SPINNERS AND THE SPUN

If a football commentator became so lost in rapturous descriptions of the tactics of a match he forgot to report the score, you would expect his career to be short. Yet to prosper as a political journalist in many of Britain's newsrooms you must put the process of politics before the point and become a kind of miniaturist who not only is unable to see the wood for the trees, but the trees for the leaves. Among the instant potboilers produced to greet Labour's victory was *Campaign 1997*, by the BBC political correspondent, Nicholas Jones. His study of what was the most important election since 1979 is one of those good, bad books that unintentionally reveal a culture that cannot recognise its own futility. At one level, Jones is a brave man. For 270 pages he betrays private conversations with abandon and records how the parties' spin doctors manipulated the news agenda. This may not make him popular. The freemasonry of Westminster compels reporters to hide their sources by using weasel phrases such as 'it is understood' or 'a senior minister said'. Discretion protects Peter Mandelson, say, from having to stand by the words he mumbled in Robin Oakley's ear if they prove inconvenient the next morning and gives Oakley and his colleagues the kudos of being members of a priestly caste with a monopoly of interpretation of the Delphic whispers of power. I have my suspicions that now propagandists like Alastair Campbell have grown far more important than mere ministers, they do not object too strongly to public recognition of their labours and status; but, none the less, Jones broke the Westminster code and for that he should be congratulated.

Yet his audacity has no purpose. Jones has produced a 100,000-word non-political political book. He admits to having no opinions himself. He and his colleagues probably wanted Labour to win. But 'the sentiment was largely apolitical': a Blair victory was simply a better story, he tells us, because the Tories seemed washed out. As the Corporation is required by law to be impartial, Jones's neutrality may be proper. But his intellectual emasculation deprives politics of content and shows you do not have to search for connections between causes and consequences to make it in the Whitehall-Media nexus.

Our connoisseur of spin is seen at his most blinkered in an analysis of how Gordon Brown declared to the press his commitment to stick to Conservative tax levels and spending targets. It was the moment when the Labour Party guaranteed that however the electorate voted, conservatism would remain in power. The consequences were profound for those who wanted better public services and less squalor and meanness. In effect, Brown announced that a permanent government of the right had been installed without opposition and the hope of change.

Jones begins his account of this pivotal moment in modern history by recommending that all lovers of the noble media game should applaud the skill of Brown and his aide Charlie Whelan – in much the same way as true cricket fans from all nations can put aside their loyalties and appreciate the technical glories of Shane Warne's action. 'One could not but admire the sheer effrontery with which Labour eventually succeeded in marshalling the news media into greeting Brown's promise with such uncritical acclaim,' he says at the beginning of a description of how Whelan fibbed to build up expectations before Brown's announcement. The 'covert orchestration of the news coverage' was 'risky', but worked like a dream. The narrative tension mounts as speculative and inaccurate weekend coverage serves its purpose. Brown goes on the *Today* programme on a Monday to reveal his tax cap. A frustrating James Naughtie does not understand his role and is 'in no hurry to get to the point'. At last he mentions tax in passing and Brown seizes the cue and 'leaps in with the answer' at – we are told – 8.17 am, precisely. The media goes wild. The *Evening Standard* clears its front page. The BBC rewrites its bulletins. The Conservatives are nonplussed. The Conservative press is delighted, as so it sodding should be. A few journalists resent being deceived, but most agree with *The Guardian* that Labour had 'spun it beautifully'. A modest Jones lets slip that his own reports that day pleased Whelan, who 'was chuffed [with Jones's] tremendous coverage'. And that is it. No consideration follows on what Brown's U-turn meant for the sick, the unemployed and the parents dependent on state schools; no musings disturb the reader on what choice is left in British democracy.

Jones is worth reading not because he is an entertaining dolt – as far as I can see he is one of the more intelligent political correspondents – but because he exemplifies a style of reporting in which the trivial is political, and where Alastair Campbell and Peter Mandelson become national figures because of their mastery of the news 'agenda', not for their political ideas, which are strikingly reactionary.

The standard explanation for the current fascination with political tactics is that spin has grown in inverse proportion to the decline of deference. The breakdown of traditional restraints has produced a generation of journalists inspired by Woodward and Bernstein. The news industry has become a monster employing thousands of iconoclastic and educated hacks who see themselves as just as clever as the politicians they cover. It is no longer enough for politicians to charm a few editors and proprietors and convince them of their probity or usefulness. There are just too many outlets hungry for scandal and exclusives. A story suppressed in newspaper X will appear on television station Y. Parties must protect themselves from the incessant pressure by hiring professionals who can coax and occasionally batter back a beast whose natural instinct is to devour them.

No one who has seen the press pack at work can doubt there is more than a grain of truth in the above. But do you detect a self-serving note and hear the faint thuds of backs being slapped? For politicians, the conventional wisdom feeds professional self-pity. They are honest men and women, public servants no less, doing their best in incredibly difficult jobs no journalist could hope to hold down, while all the time facing hostile fire from irresponsible scribblers who have been elected by no one. As for the hacks, they are brave seekers of truth rather than media bureaucrats; investigators who uncover the facts without fear, favour or thought of the consequences. There is no need to worry about the concentration of media ownership in the hands of a few rich and right-wing men because a free market in news ensures no monopolist can keep the truth from the newsagent's shelves.

Yet Michael Brunson and Robin Oakley would have looked well in periwigs at Louis XIV's court, and I'm waiting for the day when psychiatrists publish a study of the Stockholm syndrome among Murdoch and *Mail* journalists, so deferentially do they follow their proprietor captors' orders to praise client politicians. We cannot be living in a great age of investigative journalism when its few practitioners bemoan the reluctance of news organisations to investigate anything apart from the sex lives of just about everyone. The dominant mode of media discourse is the language of professionalism. Obeying orders and doing your job are grounds enough to dismiss questions of value and intellectual responsibility. It is not only in the BBC where it is the height of bad taste to ask journalists if they believe in anything at all. Nor can spin doctors pretend that they are neutral defenders of parties. The salient features of New Labour's successful and admired propagandists are their viciousness and shallowness and conservatism, as the following cases will, I hope, show:

An *Observer* journalist I know, who has spent her life working under Conservative governments, was delighted when Labour won. She was invited to a get-to-know-me reception by Frank Dobson, the new Health Secretary. As she entered the party, she thought how refreshing it would be to natter with a minister she respected. She was canny enough to realise there were professional advantages to being in sympathy with the government. It is occasionally handy to be a trusted friend of the powerful and receive exclusive previews of forthcoming initiatives which can be swiftly reprocessed and delivered to a grateful newsdesk. For 18 years she had seen her rivals on Conservative papers enjoy intimacy with Whitehall while she was left in opposition to dig out her own stories. It wasn't that she wanted to become a courtier, but the thought had occurred to her that it would make a change to receive the odd gift-wrapped story on a slow day.

The air inside was cold. Dobson's spin doctor buttonholed her. She was in serious trouble. Her fault was to have written that Labour was going to carry on with Conservative plans to close the Edgware Hospital in North London, even though all its candidates in the surrounding constituencies had promised to keep it open when they won their seats at a general election a mere fortnight earlier. You can't hide the closure of a hospital – ambulance drivers and the sick notice if there is no one to meet them. But her brief, straightforward statement of facts that could not be concealed cut no ice. She had 'two chances', she was told, and had 'blown one'. If she produced another unauthorised article, all stories from the department would go to her rivals on the right-wing *Sunday Times* instead. My friend considered the Faustian pact. She was briefly tempted, but then collected herself and returned to opposition with a sigh.

As Tony Blair consolidated his grip on the Labour Party, he had one genuine comrade on Fleet Street. Andrew Marr, then the editor of the *Independent*, did not support New Labour because his proprietor told him to or because he thought a Blairite line would be good for sales, but out of intellectual conviction. He and the Labour leader were friends and dining companions. Marr offered him the essential service of a sympathetic public dialogue, which all politicians need. During the election campaign, Marr's warm feelings were briefly tested by a craven and jingoistic article the supposedly pro-European Blair dumped in the *Sun* on St George's Day. The Labour leader sounded like a drunk Michael Portillo as he ranted: 'On the day we remember the legend that St George slayed a dragon to protect England, some will argue that there is another dragon to be slayed: Europe.' Marr noted that Blair was speaking in bad faith and the 'some will argue' was a weasel phrase slipped into an otherwise xenophobic article. Blair was pro-European to a Europhile audience while delivering anti-European 'nostalgic flag-waving Gormenghast politics' to sceptics. The similarities with John Major were boringly familiar. Marr's piece was friendly criticism rather than a polemic. 'No one is suggesting that the Labour Party today is in anything like the same state as the Tories when Major became leader,' he added. But his exercise of critical judgment was too much for his friends. Alastair Campbell demanded that David Montgomery, who controlled the troubled paper, fire him and, shortly afterwards, he was sacked.

In the summer of 1998 the *Observer* ran an undercover investigation into the links between New Labour, big business and young Blairites who were making fortunes in the lobbying game. Greg Palast, an American reporter, came over and posed as the representative of a corporation seeking favours from government. What he found created a scandal because it forced readers to understand that an administration which attached the epithet 'people's' to everything it did, lived in a right little, tight little world. As Derek Draper, a lobbyist and close friend of Peter Mandelson, incautiously explained to Palast: 'There are 17 people who count, and to say I am intimate with every one of them is the understatement of the century.' He went on to admit he wanted to 'stuff my bank account at £250 an hour.'

Draper introduced Palast to Roger Liddle, the Prime Minister's policy adviser, who said that Labour lobbyists and, by extension, clients who could afford £250 an hour, were held in the highest regard in Downing Street. 'There is a Circle,' he told Palast, 'and Derek is part of The Circle. And anyone who says he isn't is An Enemy. Derek knows the right people.' Palast asked if he could introduce him to politicians who might be helpful. Liddle handed him his card with his home number scrawled on the back. 'Whenever you are ready, just tell me what you want, who you want to meet and Derek and I will make the call for you.'

Other New Labour lobbyists, spinning in a revolving door between Whitehall and commerce, described how a compliant government was entirely devoid of ideas. My favourite moment came when Neal Lawson (a former aide to Tony Blair, and a wonk who is invited to Downing Street seminars to develop Third Way ideology) explained what the new theory for the new millennium meant in practice. Lawson earned hefty fees by playing on what he called 'politics without leadership'. Principles had no place in New Labour, he said. They had been replaced by 'non-ideologically contaminated decision-making,' which was easy to exploit because on the big issues 'they don't know what they are thinking. Blair himself doesn't always know what he is thinking'.

No sackings followed Palast's revelation. There is no mechanism in Britain that might allow an investigating magistrate to examine, for example, Roger Liddle's telephone and bank records. Instead, Labour and its media allies turned on Palast. Inevitably, Peter Mandelson, a friend of Liddle's as well as Draper's, led the attack. 'I think what the *Observer* has done is fall foul to a man with a very strong agenda of his own who has based his story on some very slipshod research,' he said. Few people inside the paper treated his outburst seriously. Slipshod research? The report took six weeks to compile. The damning quotes from Liddle, Draper and the rest were either on tape or in notebooks. In all the face-to-face meetings bar one, Palast had a witness present. The facts were of no interest to the party's mouthpiece, the *Mirror*. Under the headline THE LIAR, it trumpeted: 'Exposed: Damning US Court Verdict on Sleaze Reporter.' Palast had been dismissed as 'perverse and biased', it reported. Judges in New York 'were so angry at unfounded accusations' that they rejected his testimony 'in its entirety'.

Palast has worked for the *New York Times*, the *International Herald Tribune*, *The Guardian*, the *Observer* and the *Financial Times* and won shelf-loads of awards. He was an internationally respected authority on energy policy with a reputation for defending consumers against private power companies. Jack Cunningham, Margaret Beckett and other Labour ministers had taken his advice in the years before the general election.

If you knew nothing about him, the *Mirror* appeared to undermine fatally the credibility of the reporter and, for this was the intention, his story. On the night the paper went to press, we tried six times to give the tabloid information vindicating Palast. The man labelled by Mandelson as having an anti-Labour 'agenda' had been asked by the government to draw up legislation, we said. He had investigated alleged racketeering by the American utility company Lilco, we continued. And, yes, in this long case, in which Palast successfully advised Suffolk County, New York, on how it could sue to stop residents having to pay higher taxes to the private energy company, one conservative judge did abuse him. The judge's decision had been overturned on appeal and Wayne Prospect, the Suffolk County legislator at the time, had said: 'Greg Palast was an outstanding consultant. Unfortunately, the judge completely misunderstood the facts of the case. In my opinion, he [the judge] should have been retired some time ago because of borderline senility.' This was not a message the paper wanted to hear. The fix was on. 'It's no good,' said one embarrassed journalist. 'Whatever evidence you've got, it won't make any difference. They just don't want to know.' The *Mirror* was working with the government and planned an ambush. Draper was given an early copy of the paper to spring on Ben Laurance, the *Observer*'s business editor, on *Newsnight*. The Labour Party assumed that Laurance would know nothing about the New York case and be caught off guard and looking foolish on television. The rest of the press would assume that the *Mirror* accusations were true. The

Observer could have rebutted the charges in the morning, but by then the damage would have been done. Fortunately, Laurance was tipped off and discussed the judge's senility – to the mortification of Draper, whose attempt at a political comeback was over.

But Labour was not finished with Palast. At that year's party conference, he was sent to interview a leading councillor. The hotel receptionist told him to wait in her room and gave him a key. The next day's *Mirror* denounced him as a sex pest and a prowler. At the time of writing, Palast's lawyers have secured one tranche of libel damages and are expecting more.

These three incidents have much in common, and the tired phrase 'control-freakery' does not begin to cover the ground. First there is – wouldn't you say? – a distinct lack of principle behind Labour's media operations. As in the old Communist Party, past beliefs and commitment are irrelevant, and cretinous loyalty is all. Left-of-centre journalists are expected to swerve blindly with every contradictory turn in the party line and be able to believe Europe is Britain's salvation one minute and an infernal dragon the next. Failure to be flexible may be punished with, in Marr's case, demands for your head, or, in Palast's, character assassination. The intellectual cowardice demanded by the party explains why New Labour, a massively successful political movement, has yet to produce one political journalist of distinction. You can't write well with one eye looking over your shoulder.

Second, most of the government's hostile fire is turned on leftish hacks. Nearly every minister has said at one point that he prefers the *Daily Mail* to *The Guardian*, and it is this bias in Labour spin that connects the squabbles to wider politics. The propaganda and backstabbing is used to convince a right-wing media that Labour is sound; that it is a new Conservative Party that reserves its visceral hatred for those who were foolish enough to support it in the press, constituencies and polling booths.

Observer and *Tribune* 1998

ONE ENDING BAD,
TWO ENDINGS GOOD

George Orwell spent his life fighting against the 'smelly little ortho-
doxies which are now contending for our souls'. He delineated the
lies and murder of imperialism, capitalism, fascism and Stalinism so
successfully that we automatically attach the adjective Orwellian to
propaganda. 'The Prevention of Literature', his defence of intellectual
honesty, described how dictators and press barons conspire 'to turn the
writer, and every other artist as well, into a minor official working on
themes handed down from above'. Orwell refused to succumb, believing to the end that 'imagination, like certain wild animals, will not
breed in captivity'.

Animal Farm was written in 1945, the most inappropriate moment
possible from the official point of view. The Soviet Union was a courageous wartime ally, and T. S. Eliot among many other publishers did
not think that this was quite the right time for a ferocious satire of
Stalin. (An American house, preferring rank stupidity to censorship,
said it did not want *Animal Farm* because experience had shown that
it was 'impossible to sell animal stories in the US'.) A decade on, the
Cold War was at its height and Orwell's reputation was transformed.
Everyone who had previously snubbed him found it politic to agree that
Animal Farm was a work of genius, a brilliant parody that should be
taught to every schoolchild in the country, smuggled into Eastern Europe
and transferred to celluloid for posterity. It entered cinema history and
is celebrated to this day as the first full-length British cartoon.

The novel's progress should be a touching story of integrity tri-
umphing over censorship, were the orthodox account not junk. Investigations by the historian, Frances Stonor Saunders, suggest the 'British'
film was controlled by the American CIA and its front organisations,
which changed the ending to ensure that Cold War propaganda was
given to the audience and no hint of criticism of the West appeared.
Casual viewers may not be too surprised by her, well, Orwellian

conclusions. You do not have to look too hard to spot the differences between the film and the book. As generations of readers know, the animals in the novel rise up and throw out the capitalist farmer who oppresses them. Napoleon and the leaders of the revolutionary pigs become a new exploitative ruling class. By the final scene, the transformation is complete. The pigs are in men's clothes and invite their human farmer neighbours over for a party. Farmers and pigs drink, brawl, gamble and agree they have a common interest in keeping the lower animals and lower classes down. The 'creatures outside,' reads the last sentence, 'looked from pig to man, and from man to pig, and from pig to man again; but already it was impossible to say which was which'.

I'm sorry if I'm labouring the obvious, but the book's message is that the communist pigs were so rotten they were indistinguishable from capitalists. In the film, Orwell's conclusion is dropped. The audience is not permitted to feel the capitalist farmers and communist pigs are on the same vile level. The farmers are air-brushed from the last scene. Instead, the watching creatures see only the pigs enjoying the corrupt fruits of exploitation – a sight that impels them to storm the farmhouse and mount a successful counter-revolution.

Stonor Saunders has assembled an intriguing collection of documents to show that the perversion of *Animal Farm*'s message may not be the result of the film industry's perennial desire for happy endings. Every piece of evidence he can find points to the conclusion that the twisting of the plot was a CIA operation. She noted that Howard Hunt, former CIA agent, Watergate conspirator and one of the world's worst thriller writers, said in 1975 that *Animal Farm* (the movie) was run by the CIA. As it is unwise to take Hunt's word on anything, she looked at *Animal Farm*'s backers. The director, Louis de Rochemont, came from Hollywood. He had previously given the world *Walk East on Beacon*, a reds-are-coming yarn in which the brave FBI men smash nests of commie spies. Sonia Orwell sold the film rights to two Americans – Finis Farr and Carlton Alsopp. Both worked for the Office of Policy Coordination, which was paid for and staffed by the CIA and instructed to conduct covert and deniable operations. (Orwell's capricious widow insisted that they must get her a date with Clark Gable before she would sign the contract). Finally, she used the American Freedom of Information Act to unearth a memo from the Psychological Strategy Board (another CIA disinformation service). It was written in response to the anxieties of a Washington espionage bureaucrat called Wallace Carroll. Records at the Public Information Research, an American database where all available evidence of CIA activities is stored, reveal that Carroll was a well-connected cold warrior. He worked as a US propagandist in wartime London and was a consultant to the US government on defence, propaganda and psychological warfare during the Fifties. The memo is dated 23 January 1952 and shows that an early draft of the script of *Animal Farm* was in the hands of the CIA. The spies were unimpressed. 'Wallace Carroll's note asked whether I would go through this script and tell you whether I thought this would make a useful film,' the memo reads. 'I have read this script and so has John Anspacher and we both feel that the theme is somewhat confusing and the impact of the story as expressed in cartoon sequence is somewhat nebulous.' The critique concluded: 'Although the symbolism is apparently plain there is no great clarity of message.' Shaw, with laudable academic caution, says he cannot prove beyond reasonable doubt that the memo led to the inversion of Orwell's final scene, but his circumstantial evidence is very impressive and, in my view, pretty damn conclusive. Why else would the American secret services have read the script for its propaganda value and been involved in commissioning the film?

The 'message' of the original version of *1984*, another 'British' film that also appeared in 1955, was also given greater Cold War 'clarity'. In the novel, the rebellious Winston Smith is defeated and forced to love Big Brother. In the movie, his defiance survives brainwashing and torture. The film closes with Smith chanting 'Down with Big Brother!'

When the film's surviving animators were told the story, the elderly men and women greeted the news glumly. There is no evidence that they or Sonia Orwell knew about the CIA connection. Some angrily contested his conclusions, others felt like virtually everyone else who discovers they have had dealings with spies: duped and a little dirty.

The findings cast light on the continuing debate on what Orwell would have written if he had not died in middle age. Conservatives on both sides of the Atlantic claim that he would have become one of them, a lover of nuclear weapons who moaned about the unions while reading the *Daily Mail*. He was, after all, willing to denounce Communist writers to the British government just before he died in 1950. Their dusty platitudes ignore Orwell's anti-Stalinism and life as a member of the independent left. In one of his last essays he said he wanted 'a Socialist United States of Europe', free from the domination of the Soviet Union and America. Those who continue to believe that Orwell was in the process of becoming a supporter of the Pentagon can now see that when the CIA got hold of *Animal Farm*, it did not like what it saw. A really 'useful film' could be produced only by turning the most independent of writers into a minor official whose themes were handed down from above.

Observer April 1998

THE DISCREET CHARM OF THE BOURGEOISIE

For a party whose policies are tailored to snake round every bulge and crevice of bourgeois prejudice, New Labour has the disconcerting ability to flummox its critics with prolier-than-thou invective. Democrats who ask what has happened to its commitment in the 1997 election manifesto to deliver a Freedom of Information Act (and in the 1992, 1987, 1983, 1979 and 1974 Labour manifestos for that matter) are dismissed as elitist members of the 'chattering classes' by Jack Cunningham, the working-class hero coordinating government policy; as nothing more than 'Chianti drinkers' lounging in their Tuscan villas, by a street-fightin' Labour MP in the *Financial Times*; and 'middle class wankers' by Alastair Campbell, the grammar school boy who became the Prime Minister's £87,000-a-year spokesman after writing pornographic stories for the dirty old readers of *Forum* magazine. Plain, decent people had no interest in becoming informed and self-confident citizens and were happy to remain the subjects of Elizabeth II, her heirs and successors.

New Labour did not always wear its cloth cap with pride. In 1996 Tony Blair was the middle classes' most spirited onanist. A severe case of Portnoy's complaint compelled him to assert that freedom of information was not one priority among many for his party but 'absolutely fundamental to how we see politics developing in this country over the next few years'. Destroying official secrecy would encourage voters to trust politicians and end their 'disaffection' with their leaders. He wanted to limit state censorship because he was concerned with 'genuinely changing the relationship in politics today'. Trust was then Blair's watchword. For his liberal-left supporters this was a soundbite with mixed consequences. After four election defeats, Blair insisted the electorate had to trust him not to reverse Conservative tax and spending policies. But after the Major administration had been pickled in a septic tank of scandal, the voters must also be able to trust him to be honest, clean and, above all, open. Those who could barely be civil when asked to accept the accommodation with Thatcherism consoled themselves with the happy thought that Blair would begin the overdue task of reforming an imperial British state that had lost an empire but found the role of keeping its last restless natives in the dark congenial and essential. Blair appeared to recognise Whitehall's colonial attitude to the supposedly – although not legally – sovereign people. At the climax of his speech to constitutional reformers he said official secrecy was 50 years behind the times. An increasingly educated and demanding populace viewed it with abhorrence. It ensured incompetence and worse went unpunished. Freedom of information would enable the public to own the work done in its name and with its money. The modern leader promised to sweep secrecy aside and allow 'politics to catch up with the aspirations of people by delivering not just more open but more effective and efficient government for the future'.

Two years on, the chances of a worthwhile freedom of information act becoming law range from the slight to the microscopic. Eventually there may be a bill presented to Parliament with the words 'information', 'freedom' and 'of' somewhere in its title. But Labour has already ruled that the work of the security services, police, prisons, Department for Social Security, Immigration Service and privatised utilities will be excluded from any reform.

Cynical wisdom holds that no party willingly disseminates information after it has experienced the joys and burdens of office. Freedom of information is a measure delivered within months of a new government taking power or not at all. And, as ever, the corruption of power is part of the explanation for Labour's treachery, but so is the corruption of defeat. In the same month Blair gave his passionate defence of glasnost, Peter Mandelson was telling a different story to the Campaign for Freedom of Information. The act 'may have to wait,' said Mandelson, because it failed to answer the problem of declining public faith in government. Good politicians were a far better answer. Mere laws were no substitute for ministers who behave with 'honesty and openness' – ministers such as himself, since you ask. The paternalism of the old establishment had found a new champion. The system worked well, Mandelson implied. Criticism should be directed at the odd rotten apple and change confined to replacing corrupt Conservatives with honest Blairites. The case for a legal right to know that can be exercised by citizens regardless of whether the government is good, bad or – as so often – indifferent did not convince him.

Mandelson's influence is so pervasive he has turned the label 'control freak' from an insult from the hippy fringe to the platitude of choice for mainstream pundits. His dominance of the party's presentation and, by extension, its policies (in the final analysis, style and content are one) was only possible because Labour's run of defeats left it willing to do anything to stop the often far-right and largely foreign-owned press tearing it apart. The tight little tactics of agenda manipulation and black propaganda continued into government. New Labour's special advisers, whose only skill is spinning on behalf of their masters, have replaced civil servants as the most significant members of Whitehall departments. The party lobbies gutless editors to fire unhelpful journalists. In Scotland, Wales and London, the only candidates it will allow to stand for election are mediocre apparatchiks. Loyalist MPs and ministers frightened to speak in Cabinet willingly receive instructions from the whips on what to do and say on their pagers. (I considered writing a guide to making it in New Labour politics called 'Do you dream on message?' after a Labour MP told me that four colleagues had refused to join a charity swim because jumping in the water would require them to remove their bleepers for an hour. I vainly studied his face for a hint that he was joking.)

Many have commented on the paradox of such an anal party opening up government. The seeming contradiction has now been resolved. David Clark, the minister who was put in charge of freedom of information, was fired in the summer reshuffle. He had been the subject of continuous abuse from brave, anonymous sources who whispered poison to equally courageous political journalists. Clark believes that the liberal position he defended in disputes with Mandelson was not, on reflection, the smartest of career moves and worries about what will happen to the gains he made now his enemies are in control.

Clark had produced a white paper before he was knifed that, although excellent in parts, had several flaws. Jack Straw insisted that all information on law enforcement must be excluded from any bill. His victory ensured that the most trivial questions about policing – why a 999 call was not answered, how many officers were on duty at a football match – will be official secrets. Straw was tough. 'If you openly provide intelligence about the total number of police officers available, then that would be used by criminals,' he told an audience of MPs who could not keep the sneers from their lips. Even in the USA, where

Straw finds so many of his barbaric ideas, freedom of information covers law enforcement. Openness, however, is the one American import Britain cannot receive. Secrecy must remain in place to check the ever-present menace of Russian gangsters, Colombian drug barons and British citizens with ideas above their station. Straw confessed that the high office of Home Secretary instilled a certain bias. 'The Home Office deals with areas of very sensitive business,' he said. 'It is about law and order. National security. Keeping 63,000 people in prison who do not want to be there.' He was, he added, in a business with 'genuine secrets'. Such macho sentiments, which owe much to the influence of cheap thrillers, are shared by interior ministers across the world. They are not in themselves surprising. What was shocking was that Straw, the leader of the authoritarian faction in the Cabinet, was given the responsibility for freedom of information when Clark was sacked. The postures of a bespectacled Whitehall hardman will determine what liberty the state will allow its subjects, and it is not difficult to read his small mind.

One of the virtues of Clark's proposals was that outside the large world of law enforcement, information would be censored only if civil servants could prove its release would cause 'substantial harm'. In his evidence to the Commons, Straw dropped a strong hint that he preferred what is known in the jargon of constitutional reform as the 'simple harm test'. This far more restrictive definition allows bureaucrats to suppress documents when, in their considered view, and after all relevant factors have, of course, been taken into account, the opinion may well be formed that their release may, somehow, and at some unspecified date in the future, just conceivably harm someone or something or somesuch.

The full subtlety of the simple harm test is being revealed daily. New Labour idealists must have hoped that for all their backtracking their champions would end the days when the number of cups of tea consumed in the MoD canteen, for example, was an official secret. But petty repression continues to flourish. Matthew Taylor, a Liberal Democrat MP, asked the new and open MoD for a list of the titles of its technical reports on hydrodynamics. In theory, they were available to the public, but in practice you can't know what papers there are to read if you can't look at an index. John Spellar, the Labour Defence minister, replied: 'I am withholding the information. While the individual reports are unclassified, a composite list gives a broader picture and is classified.' You were allowed to read the research but weren't allowed to know what research existed to be read. The Labour backbencher Ann Clwyd asked Barbara Roche which companies in the arms industry had breached government guidelines on trading with dictatorships. British companies had been caught flogging electronic batons to Saudi Arabian torturers. Everyone who watched the activities of weapons' manufacturers suspected the two guilty firms were on the tip of a large iceberg. The Industry minister replied that if the government named names 'it would harm the competitive position of the companies concerned'. Secrecy was necessary to protect corporations that broke the law by arming tyrants.

If these examples seem arcane, consider the plight of North Sea oil workers and the vicitms of CJD, whom even Campbell couldn't call bourgeois softies. Earlier this year the Health and Safety Executive warned its employees about Dr Charles Woolfson, a senior lecturer at Glasgow University and three other reputable researchers. They 'were becoming persistent in their inquiries to HSE,' a leaked memo said. 'We wish to monitor those who appear to have an interest in HSE activities and who may be looking to exploit replies received in ways unfavourable to the HSE.' Woolfson's crime was to attempt to examine the failure of the executive to investigate the burns, poisonings and amputations suffered by North Sea riggers. In a Kafkaesque flourish, the HSE concluded without irony that 'any contact with these people should be reported to the Open Government Unit.' Open government is now an instrument of covert surveillance.

The BSE crisis has so far killed 31 beef eaters, wrecked the cattle industry and cost taxpayers billions. As in the North Sea example, Whitehall responded by frustrating independent research that might have saved lives. In evidence to the official inquiry, Roy Anderson, a professor at Oxford University studying infectious diseases, said he was refused access to Ministry of Agriculture data for two years. When the information was belatedly released, it showed the ministry's inability to recognise that its ban on infected feed was not working resulted in 250,000 cows going mad unnecessarily. If there had been no secrecy 'the size of the epidemic would have been significantly smaller,' the professor said. Sir Kenneth Calman, the former chief medical officer, added that Maff systematically misled the public.

Now, maybe I'm wrong and only the chattering classes care about mutilated oil workers and the victims of CJD. I have to admit I have never heard chatter about the hard lot of rough necks and the misery of degenerative brain disorders at Hampstead parties, but I don't get out much. Maybe Campbell and Cunningham, a former Agriculture minister, did not see the mad cow epidemic spread. Or maybe the Victorians were right about the blinding effect of masturbation on self-indulgent boys.

Index on Censorship and *Observer* September and October 1998

MOSSAD'S MEDIA

My career as a Mossad agent was short, unexciting and involved the Israeli state in the purchase of two pints of London Pride in a dingy East End pub. In all it lasted two minutes, but that was long enough for the noble arguments used by Israel to justify the hot and cold wars against the Arabs to be revealed to me in all their intricacy and glory.

In the summer of 1991 I was a journalist on the *Independent on Sunday* and would have thought myself an unlikely target for espionage agencies, if I had considered the question at all. Before the paper was taken over by a useless media conglomerate, it was a traditional liberalish broadsheet. No spy who approached it could be sure he would not be exposed:

either because we disapproved of his line of work or wanted to make mischief. My pieces were on crime, prisons and quangos; important work, I flattered myself into believing, but even my ample self-regard could not have convinced me that they would interest Middle Eastern spooks.

The one exception to my usual scribblings was a feature on mine-clearing in Kuwait in the months after the Gulf War. The subject was Paul Jefferson, a friend who was one of the best mine clearers in the world and an authority on Soviet weapons. He left the Army because 'peace-time soldiering was pretty boring' and spent his days crawling over the battlefields of Afghanistan, Angola and Cambodia at the behest of the Red Cross. Only when his finger tips were prodding dirt that might explode in his face, he said, was he truly alive. Paul delighted in offending left-of-centre sensibilities. Just before he went to the Gulf, I had him round to dinner and placed him next to a Camden woman who thought herself the embodiment of liberalism. She asked what he did for a living.

Paul: 'I'm a mercenary.'

Embodiment of liberalism (laughing): 'You mean you're a journalist.'

Paul: 'No, a soldier who works for anyone who pays.'

None of the other guests had met anyone like him before. They did not find the novelty appealing. Voices heightened into shrieks. Food was left uneaten. As the risk of violence grew, a guest tried to calm the situation.

Guest: 'At least you clear mines. That's, er, a good and peaceful thing, isn't it?'

Paul: 'Oh no, defence and offence are the same. Clear the mines and you make an attack easier.'

Embodiment of liberalism: 'You bastard.'

Paul flew to Kuwait the next day and his luck ran out. He had been hired by Royal Ordnance, which had won a £60 million contract to clear the mines left by the Iraqis. Although the privatised munitions company was happy to take the money, it had no experience of working on a battlefield and within hours of his arrival Paul realised he was in the middle of a shambles. The equipment his team was promised failed to show. Paul scavenged detonators, explosives and cable from the wreckage of the war and took what sensible precautions he could. Improvisation only got him so far. He walked into a dump for dead mine cases, which was meant to be a cleared and safe area. Two, maybe three, anti-personnel mines exploded under him. He was blinded – an awful injury for a man who would have been content to spend his days in the British Library when he was too old for action – and lost half his right leg. His men wrapped him in a rucksack to stem the blood and drove him across country. He had so many shrapnel wounds, doctors could not tell where one stopped and the next began. His first words on waking in hospital were: 'Kill me.'

Paul was liked and respected by defence contractors, while Royal Ordnance was regarded as a joke. When I wrote a piece about what had happened to him, dozens in the defence industry who would not dream of speaking to a hack in ordinary circumstances gave me all the help I wanted. Someone in the Israeli embassy noticed. A fortnight later a diplomat called and explained he had information that might help me. Would I like to meet? Indeed I would, I said, but something told me he was a spy.

Now, journalists have three views of spies:

1 Spies are glamorous. They move in a thrilling world and when they grace reporters with an audience they allow us to impress our editors by getting the magic words MI5 and MI6 into our articles. Best of all, what they say is always unattributable and nearly always uncheckable so no one can prove later that what we have printed is the self-serving trash of intelligence bureaucracies.

2 Spies are poison. Their immoral work undermines democracy. The history of every intelligence organisation shows they are as great a threat to the citizens of their countries as their countries' enemies.

3 Spies are silly. They extract ridiculous amounts of public money from gullible politicians transfixed by the glamour of secrecy and

use the cloak of national security to hide their incompetence. A close reading of the newspapers tells you more than they ever can.

I took the third view, but saw the force of the second, and decided to be careful. I placed the foreign and defence editors around the *Independent* office pub to act as witnesses in case of trouble. They took cover behind their newspapers when a small man from the embassy arrived. As predicted, he had no leads to give me. Instead he told a fascinating story about my profession. Israeli military observers were not allowed to attend many military exercises, he explained. Israel therefore paid defence journalists with access to mock battles to brief its diplomats. As I seemed well-versed in military technology, would I like a slice of the action?

I don't know about you, but I find these situations very difficult. I might have coaxed him along, found who was on the take and what he wanted me to spy on. Alternatively, I could have denounced him in an outraged voice and asked him what made him think I would spy for a foreign country. But I was just embarrassed to disappoint him. I mumbled that the Kuwait article was a one-off and, really, none of my other work would interest Israel.

'Oh,' he said.

'Uh-huh,' I replied.

It was a delicate moment. We both had full pints and nothing to say to each other. We wanted to drink them quickly and leave without making it obvious that we wanted to drink them quickly and leave. We drank them quickly and left.

In retrospect, what was instructive about the encounter was what was not said. The Israeli made no appeal to Jewish solidarity or Zionism. There was no hint of idealism or suggestion that he believed that anyone would work for Israel because they admired her leaders and applauded her policies. But then I suppose that if you are a representative of a state that has been illegally occupying other people's land since 1967, which has murdered, tortured, impoverished and expropriated those others, which has invaded the Lebanon and stood by while Palestinians are massacred in camps, which has passed racial laws and which was, at the time of my meeting, in the process of watching a theocratic faction emerge that would view with approval the assassination of a secular Prime Minister, then money is all you have to offer.

Jewish Quarterly Autumn 1997

CHAPTER FIVE

UK PLC

THE BLOOD BUSINESS

Giving blood for nothing to strangers you probably won't meet (and may well dislike if you did) is not a virtue that chimes with modern business practice. There is no market mechanism, no exploitation of the laws of supply and demand. How much would a dying man pay for the pint of blood that might save him? £100? £1,000? Everything he's got? Such calculations have never entered the minds of Britain's blood donors. The old National Blood Transfusion Service was founded alongside the National Health Service in 1948 and was based on the assumption that hundreds of thousands would give blood freely. Social scientists with a bent towards moral philosophy could argue donors gave out of altruism, or patriotism – stock went up during the Falklands War, for example; others maintained they gave out of a faint sense of enlightened self-interest – give your blood today and, with luck, other people's blood would be available when you needed it; or a sly egoism – people gave because it made them feel better about themselves. The most convincing argument was that the principle behind the NHS – that health care paid for from progressive taxation should be free at the point of demand – encouraged ideals of 'social duty and reciprocity'. The phrase is from the late Professor Richard Titmuss, the guru

of post-war welfare state theory, who wrote a treatise on blood dona-
tion 25 years ago that is still something of a democratic socialist
classic.

Last week, Stephen Dorrell, Secretary of State for Health, fundamentally altered a service that, as Titmuss realised, relies more than
any other on people's feelings of involvement with and obligation to a
wider society. In Eighties management-speak, the true dialect of the
Conservative Party, he said he would 'simplify structures' and ensure
bureaucracy was 'streamlined' so it would become more 'effective'.
His Commons statement confirmed that 300 jobs would be lost and
£10 million saved by stopping the processing and testing of blood at
five regional centres. The announcement was the culmination of 18
months of commercialisation. Since 1993, power over England's blood
supplies has been in the hands of the National Blood Authority (NBA),
a typical quango of the late Conservative period. The chief executive,
John Adey, came from an American health company called Baxter
Healthcare – which had sold its blood packs to the NHS. He was discovered combining his new job at the blood authority with a partnership in a Wiltshire private nursing home. Adey resents accusations that
the blood service is being slowly privatised. 'There's no question of
this being a business,' he said recently. 'But you do need to do some more
business-like things.' The 'things' included the selling of by-products
of plasma – the liquid component of blood – to Germany, which the
NBA described 'as our principal export market'. The next wheeze was
to arrange a £500,000 deal with the makers of Ribena, and McVitie's.
The companies would supply free drinks and biscuits at the 2.4 million annual donor sessions; in return, they would get home addresses
of blood givers and send them junk mail. A sponsored NHS, brought
to you by Jaffa Cakes, created such mockery that the deal was dropped.
Last summer the authority tried to save £700,000 by buying blood bags
from an Australian company, Tuta. Some of the bags had faulty seals
and it cost £3 million to replace them. The families of several patients
claimed that blood from the bags had poisoned their relatives.

The series of fiascos should have taught the Department of Health what many who work in the private sector already know: British managers are great at coming up with business-like ideas, but not so good at producing 'business-like things' when the time comes to put theory into practice. Senior staff in the blood service are disillusioned. They will not speak out because, under the new regime, public employees face disciplinary action if they take their concerns to the press or Parliament. One talked privately of 'uncontrolled changes', a 'dearth of talent' and a 'new breed of managers who think that sustaining blood supplies is "like selling widgets"'.

Dorrell's latest scheme will lead to stocks being concentrated in fewer and bigger centres and more blood being moved around the country. The dangers of a mix-up, when somebody is given blood from the wrong group or contaminated blood, will increase. If Dorrell's plans are to work, he needs a national computer system that can produce 14- to 16-digit barcodes, giving every blood sample in the country a unique number. No such system is in place, though people who work in the blood service had expected one to be running before centres were closed. Managers have not been able to decide which company should get the contract. So the blood service will continue to rely on existing systems, which can produce only six-figure barcodes. Since even a small regional centre runs through its list of permitted numbers in 18 months, the risk of incompatible samples from different donors having the same number is growing.

The NBA and Dorrell deny they are allowing businessmen to destroy a public asset. The minister promised his proposals would lead to centres of excellence being created and the formation of a national users' group to monitor services to hospitals. He quoted distinguished consultants who believe he is improving a service that, as its supporters admit, has inefficiencies and failings.

The one group he has failed to convince or understand are the donors themselves. Many, unable to follow the arguments about optimum efficiency in the NHS internal market, are in revolt because the Ribena farce, the proposed pricing and sale of blood given freely and the sacking of staff they know and like, just feels wrong. This year has seen an uprising among donors in Merseyside, where a regional testing and processing centre will be closed. More than 1,000 have joined a donor association. Billy Vaughan, an association member, told NBA officials he had received 300 letters from donors saying they had stopped giving because they were 'disillusioned' with the service. Sue Kilroe, a fellow activist, said she had given since she was 18, because it 'was nice to be able to help people' in a world where 'nobody does anything for free any more'. Now she was organising protests because the donors – without whose unforced generosity the NBA could not exist – had been given no power by the quango or the private management consultants it employed to run a public service.

Underlying their anger is an anguish at what is happening to the NHS. Titmuss would have sympathised. His study, *The Gift Relationship*, demonstrated the inefficiency of market principles. In the United States, where poor donors from skid row sold (and continue to sell) their blood, contaminated stocks were common. A man 'coerced' by poverty into selling blood was not going to lose his fee by telling the blood bank that he had hepatitis or, today, Aids. In Britain contamination was rarer because people gave for nothing and had no need to lie. The British were not better than the Americans; it was just that the creation of the NHS – 'the most unsordid act of British social policy in the twentieth century' – encouraged solidarity. The American health marketplace (where 400 companies collect, buy and sell blood) failed because it forced the poor to give blood out of economic desperation and, by extension, forced patients to risk poisoning.

Titmuss dominated the post-war generation of social theorists at the London School of Economics. For all his eminence and sophistication, his writings show a relatively simple pride in the NHS. The feeling that Britain may have lost an empire but had created a more civilised society was commonplace. That pride has disappeared. It is too early to say if blood donations will fall. The government maintains that there is no evidence that donors are walking away in disgust. But this year there have been well-publicised shortages. And last week, unknown to the public, stocks in London and Manchester fell to dangerously low levels. Sometimes the most effective policy for managers is to stop trying to be efficient, knock off early and go to the golf club.

Independent on Sunday October 1995

HOW TO WIN AT MONOPOLY

Liberal newspapers have their limits. Even on the *Observer*, reporters who cry, 'Hey, I've got a brilliant story about bus shelters!' are likely to feel one of the editor's long, cold looks stabbing the flesh between their shoulderblades and hear the jackal laughter of scheming colleagues. What the mockers fail to understand is that in Cool Britannia the mundane is lurid. Nothing that can conceivably make money is allowed to remain boring. Consideration of the apparently tedious subject of bus shelters necessarily leads to discussions of corruption, sweetheart deals, corporate binges, pelvic thrusts, the commercialisation of public space and the inability of an opportunist government to defend the public interest from assaults by anyone who calls himself a businessman.

Last week JC Decaux, a French company, excited the City by making a bid for an advertising firm called the More Group. If the takeover is successful, Decaux – which is owned by Jean-Claude Decaux, a 'reclusive millionaire' – will control 90 per cent of the 'street furniture' market. Street furniture turns out to be not only advert-bearing shelters, but superloos, drinking fountains, newspaper sellers' kiosks, litter bins designed in an ersatz belle-epoque style and Parisian pillars. All can be covered with posters and logos. Bringing a hard sell to every conceivable niche of public space is lucrative.

When Decaux bid for the rights to New York street furniture last year, the company estimated it could earn $1 billion a year from selling sites in the city. In theory, Britain has monopoly laws that prevent a tycoon cornering a market. But you only have to look at Tony Blair's eagerness to plant wet kisses on the thin lips of Rupert Murdoch to know the New Labour Department of Trade and Industry would sanction Hitler's invasion of Poland as a legitimate exercise in the free market in military force. Last week Decaux's PR people were confident that the government would not trouble them. They hoped their argument, that if the deal went ahead Decaux would still be a small fish in the broader British advertising pond, would be accepted.

If the DTI isn't bothered about monopolies, it is unlikely to be concerned about public opinion. From Barnet to San Francisco, Birmingham to Madrid, reactions to the arrival of street furniture have ranged from sullen hostility to near-riot. In the late Eighties, Birmingham's civic leaders made a doomed attempt to turn the glum but worthy manufacturing city into a hip sports and tourism centre. Councillors thought that advertising pillars would give Brum that continental ambience even its admirers conceded it lacked. The city was promised 550 'free' pillars that could be turned into superloos with Muzak and heated seats, kiosks or just left as eight-feet-high advertising columns. Decaux pocketed the advertising revenue while the city fathers had a £260,000 bill for installation costs.

The citizens of Nice discovered in 1995 that their council had also spent a small fortune on renting bus shelters from Decaux. It was not simply the cost (about £13,000 per shelter) that provoked disputes on the Riviera. According to a report in *Nice Matin*, Decaux was so keen to earn money from shelters with hoardings, it dumped them on roads with no bus routes. Confused tourists might wait for days for buses that would never come. In Madrid the council allowed Decaux to put up 1,500 pillars on pavements. The blind complained they kept bumping into the wretched lumps and shopkeepers said they blocked entrances to their stores. Three thousand protesters marched on the mayor's office chanting: 'Tacky! Tacky! Tacky!'

No one wants street furniture. The benefits to councils are, on occasion, non-existent. How does Decaux persuade politicians to do business? Some see opportunities for their cities to make money in honest deals. Others see opportunities for themselves. In July 1992 a Belgian court punished Edouard Close, Mayor of Liège, for accepting millions of francs-worth of campaign support from Decaux in return for pushing contracts the company's way. Jean-Claude Decaux received a year's suspended sentence for his part in the scandal. The burgomaster and his associates were given free holidays on the Côte d'Azur and in Spain, Corsica, Paris, Mauritius, Yemen, Sardinia and Senegal. 'At night, there were dinners in exquisite restaurants,' startled Belgian journalists recorded, 'after which they would let it all hang out among hip-swaying girls in leading Parisian cabarets.'

This was all a long time ago, said a dismissive Decaux spokesman. But in 1996 Pierre Cauchie, the Belgian manager of JC Decaux, was convicted in Antwerp for his part in the provision of fraudulent invoices in a political funding scandal. Last year the Mayor of San Francisco said he opposed a contract giving Decaux the rights to install street furniture in his city. He and his entourage were flown to Paris, wined, dined and presented with gifts. The mayor changed his mind. A few months ago, Decaux said it would make campaign contributions to Australian politicians if it won a Sydney contract. Tory councillors have been censured by the district auditor for failing to declare an interest in a contract to install Decaux superloos.

The political class's boosterism and enthusiasm for private–public partnerships, innovative thinking and imaginative modern solutions open up possibilities for corruption no one imagined might exist before. They have created a world where public space has become a hoarding and even lavatories must be viewed with suspicion.

If you missed this bus-shelter story, don't worry. Another one will be along soon.

Observer April 1998

GOODBYE,
MR CHIPS . . . HELLO, MR FRIES

If you had heard David Blunkett's and Stephen Byers's announcement that their standards revolution would bring high-class education to the young, you would probably have missed a detail buried in the appendices. McDonald's, the global junk food pedlar, was given ministerial permission to seduce schoolchildren. The Education Secretary and his deputy, Byers, a man whose ambition burns so bright it could power a county town, did not say as much. They confined themselves to trashing those who opposed commercial involvement in their education action zones. Teachers, elected councillors and other dinosaur deadbeats were victims of 'outdated dogma' and defenders of 'vested interests,' they said.

So lost were they in outdated Thatcherism, the hopeless numpties could not see that big businesses (which, according to a report from Cranfield University, have been given half the places on the 75 policy task forces Labour has created since the election) have a vested interest in capturing the child market, and no corporate raiding party is more *pris* than McDonald's. Blunkett and Byers are allowing the corporation to be a partner in the North Somerset education action zone and to send burger-flippers into local schools to help with English lessons. If this were the sole educational role for McDonald's, it would concern only those citizens of Weston-super-Mare who shrink from the sight of fat and spotty children. But since 1993 the company has offered teachers in all schools 'resource packs' that fill the gap left by the disappearance of expensive textbooks. Local history, one pack recommended, should be taught by getting children to 'explore the changes in use of the McDonald's site'. Music teachers were advised to encourage pupils to make up words for 'Old McDonald had a store,' to the tune of 'Old McDonald had a farm.' The English pack included such literary tasks as identifying and coupling 'Chicken' and 'McNuggets'. Soon the National Year of Reading will begin and Michael Barber,

Blunkett's chief adviser, is already bragging that the campaign will be so pervasive you will have to leave the country to escape it. The Department for Education has secured sponsorship from McDonald's and is asking it to provide free lunchboxes for children.

Should we condemn New Labour for corrupting schools by allowing McDonald's to use them as a marketplace for gullible young customers? 'That is an extremely cynical question,' said a company spokesman. 'We have always had the philosophy that we should put something back into the community.' Well, I've really tried my best, I really have, but even my cynicism cannot match the opportunism of the McDonald's marketing managers. Their calculations came out in the McLibel trial, the longest hearing in English legal history. The BBC refused to show a drama documentary on the fantastic defendants, Helen Steel and Dave Morris. Possibly it was felt impolitic to bring to a wider public a case that dissected corporate calculations and England's simultaneously oppressive and absurd legal system. For whatever reason, the failure to broadcast what happened has allowed the media myth to grow that McDonald's secured a Pyrrhic victory when it was awarded damages against Steel and Morris – whose criticisms it spent two years in court trying to silence. The case was a PR disaster for the company, to be sure, but it still won, many hacks believe. Given that the company is notoriously litigious, and, by the by, is a regular supplier of advertising revenue to the media, it is probably best to move on to the next business.

The trial record is not so clear cut. The judge did decide that a multi-national with a $30 billion (£19 billion) turnover needed to extract damages from two unemployed activists after finding against them on many points. (As so often with libel actions involving powerful men and institutions, the judge chose to hear the case alone and spared McDonald's the indignity of having to convince a jury of common people that it needed compensation for hurt feelings.) But on three issues McDonald's did not have a victory, Pyrrhic or otherwise. It lost. The court heard that its confidential operations manual instructed employees to remember, 'Children are often the key decision-makers concerning where a family goes to eat. Ronald loves McDonald's and McDonald's food. And so do children, because they love Ronald. You should do everything you can to appeal to children's love for Ronald and McDonald's.' As well as ruling that Steel and Morris were entitled to say, even in England, that the company targeted 'susceptible young children to bring in custom, both their own and that of their parents,' Mr Justice Bell found 'McDonald's advertisements, promotions and booklets have pretended to a positive nutritional benefit which McDonald's food did not match.' He also agreed that the defendants were telling no more than the truth when they said McDonald's 'paid its workers low wages, thereby helping to depress wages for workers in the catering trade'. About two-thirds of McDonald's staff are 20 or under. As Dave Morris said, McDonald's see schoolchildren as the next generation of cheap labour as well as burger-guzzling customers. New Labour, whose policy is to force the young into dead-end jobs, is obliging the company by keeping its labour supply 'flexible'.

Blunkett's drivellings and the trial transcript contradict a lazy complaint about the government. Barely a day passes without some wag writing that bob-haired and snub-nosed Blairites want to force the 'elite' tastes of Tuscany/Islington on the nation by banning smoking, drinking, impure thoughts about the opposite sex, beef on the bone, cakes, ale and other 'inappropriate' delights. Gags about political correctness are disinterred from their graves in the sad belief that they were funny the first time around. The creaking cracks miss the target because New Labour is part of a genuine elite that embraces politics, the media and business. Elite members would never dream, as Cherie Blair once sensibly said, of having the *Sun* in the house. They would be appalled if their children became Big Mac addicts or got jobs handing out fries at Burger King. Yet they are more than willing to use the fading populism of the declining *Sun* when they can to maintain their popularity and help McDonald's by bringing its marketing campaigns into the classroom.

The funny thing is that, when you then attack them, you are accused by the elite movers and Third Way shakers of being a 'liberal elitist' even though you have no chance of getting near power because you suffer from the crushing disability of not being a big businessman. We thus have an elite that embraces populism and forces the most degraded aspects of equally elitist corporations' populist diet and journalism on everyone's children but their own – while branding its principled critics as modern aristocrats. The elite–populist muddle shows that political language is now confused to the point of idiocy. Teaching children how to spell 'Chicken McNuggets' will not, I suspect, help them make sense of the cant.

Observer June 1998

PS   McDonald's went on to sponsor the Millennium Dome. Every school in the country has been invited to produce a McPlay based on 'our own town's story'. The appropriation of local histories by a multinational will be the only truly 'national' celebration of the millennium.

HOW TO BE STUPID

In the bad old days before the coronation of Master Tony, business leaders gazed on the British state education system with exasperated incomprehension. All those billions thrown at teachers, children and dinner ladies without one MBA or share option between them. What a waste! Fortunately, New Labour has recognised the special needs of executives suffering from attention deficit disorder and will allow them to profit from state schools. Michael Barber, adviser to David Blunkett, is upholding the central tenet of the political class that there is no area of life that cannot be improved by handing it over to corporate control. 'Successful companies are uniquely able to manage change and innovation,' he said as he announced business management of the government's inner-city 'education action zones'. Barber and Blunkett agreed that, in the words of the *Financial Times*, 'business does have a proven record of raising academic standards in the United States,' and should be given a chance here.

No one questioned them, although a few phone calls and a quick glance at the available research would have revealed that the 'proven record' of business involvement in American state schools prominently features collapsing standards, fiddled exam results, creative accounting and a mass experiment in the effects of forcing children to be a captive market for advertisers. Like New Labour, US cities fell for the line that private companies could, magically, improve children's performance without spending more public money and still make a profit large enough to keep the shareholders sweet. It took three years for American local authorities to discover that school corporations can merely manage the last. In 1992 the leaders of the impoverished city of Baltimore gave Education Alternatives Inc. a $135 million (£85 million) contract to run nine schools. The company promised to solve the profit problem by cutting back on the costs of administration. Once red tape had been slashed, resources would be concentrated on teaching. The efficiency savings would be large enough to allow Education Alternatives to grant itself a modest reward for its labours without costing the city an extra cent. John Golle, the firm's owner, presented a selfless front when he explained his priorities to the press. His brand of capitalism was dedicated to relieving the poor, he asserted. Asked if Baltimore would ever turn against him, he cried: 'No way, no way, no way, no way. The have-nots all of a sudden have something. Good, clean, safe schools, loaded with technology. Just try to take it away from the have-nots. Just try.' Many believed him. US hacks, politicians and Hillary Clinton played the part of gormless cheerleaders and hailed the company's management as a 'trailblazing' and 'mould-breaking' success.

I don't know if the first lady felt any shame when the truth about Golle came out, but I can find no public retraction. The lean company that declared war on bureaucratic waste spent $750,000 (£470,000) of public money on lawyers, travel and consultants and $2 million (£1.25 million) on what it called 'overheads' at a head office hundreds of miles from Baltimore. The profits from the contract helped maintain Golle's two luxurious homes and a fleet of nine cars. No one could find out how much the executive friends of the poor were taking because, as a manager from the Edison Project, another corporation that has moved into American state schools, explained: 'This is the nice thing about working for a private company . . . you don't have to disclose anything.' What was incontestable was that have-not pupil-customers were the victims of educational asset-stripping. The firm cut 25 per cent of teaching posts and children were squeezed into classes of 40. City regulations that guaranteed public money would be spent on handicapped children were ignored. The company boasted it was cutting truancy rates, while classroom attendances were falling. It told parents it had improved exam results, until the *Baltimore Sun* showed how they were being falsified. Money had to be taken from other schools to subsidise the private managers. By 1995, Baltimore had had enough of Education Alternatives Inc. and threw it out. So, too, did the school board in Hartford, Connecticut.

Edison, its rival, found a different way out of the profits problem. Instead of ripping off parents, it sold children to marketing departments. The company was founded in 1989 by Chris Whittle, an advertiser, who broke with the traditions of his trade when he came up with an original idea. Whittle realised he could make a fortune if he turned America into the first country where the state forced pupils to watch adverts. He offered American schools (shamefully underfunded, as in Britain) what appeared to be a fabulous deal. They would each get free use, although not ownership, of a satellite receiver, two videos and as many televisions as they wanted. All he asked in return was a guarantee that bulletins from his Channel One station were shown. Every day a 10-minute 'news' broadcast would be beamed in with two minutes of commercials for Pepsi, Reebok, gangsta rap, the US military, burgers,

Twix, M&Ms and – perhaps wisely after all the junk food – Clearasil. As long as the school signed a contract that stipulated that 90 per cent of children watched his package for an hour a week, Whittle allowed teachers to use his equipment for any other purpose. He was pushing at an open door. Heads were willing to sell their grannies to save money. By 1993 he had a market of eight million children which included 40 per cent of US teenagers. Advertisers were so keen on compulsory commercials they paid $200,000 (£125,000) for a 30-second slot.

You might think that children are bombarded with images during every waking moment, and a few more adverts at school could hardly be expected to make much difference. It is, after all, commonplace for advertisers seeking to avoid regulation to say that commercials are harmless. They don't brainwash, they simply inform sovereign consumers who are free to make their own minds up. Advertising is ubiquitous and as accepted a fact of life as the weather. Arguments against commercialisation, which once raged fiercely, have an old-fashioned ring. The debate seemed dead. Whittle's ironic and inadvertent achievement was to reopen it by running a controlled experiment on the effect of advertising on children's values. I suspect his colleagues in the industry would like to keep the results out of public discourse.

His promotional literature said Channel One was a superb advertising vehicle because children had to watch it. They couldn't flip between stations or leave the room. Whittle delivered 'the hardest-to-reach teen viewers'; pupils who – My God! – preferred reading or playing to watching the telly. For at the time Whittle moved into the pedagogy business a disturbingly large numbers of American children were bored with the box. Companies were like frustrated Jesuits. 'Advertisers who target teens know they watch an average of 10 hours less television a week' than adults, the station told potential customers. Channel One could catch the consumer society's truants because it stole the authority of the school for its corporate backers and turned teachers into salesmen. A jeans company advert, for example, announced that children should go to the head and get vouchers that would give them

25 per cent off their next purchase. Reebok's adverts told pupils their teachers 'were working for Reebok', which was no more than the truth when heads were following the company's instructions and signing up kiddies for Reebok trainer promotions. In an unguarded moment, David Tanzer, Channel One president, gave a further reason why schools were a soft touch: 'Teachers are so desperate to make lessons relevant that if they can get them interested through a Reebok campaign, they'll do it.'

Presented with a vehicle like no other, companies created a new type of targeted advert. Pepsi's Channel One slogans – 'Pepsi cares more than any other soft drinks company', Pepsi 'gives teens a voice' – were so successful that academics studying the effects of the station found pupils who could not tell the difference between Pepsi commercials and public-service announcements. The channel's profits were robust – $30 million in 1996 – and satisfied Whittle's investors, who included Associated Newspapers, owners of the *Daily Mail* and *Mail on Sunday* (oh come on, you must remember, the papers that rage about depraved liberal teachers poisoning pupils' minds).

The news the channel delivered was the feeblest of excuses for getting commercials into schools. Bulletins focused on the youthful anchors who received pathetic love letters at the Channel One web site. 'Hey Joel, I think you're cool, a great reporter and also kinda hot,' read one entry when I last tuned in. 'Kris don't listen to them people that tell you you look gay when you part your hair [Kris's parting is a big issue on Channel One] or wear them turtleneck sweaters, they're just jealous.' An American study of Channel One concluded adverts and news merged seamlessly and the package was a 'slick 12-minute commercial'.

There is no evidence that Channel One children were better informed than their contemporaries in schools without its satellite 'news'. But research in Michigan showed that the advertising – the station's sole reason to exist – was working wonderfully and having a disturbing effect. Pupils who watched the channel were far more likely than their peers to agree with the propositions: 'A nice car is more important than school'; 'Money is everything'; 'Designer labels make a difference'; 'I want what I see advertised'; and 'Wealthy people are happier than poor people'. In *How To Be Stupid: The Teaching of Channel One*, Mark Crispin Miller, an American educationalist, concluded that, at root, the messages in both news and commercials the children imbibed were: 'Watch.' 'Don't think.' 'Let us fix it.' 'Eat now.' 'You're ugly.' 'Just say yes'. Whittle had proved that even in a culture saturated with advertising, allowing corporations into schools warped children and undermined their education.

If you believe you're reading another discussion of the ghastliness of modern America, we should turn to what New Labour is doing to British education before you get too smug. There may not be a Channel One here yet, but our new government has shown itself to be free of elitist prejudices by encouraging corporate promotions in schools and allowing Rupert Murdoch, owner of the illiterate *Sun*, to sponsor its summer literacy campaign. In the US, the lobbying of politicians by private contractors anxious to get public funds is accepted and expected. Whittle spent $1 million trying to persuade California to let his channel into the state's schools. We may soon see something similar. Arthur Andersen, the management consultants, runs a school in California and realises the business opportunities a dissolution of the state education sector will bring. The firm is close to New Labour – its consultants worked free of charge for the party before the election. Now Labour is in power, an Andersen man is in the Department for Education setting up private finance initiatives for schools and, I'm sure, gaining useful experience.

Above all, contempt for vulgar America is misplaced because Whittle is ready to move into Britain. He sold Channel One in 1993 but kept the school management side of the Edison Project going. Blunkett's aides say he wants to give him the contract to manage one of the education action zones, and Edison is already tying up a deal with a comprehensive in Tameside and has approached education officers in Surrey,

Nottingham and Hackney. Edison's chief British salesman is James Tooley, a right-wing educationalist, and another great one for lecturing the nation in *Mail* fashion on how education went to the dogs in the Sixties. When confronted with the problem of how a company can make money from state schools without ripping off taxpayers and pupils, he raved about the profitable uses of new technology. Video conferencing and satellite links would allow a teacher to address three or more classes at the same time, he said as he unconsciously repeated a cost-cutting fantasy that has been tried and found wanting since the invention of radio. Another solution might well be adverts. Tooley is such a keen free-marketeer he condemned the Conservatives for not privatising state schools. He told me he is far happier with the new government. His affection is reciprocated. 'He gets on better with Labour than the Tories,' said a civil servant in the Department for Education.

Tooley and his Labour allies share many ideological affinities. A policeman in their heads ensures that their demands for higher academic standards never threaten the interests of their corporate sponsors. Tooley, the defender of traditional values, is able to ignore the US parents who particularly objected to the 'educational' Channel One playing Marilyn Manson, a satanic heavy metal combo whose members are named after notable serial killers and whose act includes much blood being sloshed round the stage while the lead singer eats bats. Nor does he seem to care that Whittle's old station advertised teen chat lines and the Hollywood diet of violent and brainless movies. Yet when they turn their gaze to the public sector, buttocks tighten, backs stiffen and Tooley and the New Labour establishment become the sternest of moralisers. Tooley was hired by Blair's friend Chris Woodhead, who has built his career by condemning low standards in all fields except the commercial. Her Majesty's Chief Inspector of Schools told him to investigate the value of educational research in liberal universities. Somehow academics knew what his report would say before he wrote it; they guessed that official fingers would wag at their obsessions with race, class, sex and other irrelevancies. The inquiry has not been completed, but Woodhead has surprised no one by revealing that Tooley's work in progress includes the conclusion that educational research is 'dross'. Zero tolerance in the public sector, perpetual indulgence in the private.

You won't have read much in the newspapers about the dark side of Whittle's record. Fleet Street's education correspondents' coverage of Edison has made this hardened hack weep. I will admit that they look magnificent in their tweeds, corduroys and bargains from the Monsoon sale, but I have reluctantly come to the conclusion that they couldn't manage 30 seconds of investigative journalism. Time and again they have parroted the Edison Project's PR and recycled its press releases. They don't mention Channel One, don't discuss the effect of advertising on pupils and appear not to know that research at the University of Wisconsin could find no evidence that Edison institutions were providing a better education.

Fleet Street and Whitehall are dominated by corporate values and cannot bring themselves to say that even by his (and their) crass standards, Whittle is a failure. His history has been one of decline. He was a man of lavish tastes, with an expensive wife, the niece of Gianni Agnelli no less, and three homes. In the early Nineties Whittle executives were receiving salaries of £250,000 plus, and their boss regularly threw parties costing £75,000 a bash. He built a mock Georgian company HQ at Knoxville in Tennessee. Locals commemorated its garishness by naming the pile Whittlesburg. Since he sold the advertising channel, his reputation as a go-getting entrepreneur has taken a battering. His plans to transmit a drug company-financed commercial television service to patients in American doctors' surgeries, came to nothing. Debts built up and the company's ambitions collapsed. In 1994 the Edison Project predicted it would soon manage 1,000 American schools. It currently manages a mere 25 and has yet to make a profit. In other words, a Labour government is throwing a lifeline to a struggling firm whose chief claim to fame is that its founder helped stifle the spirit of millions of American children. Call me a fuddy-duddy if you must, but am I missing something? Isn't this what used to be called a story? And doesn't the arrival of classroom corporations require that a little consideration is given to questions of principle and policy?

Alex Molnar, Professor of Education at Wisconsin University, provides it when he concludes a powerful investigation into American education — *Giving the Kids the Business* — with the thought that state schools cannot be run for profit because they provide education to parents who cannot afford it individually. 'The market can offer no guidance on matters of justice and fairness that are at the heart of democratic civil society,' he writes. 'Left to its own devices, the market is as utterly incapable of making high-quality schools for every child as it is of providing a job for every American who needs one.'

Observer 1998

BOARDROOM REVOLUTIONARIES

When I was a student there was a popular caricature of an unbending Marxist who refused to give money to starving beggars because charity ameliorated the contradictions of capitalism and postponed the day when revolution would sweep the land. I thought the joke was just that, but now . . .

We move to Trafalgar Square on 31 March 1990. Mark Steel, the comedian and writer, was watching the Metropolitan Police fail to contain tens of thousands of demonstrators. The anti-poll tax riot led to the biggest campaign of civil disobedience since the war as well as the fall of Margaret Thatcher. Next to Steel was a commissar from the Revolutionary Communist Party, which dismissed those who fought a tax that took from the poor and gave to the rich as wet liberals. 'There's nothing to be concerned about,' he sneered down a phone to head office, 'just a bunch of middle-class kids playing about.' The revolutionary party also despised Anti-Apartheid for 'helping capitalism' by supporting sanctions against South Africa, and had nothing but contempt for the NHS. At about the time of the poll tax revolt, Yunus Baksh, secretary of a Unison branch in Newcastle upon Tyne, was organising protests against cuts in funding. At one, members of the RCP handed out leaflets denouncing the cause of better pay for miserable cleaners and porters. Nurses were jostled and abused when they asked whether the NHS was really an instrument of the repressive state. After a second demo, Baksh and ambulance drivers worried about their jobs met members of the party in a Newcastle pub. The comrades shouted at Baksh and punched him in the face. You might think that a tiny group of cranks – so far gone it agreed with the *Sunday Times* that Aids was a 'gay plague' that could never be contracted by heterosexuals, and opposed rallies against the British National Party – would be a footnote in political history. But today the RCP is the acme of fashion, all the rage. Join it, my dears, and see the doors of the media, big business and high culture open when you ring.

Looking good was always a revolutionary priority for the RCP. A man, who asked to be called 'John' because he did not want to be troubled by his former friends, said supporters had to serve an apprenticeship with a handler who monitored their progress. They were allowed to become full members only when they had shown they had imbibed the correct ideology by sitting an exam on the party's theory. 'If you passed you got a clothing allowance,' he said. 'You had to be attractive, trendy, so you would go down well when we tried to find wealthy recruits at the Edinburgh Festival and outside Sloane Square tube.'

The party stopped active work in the early Nineties. Adherents clustered on its magazine, *Living Marxism*, which was renamed *LM*. Last year Channel 4 broadcast *Against Nature*, a three-hour series devoted to *LM*'s theme that environmentalists are modern Nazis who throw fabricated concerns about global warming and the mass extinction of species in the way of progress. The green movement isn't sacred and should be able to answer hostile questions, but viewers would have known where

Against Nature was coming from if they had been told that the assistant producer, Eve Kaye, was a coordinator of *LM*, and that the director Martin Durkin described himself as a Marxist. (He denied any link with *LM* but followed its line.) The documentaries quoted two 'independent experts' who praised human cloning and condemned sustainable development in the Third World as a Western conspiracy against the wretched of the earth. One was John Gillott, *LM*'s science correspondent; another was Frank Furedi, *LM*'s star columnist and all-round media don from Kent University. (Furedi is also known as Frank Richards, incidentally. Like Lenin and Trotsky, many at *LM* fight under a *nom de guerre*.) *LM* continues the RCP tradition of striking reactionary postures. Last week a howling book was printed by Jonathan Hunt, a second-hand car salesman turned journalist, which accused my colleagues on *The Guardian* of framing Neil Hamilton. That mighty moralist and spanker, Paul Johnson, and the rest of the *Spectator* crowd hate the paper for having the impertinence to tell the truth about Jonathan Aitken, and abuse it weekly. Even they could not bring themselves to endorse Hunt. He was, however, able to cite support from *LM* in his defence. When I dropped into the *LM* office they gave me Hamilton's home number and urged me to phone the old brute. 'He calls us his friends,' said *LM*'s James Heartfield, whose real name is James Hughes.

Last year *LM* ran a story from a German engineer-turned-journalist who defends the Serbian leadership against all-too-clear charges of murder, systematic rape and ethnic cleansing. The magazine claimed ITN had fooled the world by forging its famous pictures of starving Bosnians herded behind barbed wire by the Serbs. ITN sued and the liberal aristocracy *LM* loathes came to its aid. Harold Evans, Doris Lessing, Fay Weldon and Paul Theroux reproached ITN for a 'deplorable attack on press freedom'. Decent journalists see the British libel laws as a menace. They know that powerful frauds, such as Aitken and Hamilton, can use them to suppress awkward inquiries. Doubtless Evans and the rest thought they were defending a plucky little magazine against an overbearing media conglomerate. But as George Monbiot will point out in an article in the forthcoming issue of *Prospect*, the conflict is more apparent than real, and global capital and living Marxists can get on famously. Anti-imperialist *LM* runs pieces by Roger Bate of the far-right Institute for Economic Affairs, which believes that African countries would be better governed if they were sold to multi-nationals. This year it printed the theory of one Ron Arnold who claimed that the Unabomber was an environmentalist and – QED! – environmentalists were therefore terrorists. Arnold is Vice President of the Centre of the Defense of Free Enterprise, which campaigns against restrictions on corporate America. *Against Nature* not only featured *LM* contributors but also Reaganite economists and members of the Cato Institute, another well-endowed American think-tank that works with the British Adam Smith Institute to promote the dismantling of the Chilean welfare state by the topical General Pinochet as a model for the US and UK. All agreed with *LM* that leftie greens were endangering human happiness. The Independent Television Commission forced Channel 4 to make a prime-time apology.

The links with corporations are not merely ideological. A leaked memo is causing great hilarity in the consumer movement. It appears to show the radical Frank Furedi/Richards offering his services to the supermarket cartel. For £7,500 he will provide research that will 'educate' consumers towards a 'less emotive' consideration of food safety. Business-friendly dismissals of 'panics' about BSE and genetically modified food feature strongly in *LM*'s 'libertarian' philosophy. Furedi says that although he has received no money from supermarkets he would be willing to accept payments.

It is at this point that an obscure sect becomes an authentic representative of the spirit of an age where corporate values undermine all others. The party leaders talk of 'UK plc', as if democracy were a business and the electorate were consumers to be swindled by advertising executives (or spin doctors, as Westminster journalists call them) and chivvied into snapping up bargain buys by the shop girls formerly known as politicians. Last week David Blunkett announced a new training college for head teachers would be set up at a business school. The Education Secretary said heads were like 'managing directors of big companies' and showed no sign of knowing that managing directors do not have a duty to produce an educated public who appreciate learning for its own sake, and would be sacked in seconds if they said they did. I could quote examples for ever. I think, however, it is with *LM* that we see multi-national triumphalism reaching an apotheosis. We can now gaze on the gorgeous spectacle of corporate Marxists: the boardroom's revolutionary arm. If, that is, you can say that *LM* is revolutionary. Its spokeswoman, Clare Fox (I don't know if that's a real name), said in true Blairite fashion that differences between left and right didn't amount to a hill of beans these days, and she was far more concerned with restraints on freedom. Yet there was one organisation that supported the poll tax, low pay for hospital workers, the lifting of sanctions against South Africa, Neil Hamilton and unlimited freedom for corporations: the Conservative Party. Most put it on the right.

The Conservatives had no time for drips who gave change to beggars. Nor does RCP/*LM*. 'John', our former supporter, was out with his handler when he passed a beggar and dropped 50 pence into his hat. His minder exploded. 'Don't you realise you're helping capitalism?' he roared. 'Don't you realise you are subsidising poverty?' All John realised was that he had had more than enough of 'middle-class kids playing about', and quit.

Observer October 1998

A WORD ABOUT THEIR SPONSORS

The gala dinner at the Labour Party conference on the 29th of this month will see the social exclusivity of the Versailles court come to proletarian Blackpool. The shabby poor who voted for Tony in the hope that he would represent them won't get past the bouncers. Nor will the smarter but equally credulous delegates who suppose they have been sent to the Winter Gardens to direct government policy. Flowers, food, tables and drinks will be branded by corporate sponsors. The conference will be plastered with as many logos as a Bernie Ecclestone fag cart and look more like a trade fair than a political convention.

Which only goes to show that appearances do not always deceive. The conference has become a venue where politics comes at a price. The real movers of New Labour – businesses and lobbyists – are renting tables at £2,000 apiece. In return each firm will be served with a Labour politician to soak up the sales patter through all the courses. The undoubted belles of the ball will be executives from the American power firm Enron. They are hosting the pre-dinner drinks and will have plenty of time to simper at the Prime Minister. I suspect their advances will be welcomed. Jeffrey Skilling, Enron's chief executive, has a New Labour impatience with curbs on capitalism. 'You must cut jobs ruthlessly by 50 or 60 per cent,' he has said of his employees. 'Depopulate. Get rid of people. They gum up the works.' Amnesty International exposed degumming in India when it investigated the beatings of villagers opposed to an Enron power plant. So violent was the company's use of what in effect was a private army, it received the distinctive honour of being the subject of the only Amnesty report about a corporation rather than a dictatorship. Complaints about Enron have been logged around the world by environmentalists and prosecuting authorities. I'm sure the government will brush criticisms aside because Enron, for all its faults, has one remarkable quality: it is the global leader in squaring politicians.

There are those who propose that it does not matter how citizens vote in the United States because corporate funding of parties ensures that the political class and permanent government will always put the business interest before the public interest. Their beliefs are amply confirmed by Enron. If one man can embody the decay of American democracy, then Kenneth Lay, Enron's founder, is it. His profits come from running gas, nuclear, coal, wind, electric and water plants. He must persuade governments to deregulate and privatise to keep the money flowing. A light regulatory touch is necessary not only because Enron wants to buy public assets with the minimum of interference but because it is up to its neck in the derivatives market. The firm bets on what the weather, and thus the demand for its power, will be. Governments made nervous by Nick Leeson might ask agitated questions were they not calmed with campaign donations when they are in power and well-paid jobs when they retire. Enron gave generously to George Bush's campaigns. When he lost the 1992 election, two Bush cabinet ministers and his former director of operations were hired by Enron, and Bush's sons lobbied for the company in Argentina. The Commodity Futures Trading Commission, which is meant to control the US energy industry, was keen to free power companies from the shackles of regulation. It proposed exempting them from fraud legislation. Three months after Wendy Gramm, the commission's chairwoman, decided that the law, like taxes, was for the little people only, she left for a job on Enron's board. Tom DeLay, a Republican representative, was the crudest recipient of the company's dollars. He introduced a bill to Congress to deregulate the electricity industry. The link between campaign donations to DeLay and his support for private energy corporations was so brazen that Washington wags nick-named his measure the Enron Bill.

In the true spirit of permanent government, Republican Enron executives have been happy to fund Democrats. Master of corruption that he is, Bill Clinton did not even have the decency to wait to be seduced but took the initiative when he came to power in 1992 and practically begged Enron to suborn the Democratic presidency. He ordered Mack McLarty, his chief of staff, to do all he could to help Enron, and DeLay became a presidential golfing partner. Clinton's support for Enron was vigorous. Mozambique's minerals minister said America threatened to withdraw all aid if he did not allow the company to exploit natural gas reserves. In the 1996 presidential election Enron slipped $142,000 to Clinton's campaign. Enron denied the money was payment for services rendered. Clinton had merely wanted to promote a great American company. Make of this what you will, but in all the company has put $3 million into campaign funds since 1988, according to an invaluable Washington magazine, *Counterpunch*, which monitors the wholesale trade in politicians. Enron's shareholders must surely expect a return from such a substantial investment.

That the company feels it can send its buyers to deal with the board of UK plc speaks loudly to those who are concerned about the strangling of democratic choice. Admittedly, there do not seem to be too many of us about. As soon as you start questioning Labour's drive to become the party of business, some podgy pundit starts bellowing that the old trade union funding of Labour was just as dubious as the new corporate sponsorship. They do not seem to understand that no one gives money to politicians without strings. What matters to the electorate is the variety of policies on offer. When all the major parties court business, the likelihood of any government frustrating corporate desires is vanishingly small.

The process of draining democracy of content – otherwise known as the Blair project – is moving rapidly. Although its expenditure in Britain is paltry by US standards, Enron can see that a British political class is developing on US lines and is working hard to attract its attention. As well as stuffing £15,000 into New Labour pockets, it has hired one of the party's favourite consultants, Karl Milner, who left the service of Gordon Brown to work as an influence-pedlar with the lobbying firm GJW. You may remember during the cash-for-access scandal Milner bragged to the *Observer*'s undercover reporter, Greg Palast, that 'we have many friends in government. They like to run things past us some days in advance, to get our view.' He proved he was not exaggerating by producing a copy of an unpublished Parliamentary report on energy policy. Milner told Palast that he had swiped it for Enron. The company was eager to be exempted from a profit-threatening moratorium on building private gas plants the government was planning to introduce to save the remnants of the coal industry. Milner described how he would help Enron avoid troublesome regulation by manipulating New Labour. 'There are ways round it,' he said. 'The way that you go about it is that you play on the existing prejudices within the Cabinet for coal, you play on the existing prejudices within the Cabinet for competition, and you play the forces off against each other. It's intimate knowledge of what's going on that produces results in the end. That's how GJW makes money.' In return for his fee he arranged private meetings at the Treasury and with John Battle, the Energy minister.

Bipartisanship flourishes in Britain, too. Enron has hired the former Tory Energy Secretary, Lord Wakeham, and plonked him on its bulging board. He combines his services to the company, for which he receives a salary of $78,000, with the part-time job of chairman of the Press Complaints Commission, moral arbiter of the newspaper industry.

With so much money and effort being spent on wooing the people's representatives it is sad yet inevitable that services to the public have suffered. On the coast of the Arabian Sea at Dhobal near Bombay, Enron has built the sub-continent's largest power plant, with $2.8 billion of the Indian taxpayers' money. There have been constant protests from villagers who say Enron effluent is destroying their fisheries and coconut and mango trees. In June 1997, when the men were at sea, courageous police armed with batons turned on women and children and beat and imprisoned them. 'I was in the bath,' Baba Bhaleker, the wife of one of the leaders of the demonstrations, told Indian journalists. 'They dragged me out of the house and kept beating me on my back. My one-and-a-half-year-old daughter held on, but the police kicked her away.' 'Goondas' (goons) broke into protesters' homes, Amnesty reported, and warned they would be killed if they continued to oppose the station. Hundreds of women were arrested and held in stinking jails. Amnesty showed how the police had been bought by the company at $3.50 per day per cop to act as its agents and were backed up by its private security guards. The US ambassador in New Delhi, Frank G. Wisner, put enormous pressure on the Indian government to stop

Enron being thrown out of the country after the corporate riot. He got a seat on Enron's board when he retired.

Enron faces charges in Puerto Rico after a propane gas plant blew up. Closer to home, two British workers at Enron's Teesside plant almost died from burns after a fuel explosion. Magistrates fined the company £10,000 for failure to exercise due care.

The company's environmental record is predictably ghastly. In the American state of Oregon, Enron inherited an abandoned nuclear plant which had had the right to take water from local rivers. Frank Gearhart, an Oregon environmentalist, reports that Enron is now selling those rights, which were only given on condition that the extracted water was used in the plant. He predicts rivers will dry up in the summer. His fellow green activist, Jody Robindottir, added: 'Enron has countless environmental problems. Everywhere they go they destroy the infrastructure.' In Louisiana, Enron's gas plant contaminated drinking water with lead. In Florida the company was fined for pollution so gross the state government said it was 'the worst environmental damage from a single project' it had ever seen.

After all of the above, I'm sure you won't be startled to hear that Enron's visit to Blackpool coincided with a bid for Wessex Water. The Trade Secretary, Peter Mandelson, must decide whether the company will have monopoly control of the water supply in southern England. Will he look at Enron's record in India and the US? Will he declare a conflict of interest and say that civil servants must decide whether the takeover goes ahead? If you think the answer to either or both questions might be yes, you really don't understand how the permanent government operates.*

Observer September 1998

---

* It was no in both cases.

LIFE IN THE REAL WORLD

Eamon Coyle is gay. He isn't an Outrage! closet-emptier who will shout 'I'm homosexual' from the rooftops, but he will briefly discuss his private life if you ask while at the same time thinking it's none of your business. His modest openness may not meet the requirements of daytime TV but does mean that his sexuality cannot be used to blackmail him. Which is just as well because Coyle worked at Harrods until he was forced out in 1995, and Mohamed Fayed knows all there is to know about intimidation. Coyle made himself a target by telling what he knew about the Fayed way of human resource management and received a bully's ultimatum: mess with me and you'll suffer, obey me and I will be your friend.

Fayed looms large in the British imagination. His endless battle with Tiny Rowland and his attempts to overturn the Department of Trade and Industry report that branded him a liar have resulted in the well-merited destruction of the careers of Neil Hamilton and Jonathan Aitken. Fayed took his case against the DTI inspectors and the judges – who upheld their conclusion that he lied when he fought Rowland for control of Harrods – all the way to the European Court of Human Rights. His claim for British citizenship is heading in the same direction. And when a drunk driver in Fayed's employ took his son and his son's girlfriend for a drive in Paris, there was a crash and Diana Spencer, for reasons I don't pretend to understand, became a saint for a while. With the monarchy, law, City, Parliament and Fleet Street all caught in his grand feuds, it is worth remembering that the tactics used by Fayed against Coyle and others are unexceptional. Thousands of workers in unglamorous firms receive comparable treatment.

Coyle began a career in security as a policeman in Ireland. He moved to London and joined Harrods in 1979 as a store detective. He was promoted quickly and became the deputy security director. He slipped up in 1990 when he was convicted of a trivial charge of criminal damage and was fined £100. He told his superior, Major Bob Loftus, about the conviction and that seemed to be that until 1995, when Coyle investigated allegations that Harrods staff were moonlighting. When he dismissed a former Metropolitan Police detective sergeant, the sacked investigator found out about Coyle's conviction – which was meant to be secret – and used it in an appeal. Coyle went and Loftus soon followed. Since their resignations, they have talked at length, and with impressive and confirmable detail, about how Fayed ran Harrods as a corporate secret state. Scores of employees were bugged because Fayed doubted their loyalty. Michael Cole – Fayed's spokesman – executives, secretaries, bodyguards and, above all, officers of Usdaw, the shop workers' union, were tapped. The security department ran a hi-tech system that could record three different calls – a section manager being indiscreet about his sex life, another moaning she was a victim of discrimination and a third complaining about a manager – at the same time.

Coyle and Loftus went on television in December 1997 to discuss the company's paranoid authoritarianism. On 19 January, Michael Rogers, Harrods' legal director, wrote to Coyle saying he had a company training video that had been taped over and showed Coyle being 'intimate' with a boyfriend in a company flat. 'I think it best not to describe in this letter the contents,' sniffed the lawyer with a combination of coyness and menace. He told Coyle Harrods would go to the police and charge him with theft of the tape, but then dangled a carrot in front of him. Before Harrods phoned 999, it wanted to hear his 'input'. Coyle was asked to give the store 'observations' that may be 'relevant' to Loftus's claims about the bugging of staff and could help Fayed's 'legal proceedings' against the Major. In other words: cooperate or we'll set the cops on you. Coyle ignored the letter. Loftus was a friend and he could not see how anyone might imagine he had committed a crime. He had made a video on one of his own tapes as a memento of an affair and suspects a copy was made in Harrods when it split and he asked a colleague he thought he could trust in the TV department to repair it.

Harrods wasn't bluffing. It called Scotland Yard, and London's finest – with all the crimes of a great and dangerous metropolis to investigate – came running to arrest Coyle. Now let's assume the Harrods management is telling the truth and Coyle did tape over a training video. It is a hard assumption to make, I grant you, after Coyle's firm denial, the DTI's conclusion that in Fayed's world 'lies were the truth and the truth was a lie', the record of covert operations against staff that makes Coyle's story about his tape being copied more than credible and the reports from Fayed about Di giving dying words she appears to have been in no condition to utter. Yet even if we pretend that Harrods is being candid for once, it is still very hard indeed to understand why the police should care. Harrods has the tape back in its possession and might record any training instructions on it. At most Coyle has put his former employer to the inconvenience of taping on fresh corporate guidance on how to dispense perfume or ignore the fact that your manager is bugging your phone. But the police care very deeply about this most trivial of alleged crimes – as they have cared deeply before. A former finance director, Graham Jones, was hauled off a plane at Heathrow, for instance, and detained by the Met after a spurious fraud complaint from Harrods. A former managing director was held in prison in Dubai on trumped-up charges from Fayed. He sued Fayed and won. There have been many other complaints from Harrods to the Met against employees, from senior executives to cleaners. All the accusations were rigorously investigated and all later withdrawn or proved false. Every victim of unwelcome police attention had crossed Fayed. Mess with us and you know that we will have something on tape you wouldn't like to come out. Mess with us and the police will pick you up and, if we've fired you and you're looking for a new job, you wouldn't like prospective employers in the conservative world of retailing to hear about that, would you? Even the unflappable Coyle is worried that a copy of his video will get to a tabloid. I can't see why the papers would be interested, but that's not the way you think when the screws are being turned.

I phoned my old friend Michael Cole to discuss these and other issues. When I last spoke to him in the days after the Paris smash he had told me he loved Fayed like a father. His secretary said he had just resigned and no one else could answer my questions.

If Fayed is a monster the police are more than happy to serve, he is not a lone brute in the jungle. British Airways set private detectives on its workforce. The wives and children of striking workers at the Magnet Kitchens Factory in Darlington have been threatened with legal action by Clifford Chance, Magnet's fantastically wealthy firm of City solicitors, for organising a peaceful protest on a public right of way outside the luxury home of the company's chief executive. Private security forces and a legal system that regards workers' rights as illegitimate have allowed coercive surveillance to become a standard management tool. Security cameras and computer systems that can monitor the number of times each and every worker hits a key have made spying as much a problem for the average office worker as for the employees of the phoney pharaoh.

All of which puts into perspective Tony Blair's desire to water down New Labour's commitment to give staff the right to vote for representation by a union. Blair and the Downing Street Policy Unit have accepted the Confederation of British Industry demands that a union must not merely win 51 per cent of votes in a recognition ballot but the support of 40 per cent of workers eligible to vote (a rule that would lead to nearly all MPs losing their seats if it were enforced at general elections). The unions protest that the concessions will make it easier for executives to use intimidation to scare employees from voting for union rights. Blair, rather impertinently, told the TUC last year that trade unions must 'live in the real world'. As I look at a Prime Minister, whose life has consisted of public school, Oxford, the Bar and the Commons, and gaze at the New Labour benches filled with the prim shapes of professional pols, place-seekers, flatterers, gutless wonks and Stepford Wives, I wonder they really have any idea of just how real the real world can be.

Observer February 1998

GENETICALLY MODIFIED
GOVERNMENT

To the literal-minded, the controversy stirred by the demand by Monsanto that its weird science should be licensed in Britain is easy to resolve. No one from bedraggled green activists to the most conservative patrons of the Sainsbury's ready-shredded salad counter wants genetically modified food. The government should ban it and turn to more pressing issues. I'm sure all readers prospering in the fixing business will be relieved to hear that the naive notion that democratic politicians must respond to the will of the people has been dismissed for the sentimental tosh it is. As the courts impose ferocious penalties on its critics, as magazines reporting the history of the US chemical company are pulped and as Washington and New Labour lobbyists turn their charm on a receptive Whitehall, Monsanto can gaze with satisfaction on the gap between democratic theory and practice.

The company's authoritarian successes may confuse those who remember its touchy-feely advertising campaign of the summer. The firm promised to supply readers with the addresses of critics of the food industry because: 'We believe that food is so fundamentally important, everyone should know all they want to about it.' One critic is the *Ecologist* magazine, a small well-researched journal, which sent an issue on Monsanto to its printers, Penwell's of Liskeard in Cornwall. The special edition promised to be a fascinating read. The magazine planned to show how Monsanto manufactured Agent Orange, the poison the Americans carpet-bombed on the Vietnamese. Various learned authors reported that for all the claims of openness – 'Food biotechnology is a matter of opinion,' its adverts continued, 'we believe you should hear all of them.' – the company suppressed discordant voices. When American farmers marketed their milk by saying it was free of a bovine growth hormone Monsanto produced called rBGH, the company sued them. The hormone has been banned in Europe and Canada because of fears of a link to cancer. Politicians in the US state of Vermont were threatened with legal action when they insisted that milk with the hormone must be labelled. British consumers who believe that clear labelling will give them the choice of not buying genetically modified food should take note. Genetically engineered soya beans are already being imported from America, and no label tells us they are mushed up in our processed meals. Supermarket customers are unlikely to learn about the dodging of labelling regulations from the *Ecologist*. The printers told the editor, Edward Goldsmith, that they had destroyed the entire issue because they feared a libel action. They had contacted the 'open' company and were informed that they would be included in any defamation charges brought against the green journalists. Goldsmith found another printer and republished the magazine at considerable expense, but W H Smith and John Menzies, Britain's leading newsagents, refused to stock it because they were also frightened Monsanto would set the lawyers on them.

Other critics have had sweeping punishments. Six members of a direct action group with the anarchic name of GenetiX Snowball received injunctions against trespassing on Monsanto test sites after they tore up crops. The High Court orders sound fair enough until you learn they will also be liable for attacks on Monsanto sites by other members of the group or complete strangers. Yet, strangely, the harsh authorities are reluctant to treat the company with comparable severity. Oil-seed rape from a Monsanto experimental site in Lincolnshire contaminated nearby plants because the buffer zone around the rape was too narrow. The Department of the Environment has failed to say if it will threaten executives with fines and prison sentences for breach of food regulations.

The most striking court cases come from the United States. They show that to be worried about genetically modified food you don't have to believe the scientists who warn that Monsanto's pesticide-resistant crops will lead to new breeds of super weeds and meals that will be difficult to stomach. The company claims that its crops will feed the starving; the same advertising campaign that announced it wanted a thousand modified flowers to bloom in the garden of free debate also promised a new green revolution that would eradicate famine. Monsanto's few friends have been won over by this altruistic propaganda. The copywriters failed to include an alternative take on Monsanto's effect on farming. The American experience suggests that gene technology is driving Monsanto and its competitors to create agribusiness monopolies that will put farmers everywhere over a barrel.

Genetically modified foods have great exploitative potential. Bacterial and insect genes are spliced into crops to make them resistant to one particular herbicide, Roundup, manufactured by Monsanto. Users of the seeds can quickly become a captive market for the pesticide. Farmers will be unable to take seeds from their crops and replant them the next year. Monsanto hopes to make prudent management of crops impossible and has taken over a rival biotechnology company specifically to get its hands on what is charmingly called the 'terminator' gene. The terminator is a genetically engineered suicide mechanism taken from bacterial DNA which makes the next generation of seeds poison themselves. As Alan Simpson, Labour MP and critic of the biotechnology industry, says, for the first time in history farmers will be prevented from saving seeds and be forced to pay an annual 'feudal levy' to Monsanto each time they sow a crop. While they wait for the terminator to arrive, Monsanto has developed a novel legal concept: seed piracy. It has hired private detectives to investigate 475 cases of American farmers suspected of taking and replanting seeds from their crops. The US courts have fined offenders as much as £20,000 each. Again, British farmers should take note: life is being privatised, patented and ringed with copyright lawyers.

Whether the government will pay attention is another matter. Leaked internal market research from Monsanto revealed that public confidence in the company had collapsed, and even the supermarket cartel was angry at being conned into selling unlabelled modified food. The only group that was a sympathetic audience for the corporate spinners was – and why the hell am I still surprised by this? – 'opinion-forming'

Labour MPs. The company is using every available tactic to influence the government. Bill Clinton, a Monsanto client, has lobbied Tony Blair twice to allow Monsanto into Britain – statesmen apparently have the time to discuss such vital issues – and the company has followed up the presidential initiative by hiring David Hill, a former New Labour spin doctor turned lobbyist, who calls his old friends on its behalf.

By contrast, Simpson's criticisms of corporate influence have earned him the unbending hatred of the Labour leadership. A hack who recently went to Number 10 saw a copy of the lefty magazine *Red Pepper*, featuring an article by Simpson. He asked one of Prime Minister's aides what he thought of him. 'Simpson's a bastard,' came the reply. 'Suppose people start listening to him. It could wreck everything.'

Observer November 1998

PS   In February 1999 GM food finally faced criticism. The recruitment of a score of members of the Clinton and New Labour administrations was subjected to overdue scrutiny. Tony Blair dismissed Monsanto's critics as 'tyrants' and 'scaremongers'.

CHAPTER SIX

FOCUS GROUP FASCISM

HOWARD'S BEGINNING

How should those who feel wholly or vaguely Jewish react to the Conservatives' penalties on refugees fleeing to these shores? Or, to be blunter, how should they respond to a Jewish Home Secretary kicking destitute asylum-seekers during the heated build-up to an election in which Tory strategists hope race will 'play well' for the party in the tabloids?

For many well-bred people it is faintly disreputable to examine Michael Howard's family. That the Home Secretary owes his current eminence and probably his life to an often unsatisfactory but occasionally vibrant liberal British tradition is an irrelevance. Ministers should be judged on their policies not their ancestors. Howard himself shares the minimalist position. He keeps discussions about his past short and uninformative. A profile in *The Guardian* is typical of a dozen in the files. 'I think he was a bit taken aback when I asked about his family history,' the interviewer reported. 'Yes,' he quoted Howard as saying, 'it was true his grandfather came from Romania. (Pause.) Yes, his father's family had settled in Wales.' And on his mother's side? 'He said her family was "also from Eastern Europe".' And that is all the newspapers have got from him. Now of course, politicians have no duty to answer personal questions. Jewish politicians may well be wary of residual (or not so residual) anti-Semitism and anxious to steer the conversation away from their backgrounds. Yet when all the respectable caveats have been made, the fact remains that Howard is far more closely connected to the flight of refugees from fascist Europe than his vague statements to the press suggest. As Britain at his instigation introduces the harshest asylum regime in recent history – a regime that would have sent the Howard family to a concentration camp if it had been in force earlier this century – all but the most rigorously logical minds may wonder why the personal has had so little impact on the political.

Solid information about Howard's past is hard to come by. A picture of sorts can be glimpsed in the birth, marriage and naturalisation certificates at the Public Record Office. Michael Howard was born Michael Hecht in Llanelli 54 years ago, the son of a draper. It was not his grandfather who escaped from Romania, but his father. Bernat Hecht was born in a Romanian town called Ruscova on 13 November 1916, according to his naturalisation documents. His surviving friends describe him as a handsome, hard-working and easy-going man who arrived 'just before the war' – recollections that fit with the history of repression in the Balkans and magnanimity in Britain.

Romania had a native strain of anti-Semitism that needed little inspiration from German Nazism. All minorities were guaranteed equal treatment by the 1923 constitution, but civil rights did not survive the great depression. The fascist nationalists who were to form the Iron Guard demanded that the pure Romanian peasantry must be protected from the alien 'Judaisers' who were not only cosmopolitan corrupters of virtue but conspirators responsible for the slump. Both the Iron Guard and the equally racist League of National Christian Defence prospered as recession deepened. Anti-Semitic laws passed in 1937 deprived thousands of Jews of citizenship. A 1940 Statute of the Jews prohibited mixed marriages. After the Axis invasion of the Soviet Union in 1941, mass slaughter began. Historians emphasise that the desire of Marshall Antonescu, the war-time dictator, to demonstrate his independence from Hitler meant 'only' 300,000 or so of the 800,000 Romanian Jews were murdered.

The odds were long but not unbeatable. Renée Woolf, Michael Howard's cousin, says Bernat's brother, Wally, and sister survived the concentration camps and found asylum in Britain after the war. Hecht did not have to roll the loaded dice because a Jewish family on the Western edge of Europe got him out. The Landys of south Wales (descendants of refugees from Tsarist Russia) brought him to Britain. Hecht met Hilda Kershion, a Landy cousin. In 1940, aged 28, she married the penniless 23-year-old. Her new husband went into the family's drapery business and enjoyed an unusually peaceful domestic life by the standards of the Forties. Their son Michael was born in 1941. Hecht became a British citizen in December 1947. On 8 January 1948 Hecht took the oath of allegiance. He changed his name from Bernat to Bernard and Hecht to Howard. Young Michael Hecht became young Michael Howard.

The Landys could rescue a man they had never seen by exploiting one of the few loopholes in Thirties immigration law. Between 1933 and November 1938, just 11,000 German Jews found refuge in Britain. With the same cruel-to-be-kind tone Howard and John Major deploy today when they insist they must be tough on allegedly 'bogus' asylum-seekers to prevent a racist backlash against British blacks and Asians, the Conservative politicians of the Thirties said refugee numbers must be limited to avoid fanning the embers of indigenous fascism. They were doing it for the good of the victims, like every master who has flogged a boy. It's not that we are prejudiced ourselves, they implied then (as now), we merely want to protect minorities from an unsophisticated and, frankly, barbaric electorate who lack our humanity. Most Anglo-Jewish leaders in the Thirties shared the unwillingness to let in foreign Jews and were equally concerned about an anti-Semitic reaction. But they did what they could in a few cases, and in 1933 set up a system that allowed a handful to escape. The government received guarantees that a refugee from Germany would be managed by British

Jews who would feed and gainfully employ him until he moved from Britain. Whether the refugee stayed for a year or for ever, he must be supported by sponsors who ensured he was not a burden on the state. When a relaxation came, it was the result of pressure from the supposedly brutish public. Newsreel pictures of *Kristallnacht* inspired general disgust. The Home Office responded by issuing more visas. About 40,000 Jews found sanctuary in Britain between November 1938 and the start of the war. Bernat Hecht almost certainly arrived in late 1938 or 1939 after the softening of the rules. Liberalisation did not end the requirement that Jews find sponsors, as pitiful advertisements in the *Jewish Chronicle* show. 'Urgently seek for uncle (55) in daily danger, fearing Dachau, generous rescuer providing short term guarantees until emigration overseas,' reads one from February 1939.

Whether Hecht would have reached a safe haven if his son had been in office at the time is a very personal political question. You might, if you had the subtle mind of a modern Home Office bureaucrat, dismiss the Jewish refugees of the mid-Thirties as economic migrants and shamelessly bogus asylum-seekers. The sponsorship and start in the family business the Landy family gave him would be treated with intense suspicion today. Asylum-seekers are not allowed to work for their first six months in Britain and need the permission of the Home Office to get a job thereafter. The regulations are designed to prevent economic migrants who want to better their lot by working from getting past the immigration desks at Heathrow. Having relatives who promise to support you, or knowing a family with unmarried daughters, is fatal: conclusive proof that you are a cheat searching for a marriage of convenience that will force the government to give you residence, rather than a refugee with a genuine fear of persecution. In any case, our time-travelling Howard adviser might continue, how genuine were the fears of men like Hecht in the Europe of the Thirties? There were, to be sure, concentration camps in Germany and discrimination in Eastern and Central Europe. But no 'final solution' was in place and there were no mass killings. Hitler's law enforcement methods were admired. Only the outbreak of war prevented Sir Norman Kendal, the head of Scotland Yard, from accepting an invitation to tour Dachau and learn about modern crime control from Nazi policemen. Could every Jew who came to Britain prove that he or she would be tortured if they were deported? Did their fears of disaster have any real grounds? Or were Jews slyly exploiting a little local unpleasantness to secure admission to Britain? If the reader finds this fantasy far-fetched, consider what the modern Home Office is saying about refugees from Africa and Bosnia (of which more later). If, as is more than probable, Bernat Hecht arrived after November 1938, the contrast is greater. Michael Howard's father would have benefited from a generous relaxation of the immigration rules – a generosity his son despises as weakness.

The Home Secretary rejects such comparisons. Real refugees have nothing to fear, he says. He only wants to protect a charitable nation from swindlers who play on our kindness to strangers and live off a welfare state whose reputation for open-handedness has spread round the globe after 16 years of Conservative rule. This country had become 'far too attractive a destination for bogus asylum-seekers and other illegal immigrants,' he told the Commons. Britain would continue to be a beacon to dissidents, but a new 'fair but firm' system was needed to ensure the country was a 'haven not a honey pot'.

At first glance, Howard's restrictions seem justified. Between 3,000 and 4,000 people a year claimed asylum in the mid-Eighties. In 1989 the figure jumped, and despite significant swings has never fallen below 20,000 since 1990. In 1995 about 40,000 claimants arrived and presented themselves as a welcome target to right-wing pundits and politicians who had lost trade unions, the Soviet Union and CND and were short of menaces that might provoke the righteous hatred of their followers. Undoubtedly there are desperate people among them who, for all their miseries, are not going to be shot if they are sent back home. Their lawyers – if, that is, they can afford or find lawyers – can be confident that once their clients are in the country applications for asylum can be dragged out for years. They know the Immigration Service,

the most incompetent department in Whitehall, may well give up eventually and let them stay.

Yet everyone who knows refugees, or has the imaginative sym-
pathy to put themselves in their place, argues that Howard's claim that
Britain is being flooded with cunning crooks is a vicious and self-serving
myth. To understand their anger you must look beyond the figures.
Astute readers will have remembered that 1989 also saw the fall of the
Berlin Wall and the beginnings of the break-up of the Soviet Union and
Yugoslavia. The years since have witnessed the virtual disintegration of
Mobutu's Zaire and the actual disintegration of Somalia, military despo-
tism in Nigeria and civil war in Kashmir. All-too genuine refugees have
poured out of all these countries. Most just cross the border and wait
for better times. Impoverished neighbouring states have to cope. You
would never guess from the militant self-pity of the British right that
nearly all refugee crises are borne by the Third World, not the First.

Howard implies that a touch of authoritarianism is necessary because
the system is lax. On this reading the tiny minority of the world's asylum-seekers who reach Britain are welcomed by soft-hearted border
guards who take fairness to the brink of licence. The Home Secretary
forgets to mention that only one in four asylum-seekers is granted permission to remain and that his civil servants have devised rules to con-
found refugees with an ingenuity that would have dazzled Kafka.

In 1992, 5,000 Bosnian Muslims — whose treatment at the hands of
Serb and Croat ethnic cleansers should ring bells in most Jewish heads
— made their way to Britain. The numbers were insignificant when compared with the hundreds of thousands who ran to Germany, but they
were too high for the Home Office to bear. The Immigration Service
decreed that no Bosnian could travel to Britain without a visa from a
British embassy. There is no British embassy in Bosnia. If Bosnians
crossed a border and went to the British embassy in Vienna, for example,
they would be caught by a new Catch 22. When they entered Austria
they were stepping on the soil of what the Home Office calls a safe
country. Asylum-seekers must make a claim in the first safe country

they reach. If they carried on from Vienna to Heathrow or Dover, they would be turned back and told to put their case to the Austrians. (It is worth pausing at this point to honour a Civil Service, well informed on the Balkan massacres, that coolly set this unbeatable trap.) The stratagem was a brilliant success and the trickle of refugees from Yugoslavia dried up. Through the Nineties, Britain refused to intervene against the Serbs while turning away the victims of the killing fields it tolerated.

Or reflect on the case of Nigeria, whose treatment of Ken Saro-Wiwa created an international scandal. If Howard is right, bogus economic migrants should have been pouring into Britain since 1986 when an oil price crash wrecked the Nigerian economy.

Virtually no one showed up. Immigration officers were spared the need to call for Yoruba-speaking interpreters until 1993, when the military ignored the results of a general election and terrorised its opponents. Everyone from Amnesty International to the US State Department recognised that the subsequent persecution forced thousands into exile – everyone, that is, except Howard. His department succeeded where the civilian opposition failed, and turned Nigeria from a tyranny to a democracy that might inspire the continent. Immigration officers were supplied with a Home Office analysis of Nigeria which they used to determine whether asylum-seekers were genuine or bogus. The briefing held that Nigeria was a country where 'rights are generally respected', the 'unfair trials' of opponents were unknown and minorities faced no special persecution. Armed with this soothing assessment, the Immigration Service went to work. Of the 2,500 Nigerians who arrived seeking sanctuary between the 1993 declaration of martial law and October 1995, only 19 were given permission to stay. Were the 2,481 others bogus? Or were they victims of the elite's determination to ignore evidence of oppression and sustain itself in power with a touch of populism and a hint of racism? Or were they, like Bernat Hecht, refugees who felt a cold wind on the back of their necks and got out before it was too late? Almost by definition successful refugees are those who leave before the police knock on the door and provide evidence even the Home Office can't ignore of 'a genuine fear of per-secution'. This then is the honeyed system Howard believes is a soft touch, a system built on either stunning stupidity or active mendacity, that pretends dictatorship does not exist in Nigeria and uses malicious tricks to keep out Muslim Bosnians. The Cabinet now wants to go further. The regime will be hardened by removing benefits from asylum-seekers. As we have noted, they are not allowed to work in the drapery trade or, indeed, any other business. Their career choices appear to be the black economy, prostitution, crime, beggary or star-vation on the streets.

Howard's civil servants say he is not a racist. But his party is more than happy to have race in the air as an election approaches. The last assault on 'bogus' asylum-seekers was just in time for the 1992 elec-tion. Now that the next campaign is in sight, Andrew Lansley, a for-mer director of research at Conservative Central Office, has said John Major can defy all expectations and beat Tony Blair if he harped on the public's 'negative perceptions' of Labour. Race was one likely-looking negative. 'Immigration was an issue which we raised successfully in 1992 and in the 1994 Euro-election campaign,' he said. It 'played well in the tabloids and still has the potential to hurt.' Jack Straw, who has a German Jewish great-grandmother, responded to Lansley by saying 'it is obscene that, of all people, Mr Howard, whose family directly benefited from liberal refugee laws, should allow asylum and immigra-tion to be used in political stunts. Like many people in Britain, Michael Howard is descended from immigrants, and so am I.' Even Jewish leaders who find Howard hard to take were wary of Straw's criticism, preferring to say that the Home Secretary is a member of the Cabinet, implementing government policy. Whatever else Jewishness is, it is not a political programme.

I can see their point. The history of Israel shows that past persecu-tion does not produce toleration. Quite the reverse. But I'm not sure that Howard can get off the moral hook so easily. The spectacle of a man who cannot see his father in the faces of the Bosnians and Nigerians his department rejects is risible and repellent and leaves him open to pointed questions about his choice of friends and enemies. For decades Gore Vidal has brilliantly satirised (and probably immortalised) the American Jewish intellectuals Norman Podhoretz and Midge Decter, who moved to the right and embraced conservative bigotry. How could they recycle every prejudice against homosexuals when there is 'no difference in the degree of hatred felt by the Christian majority for Christ-killers and sodomites?' he asked. In Britain lining up with the right also gets you into strange company. The House of Lords is, preposterously, held up as a check on arbitrary government. Yet in the 11 years of the arbitrary Thatcher administration, the only measure the overwhelmingly Tory Lords rejected was a War Crimes Bill to bring elderly Nazis to trial.

Psycho-journalism is a futile game. Yet is it at least possible to speculate that an ambitious and assimilated Conservative politician might wonder what vistas would be open to him if only he could be seen as a real Englishman? Might he be tempted to prove that he is not alien by turning the screws on aliens? I was struck by the report of one of my colleagues who discussed Howard with a Conservative whip recently. One 'problem' prevented Howard leading the Tory party, the whip said. The problem was that he was Jewish. Howard and other Jews can get into the Cabinet without great difficulty, yet, somehow, the mutterings in the Conservative Party start when the biggest prize is on offer.

The importance of Englishness is likely to grow in the coming decade. A new government will devolve power to Scotland and Wales. Southern conservatives are already reacting by playing with replacing the old, multi-national British identity – which gave Asians, blacks and Jews a tolerant fable they could exploit when the going got rough – with an exclusive English nationalism. For the moment race is impinging on politics in the loud campaign to keep out refugees. Any Jewish politician who adds his voice to the clamour must, inevitably, be asked what would have happened to him if the new authoritarianism had been in place in the Thirties. And, with an equal inevitability, the answer will be that he would have been shut out and left to die.

Jewish Quarterly December 1995

OEDIPAL POLITICS

More on the appalling effects of the Oedipus complex on the Party of the Family. After Michael Howard banned refugees from Romania – from where his Jewish father fled to escape Nazism in the Thirties – the history of Michael Portillo was discussed at a reunion in Madrid of members of the International Brigades. A few of the old comrades knew Portillo's father, Luis, a Spanish socialist, pacifist and official in the Republican government overthrown by Franco. He, too, escaped murderous fascists by finding asylum in Britain in 1939. Members of the brigades and Spanish republican exiles in post-war Britain remembered seeing Luis and young Michael at a Spanish cultural centre in west London. They enjoyed dangling the infant from their knees. 'I wished I'd dropped the bugger on his head when I had the chance,' said one.

Harsh words. But no harsher than Portillo's denunciation of the cynics undermining Church, State and Crown with their alien critiques of all that was wonderful in Britain. Among the intellectual knockers and 'poison pessimists' he wanted to take out were socialist refugees who sounded very like his father. 'Since the time that Marx and Engels lived in Britain we have tolerated, even encouraged, those with anti-establishment views to settle here,' he snarled. Parents beware. If your children show an interest in Conservative politics, disinherit them, change the locks and invest in body armour.

Observer November 1996

UNORIGINAL SHOCKERS

A fantastic new game is enlivening fun fairs and amusement arcades. Original Shocker is a replica of Old Smoky – the electric chair in whose hard, wooden arms dozens of convicts have been killed in Florida. (A majority may even have been guilty.)

Sensation-seekers pay £1 to be strapped in. They hang on to steel handles that send ever more violent shocks up their arms. If they can manage to stand 2,000 'jolts', smoke comes out of the back of the machine and they receive a certificate acknowledging their achievement. Novas Productions has attracted buyers who see the chair as a policy statement as well as an entertainment. 'Magistrates can send offenders up here and we'll give them a blast,' gurgled Bill Haslam, the manager of the Way Out West Park in Southampton's Ocean Village. 'It's a spectator sport, really,' explained a spokeswoman for the Trocadero fun palace in central London. 'As soon as someone gets on the chair, a crowd gathers.'

Only the puritans at Amnesty International have complained. The electric chair is a modern version of auto-da-fé. Instead of being consumed at the stake, the prisoners' innards are fried inside.

Alas, modern technology has its limitations. Technical problems can keep a prisoner alive and cooking for a good 30 minutes. The American state of Georgia thoughtfully provides sick bags for witnesses who find the resulting screams and smells unsettling. 'The idea of trivialising this process and turning it into a game is in bad taste,' said an Amnesty spokesman. But what do spoilsports know about taste or style? Electric Shocker should be installed at the taxpayers' expense as an executive toy in Jack Straw's office. It would be a useful reminder of the consequences of New Labour's apostasy.

The current issue of the *Jewish Chronicle* reports that Straw will revive a backbench Conservative bill from the last Parliament, which modestly proposed that 150 years of liberty should be junked and anyone 'conspiring' to overthrow foreign regimes, including tyrannies, should be charged in the British courts with inciting rebellion. The *Jewish Chronicle*?

A strange place to make such a momentous statement. I suspect Straw thought its readers, worried about Hamas and Islamic Jihad, would make a suitably tame audience that wouldn't ask what would have happened to Karl Marx, Charles de Gaulle and African National Congress leaders under Straw's law. New Labour is great at product placement, if nothing else. In a letter to the Jewish Board of Deputies, the Home Secretary said he was giving the Tory bill 'careful consideration', even though care and consideration were notable by their absence when the Conservatives tried to make conspiracy against foreign dictatorships an offence. Their measure was a sop to the Saudi monarchy after Michael Howard botched his attempt to exile the dissident Mohammed al-Mas'ari to a Caribbean island where he could not imperil the arms industry's deals in the Middle East. If Straw has his way, British citizens supporting the opposition in Saudi Arabia, Iraq, Indonesia or any other dictatorship, by exercising what they assumed was the right to free speech, may be prosecuted. (The small print of the Conservative measure explicitly included the communication of messages to a foreign country as criminal incitement after exiles faxed propaganda to Saudi Arabia.) The real victims will be asylum-seekers. If convicted, they will be deported. As 94 countries retain the death penalty, some will meet an executioner on their return home. In opposition Labour backbenchers wrecked the Conservative bill, claiming it would 'criminalise those who work to organise and inspire the overthrow of tyranny around the world'. Now their own government is criminalising the enemies of criminals.

David Jones, the managing director of the Original Shocker factory, has one regret. 'Unfortunately we can't use real electric shocks because of health and safety regulations,' he moaned. The chair is a gruesome imitation which vibrates instead of electrocuting. In government, New Labour, too, is an imitation of what has gone before. As Straw decides to keep Conservative boot camps, kiddie jails, electronic tags and attacks on asylum, you need to ask what exactly is so new about him.

Observer August 1997

HOCUS BOGUS

Tomorrow two versions of law and order will be on show at Oxford Crown Court. Jurors will see conventional justice in action when they hear nine refugees arraigned on charges of rioting at the Campsfield detention centre for asylum-seekers. The hearing will be in public. Evidence will be weighed on its merits and the learned judge will gravely explain that it is a cornerstone of British liberty that no one can be sentenced to a term of imprisonment unless found guilty beyond reasonable doubt by twelve good people and true. Just occasionally, however, the court may catch a glimpse in the testimony of suspects and guards of another justice system, in which life behind razor wire is monitored by the video cameras of privatised, secretive and arbitrary authority.

The defendants were imprisoned in Campsfield – interned is a better word – without trial on the whim of immigration officers. Their only crime was to exercise a right guaranteed by the United Nations to ask for asylum. Britain is a signatory to the UN refugee convention and proclaims its commitment to human rights. In practice, Britain breaches the treaty daily. You can hear the perfidy in the language used by Jack Straw to describe refugees: 'bogus asylum-seekers', 'economic migrants'. Honesty is so rare, Tony Blair and the press can get away with dismissing Kurds as scroungers even though they are not only having to fend off the attentions of Saddam Hussein but are witnessing the persecution of Hadep, a democratic Kurdish party in Turkey, and assassination attempts on human rights workers in Ankara and Istanbul. As Straw and his colleagues must have been told, there is no such thing as a bogus asylum-seeker. A Canadian accountant with a persecution complex can appeal for sanctuary in Britain. He won't get it, but you cannot prejudge him by saying that he is 'bogus' before his case is assessed, and hope to remain within the UN convention.

Nit-picking legalism and respect for linguistic clarity carry no weight at Campsfield. The prison is outside the rule of law as it is usually understood. The bogus of the Earth are delivered into the hands of Group 4, the private security conglomerate, by immigration service panels rather than independent courts. Sir David Ramsbotham, the Chief Inspector of Prisons, worried that the safety of inmates was at risk because no 'clear rules and sanctions' governed the behaviour of its guards. The defendants, who will see in Oxford their first prosecutors who cannot be confused with the judge and jury, are typical Campsfield internees. They do not know why they are being treated as criminals. (They have committed no crime: how can they?) All are black and three are teenagers. One 17-year-old is in a mental hospital after he was found hoarding anti-depressants. A 19-year-old tried to kill himself twice: first with a rope and then with a drug overdose. He's so sick no one expects he will make it to the court to hear the case against him. The crass authoritarianism of Britain's asylum law is perhaps best illustrated by a brief history of Sunny Ozidede, their co-defendant. He is from the Ogoni region of Nigeria where the depredations of Shell and the military dictatorship received a little attention after the execution of Ken Saro-Wiwa. Ozidede engaged in the dangerous pastime of protesting against the multi-national. He fled to Britain and was denied asylum. When his immigration appeal panel convened, he was in hospital suffering from injuries – sustained, he said, during torture. The hospital told the Home Office he did not have a solicitor and was in no condition to represent himself. His failure to attend the appeal was enough to condemn him to an indefinite sentence in Campsfield as a cheat who was likely to disappear if he was left at liberty. There was no trial, of course.

Amateur opportunists occasionally betray themselves with stammers and blushes. True professionals passionately believe the stories they spin, and not a flickering of an eyelid suggests doubt or shame. For the past three weeks I have been privileged to watch a show-stopping display of outraged innocence and righteous anger provoked by a short piece I wrote last month about Campsfield, the Oxfordshire detention centre for asylum-seekers. Like many others, I thought Campsfield was a disgrace. A private prison company, Group 4, makes profits for its shareholders by interning refugees. (Labour, too, opposed 'immoral' private prisons before the election, but mislaid its principles when it moved to office.) The peg for the article was the start of the trial of nine Campsfield asylum-seekers accused of riot. A shocked chorus began its song the next day. Mike O'Brien, the Home Office minister responsible for Campsfield, confirmed my belief that there is no spectacle on earth quite as ridiculous as an English wonk playing the hard man. In a letter to the editor of the *Observer*, and in about a dozen phone calls from his press officer, he said the report was 'riddled with inaccuracies'. I had 'seriously misled' readers, apparently, and proved myself incapable of reaching the British press's famously high standards of journalism. Meanwhile, Group 4's lawyers sent a threatening letter that warned they would sue if 'such articles continue to be published'.

My, my, my. The poor old editor hounded by ministers . . . Crippling libel actions in the High Court imminent . . . Slender reputation on the line. This time we must be cautious and confine ourselves to looking at what happened when the alleged rioters appeared in court. To avoid the ever-present danger of misleading the readers with inaccurate reporting, we will stick strictly to what was said at the trial and see how the Group 4 staff, whom O'Brien supports so cravenly, upheld the cause of accuracy in the witness box.

The riot began when rumours spread through the camp that guards strangled an internee when Group 4 were trying to move him to a state prison. 'Missiles were thrown at officers,' the prosecution claimed, as it painted a picture for the jury of bestial asylum-seekers trashing the jail. 'Windows were smashed, telephones and surveillance cameras destroyed, the prison shop was ransacked and the kitchen wrecked.' John Allen, a Group 4 supervisor, denied the wreckers were provoked.

His officers had done nothing that could possibly be interpreted by onlookers as an attempt to strangle an inmate. The defence produced a video showing a detainee with a Group 4 guard's hands round his neck.

Defence lawyer: 'Don't you think that seeing this, the other detainees would think that he is being strangled?'

No reply.

Finding out who destroyed the camp was not as straightforward as innocent observers might have imagined. Mo Stone, a Group 4 officer, was questioned about the smashed telephones.

Defence lawyer: 'The wall telephone was broken. Did you break it?'

Stone: 'No.'

Lawyer: 'Are you sure about that? Are you saying that if other witnesses say they saw you break the telephone that they are liars? I put it to you that you personally smashed the telephone.'

Stone: 'We did pull it apart.'

Lawyer: 'Did you tell the police that? Why not?'

Stone: 'I don't know.'

The Group 4 witnesses pretended the riot was terrifying and hinted that they feared their very lives were in the balance. Caryn Mitchell-Hill said a detainee menaced her as she confronted him alone in a prison corridor. Security camera film showed she could not have been in the corridor when the prisoner allegedly intimidated her and was, in fact, with other officers at the time. Jane Essery told the police she was frightened. The defence had a tape of her talking to her superiors after the riot.

Defence lawyer: 'You were asked [by Group 4] how you felt. To the question: "Did you feel threatened?", you replied: "No, I felt very calm, actually." Why did you tell us one thing and your employers another?'

Essery: 'I have never heard that tape and was not told it would be evidence.'

Another private warder, John Graham, said a refugee from Nigeria, Sunny Ozidede, threatened him. In court he admitted he couldn't recognise the defendant. Chris Barry, a Group 4 orderly, identified Ozidede as one of the rioters. He was forced to admit he had made a mistake, provoking an exasperated bench to intervene.

Judge: 'Let me get this straight. You are saying now: "The person I described must have been someone else"?'

Barry: 'Yes.'

Barry also claimed to have been smacked on the head, punched, kicked and sprayed with chemicals in an assault that left his shirt torn to shreds. Video footage showed a close-up of Barry after the supposed beating wearing a clean, unruffled shirt.

The parade of forgetful privatisers went on and on until even the prosecution wearied of hearing what one Group 4 witness quaintly called 'undeliberate lies'. The state threw in the towel and the judge ordered the defendants' acquittal. The clearing of their names did not save all of them from jail. To the authorities' slight discomfiture, Ozidede was found after the riot to be genuine rather than a scheming, bogus asylum-seeker who must be imprisoned without trial to prevent him absconding. His scars were consistent with his description of torture by the Nigerian military police. He was granted refugee status and left Oxford a free man. Five others were not so lucky. They were carted off to Rochester Prison, a Victorian slum. Their lawyers have no legal means at their disposal to get them out. As I said, the imprisonment of asylum-seekers is not controlled by independent judges. Their solicitors have been forced to resort to the desperate tactic of begging the Home Office for mercy. We can only wish them luck and note that what is meant to be a Labour government has become the client and eager little helper of penal capitalists.

Only a few years ago, Labour politicians worried about the creation of a penal-industrial complex in which incarceration entrepreneurs formed a powerful lobby with a clear interest in jailing citizens. That was in the bad old days. Just before the Oxford trial began O'Brien toured Campsfield and did not ask whether unconvicted men, women and children should be milked for the benefit of overpaid executives and dividend-hungry shareholders, but instead presented managers with an 'Investors in People' award. The government felt that the company's training of staff was exemplary and it was nothing if not fitting that a grateful Labour administration should register its break with the tired, discredited principles its members held in opposition and register the nation's gratitude by recognising the excellence of Group 4 with a certificate, a warm speech of thanks and the prosecution of those among its customers who had the impertinence to complain about poor service.

Observer June 1998

NO SPECIAL LOVE

MPs trudged into Westminster with minds fried by the Tuscan heat and the aromas of Chianti and Body Shop suncream oozing from their flaky skins. After a magisterial debate lasting slightly longer than the average wait at check-in our statespersons tore up the constitution and scuttled back to their villas. The inefficient tradition that everyone is innocent until proved guilty was modernised out of existence. The right to silence, a protection against torture and false confession dating from the abolition of Star Chamber was destroyed, along with the right to organise against dictatorships enjoyed by Lord Byron in the war of Greek independence. Policemen and prosecutors will henceforth decide who goes to jail. Good terrorists, on side for the time being, will not be touched. Innocent victims – the collateral damage of the bonfire of the liberties – and bad terrorists will be interned. British citizens and exiles who support the overthrow of tyranny will be charged with conspiring to commit vaguely defined offences. British justice will once again be the civilised world's favourite oxymoron.

The emergency recall of Parliament during the summer break and the tough talk of combating terrorism and 'sending a message' after the bombs in Omagh and America's East African embassies hid the spectacle of a panicking Prime Minister hyperventilating. The emergency Parliament followed Tony Blair's instructions and allowed suspects to be jailed when police officers – and MI5 agents, bravely hiding behind screens – maintain the defendant is a terrorist. Ministers got very touchy when you called the planned internment 'internment'. A judge will, they said, be in charge, and his presence will ensure the kangaroo courts aren't bounced into miscarriages of justice. But during the Gulf War Lord Bingham, now the revered Master of the Rolls, locked up dozens of Arabs because MI5 said they were terrorists. Several months later the Home Office admitted that every last one was innocent. The word of an officer will not be enough to imprison an Irishman, the spinners continued, there will have to be collaboration. On closer inspection the impressive safeguard turns out to mean this: the court will be able to assume guilt if the suspect fails to answer questions and can treat what used to be the right to silence as collaborative proof of guilt. Internment seems to be the word after all.

For a moment a faint pulse appeared to flutter in the corpse of Parliamentary democracy. Presented with a bill allowing assertion rather than evidence to jail a citizen – 'the classic hallmark of totalitarian justice', as the Labour MP Bob Marshall-Andrews said – there was just a hint of a chance the Commons would decide, for once, to revolt. MPs had little time to read, let alone debate, the powers Alan Clark nicely described as 'focus-group fascism'. A testy Tony Blair was forced to sit and listen for an hour to principled arguments I doubt he understood. Then the lobby trash staggered out of the Strangers' Bar, and good soldiers from the Labour, Tory and hopelessly illiberal Liberal Democrats benches obeyed orders and voted for repression. Not one of the aristocrats and quangocrats in the House of Lords, who claim to check on Britain's elected dictatorship, bothered to vote against the government.

While a measure that could revive support for the Real IRA in Dundalk and Armagh was whipped through, the state terrorism practised by the United States, when it blew up one of the few pharmaceuticals factories in sub-Saharan Africa, continued to receive servile backing. Try not to think about the need for medicines in Sudan, a country afflicted by famine and civil war, and try not to be too humiliated by the eager backing Britain gave to the claim that the plant made chemical weapons, which already looks like an enormous lie.

The government's response to Realpolitik at its dirtiest is to make it dirtier still. As well as bringing back internment, the addled summer Parliament created an offence of conspiring to commit terrorist acts in any foreign country, whether they are a tyranny or not. 'Terrorism will be defined very widely,' said a merry spokesman. 'All serious crimes, including damage to property will be terrorist.' You can rest assured, he added, that the law officers will prosecute only when 'it is in the public interest'. The public interest gambit is likely to mean that if refugees and British citizens oppose an arms-buying dictatorship – Indonesia, say – they could be jailed in the public interest if East Timor rebels used funds collected in Britain. But protestors who take on a tyranny that foolishly has not come to deal with British Aerospace – Afghanistan, for example, or Iraq – will find it is in the public interest to leave them alone. On these grounds Nelson Mandela would have been sent to the Scrubs for organising violent revolution in British-backed South Africa, and you might have been his cell mate if you supported the Anti-Apartheid Movement. There was no consultation. The Home Office's finest were still scribbling out a law on the back of a fag packet the day before Parliament reassembled. The pressure on them was too great and several clauses were gibberish.

The flip modern style is as uncomfortable with the idea of decadence as it is with the concept of evil. If you talk of liberty dying, you risk sounding crusty. Yet there was a time when British governments fell when they tried to do what Blair and Straw did so easily last week. In 1858 Lord Palmerston was under pressure from Napoleon III, the

King Fahd of his day, to arrest French republicans accused of plotting to kill him. Palmerston anticipated New Labour with his Conspiracy to Murder Bill. Alexander Herzen, a refugee from Tsarism, said if it was passed 'every embassy with any diligence and zeal might have thrown any enemy of their governments into prison.' Palmerston miscalculated and was confronted with mass protest. If Parliament had not killed the bill, 100,000 were ready to demonstrate in Hyde Park. 'The Englishman,' sighed a very relieved Herzen, 'has no special love for foreigners, still less for exiles whom he regards as guilty of the sin of poverty . . . but he clings to his right to asylum.' No longer. The embassies of Belgravia will be collecting the names of exiles and British citizens supporting opposition groups from Indonesia to Palestine. I'm sure their diplomats will soon be politely suggesting to Straw that failure to prosecute will be regarded as an unfriendly act when bids for the next tank contract are considered. Why shouldn't they? He is all but begging them to submit hit-lists to the Attorney General.

Neal Ascherson came up with the best reason to care. It's always worth watching how politicians treat refugees, he said, because it is then they show how they would deal with the rest of us if they thought they could get away with it. On the evidence of the anti-terrorism legislation, the dark fantasy of the political class is to suppress free speech, abandon tolerance and instruct coppers and spooks to jail anyone they imagine to be suspicious.

Observer September 1998

AFTERWORD

THE FALL OF PETER MANDELSON

In his realist classic of 1984, *First Among Equals*, Jeffrey Archer has a Labour minister from a northern constituency disappearing with a prostitute for five minutes or so. She recognises Raymond Gould and turns to blackmail once the business is done. Gould refuses to deal and she takes her tale to Mike Molloy, a *Mirror* reporter. Molloy confronts Gould, who refers him to his solicitor, Sir Roger Pelham.

A few minutes later when the phone rang again Raymond still hadn't moved. He picked up the receiver, his hand still shaking. Pelham confirmed that Molloy had been in touch with him.

'I presume you made no comment,' said Raymond.

'On the contrary,' replied Pelham. 'I told him the truth.'

'What,' exploded Raymond.

'Be thankful she hit on a fair journalist because I expect he'll let this one go. Fleet Street are not quite the bunch of shits everyone imagines them to be.'

Molloy kills the story. Gould rises to become Labour leader and – I do hope I'm not spoiling it for you – is made Prime Minister in the concluding sentence of a thrilling final page.

Critics returned to this scene after reporters from the *News of the World* showed no mercy when they set up and bugged conversations between Archer and a prostitute. The passage was still being thrown back at him in 1987, when a libel jury's award of record damages to the novelist announced that the suggestion that Archer had engaged in extra-marital sex was the vilest lie in English history. It has taken 12 years for Archer's analysis of journalism to be vindicated. The master's intuitions about the bonds of good fellowship in the Westminster–Fleet Street nexus were confirmed by the reception of Paul Routledge's very unauthorised biography of Peter Mandelson, the Labour member for Hartlepool who would like to be Prime Minister.

Routledge, an Old Labour hack, set out with an apparently impossible ambition: to do a service to the Labour movement by taking on the second most powerful man in the government. His tough talk sounded like saloon bar bragging until, to the astonishment of all who knew him, Routledge brought down Mandelson. But the minister's resignation was a messy affair for the author and an instructive one for those of us who watched Mandelson's confused allies attempt to restore order.

Routledge's dislike of Mandelson is a consequence of his trade unionism and his friendship with Charlie Whelan, Gordon Brown's former press officer. The Chancellor might appear to outsiders as the willing servant of a free-market consensus that has cracked in those parts of the world – roughly one-third – currently in recession and worse, but to Routledge and others on the left he presents his dispute with Mandelson as a fight between a democratic socialist and a gilded opportunist. Its origins, however, have nothing to do with ideology. They lie in the only act of operatic passion in New Labour's anaemic story: the moment of great betrayal when Mandelson switched from Diet Pepsi to Diet Coke and took his support from Brown to Tony Blair, thus denying his former friend what Archer would doubtless call the greatest of all prizes. It says much about Mandelson's self-confidence that he engaged energetically in the subsequent war – a campaign conducted with off-the-record briefings, the supplanting of Brownite X with Blairite Y in the fifth most senior post at the Department of Trade and Industry, and anonymous accusations from 10 Downing Street of lunacy in Number 11 – while knowing all along that the Chancellor's camp had a secret that might ruin him. 'There's a thermonuclear bomb ticking underneath Mandelson,' Whelan whispered to lobby correspondents as Routledge's publication date grew closer. 'It's going to blow him away.'

In 1996, when he was living on £46,000 a year, Mandelson borrowed £373,000 (eight times his MP's salary) from Geoffrey Robinson, an industrialist Blair put in the Treasury after New Labour's victory. Robinson's fortune had been inflated by dealings with Robert Maxwell and the Channel Island tax havens, and a legacy from a satirically named Madame Bourgeois, a Belgian heiress. He had no political base in the Commons and may have felt it politic to bankroll Blair's closest ally. Mandelson did not declare his enormous loan, acquired on such preferential terms that it was a gift by any other name, in the register of MPs' interests. The Secretary of State for Trade and Industry also forgot to mention the debt to civil servants in his department when they began an investigation into Robinson's affairs. This was careless. Robinson had been close to Blair – the Prime Minister and First Lady took their children on holiday to his Tuscan villa – but by December, his loyalties were clearly with Brown. He had been all but finished by successive scandals. As his reputation was shredded, the Brownites were tormented by suspicion. Unnamed 'sources', who were everywhere at the time, pointed out that several of the anti-Robinson exposés were written by Blairite journalists. It is possible Robinson may have decided to take Mandelson down with him. More plausibly in my view, Robinson calculated that Blair would never desert Mandelson: by tying their names together, he would let Number 10 know that his dismissal was sure to raise pertinent questions about Mandelson's fitness to remain in office.

In any event, Routledge had a story to tell and he sent it to his publishers. No one who knows the book trade will be surprised by the sequel. Presented with a sensational document and an urgent need for secrecy, Simon and Schuster posted a proof copy to Routledge at the *Independent on Sunday*'s office in the House of Commons, which wouldn't have mattered if he hadn't left the paper a year earlier to join the *Mirror*. The envelope was opened and its contents read. Instead of stealing a friend's work and sharing it with his or her readers – a disgraceful Fleet Street habit, but one sanctified by tradition – the culprit went to Mandelson and gave him a summary of Routledge's findings. The detail of what was later leaked suggests that photocopies of the most damaging pages were given to the minister along with a promise to say nothing and leave this one to him. Rival papers later named the *Independent on Sunday*'s political editor as Mandelson's nark. She denies being a government spy, and may be telling the truth. I can think of at least five journalists in Westminster who would rather protect Mandelson than publish the scoop of the year. Not all my colleagues are shits.

The Guardian, like many papers before it, was investigating how Mandelson could afford to purchase a Notting Hill home, have it done up by a minimalist designer with a maximum rate-card, while buying a £70,000 house in Hartlepool, dressing in Savile Row suits and patronising the best restaurants. (The questions have still not been answered, incidentally. We now know that as well as receiving £373,000 from Robinson, Mandelson had a £150,000 loan from the Britannia building society and £50,000 in a Coutts account. There was no family money. His grandfather, Herbert Morrison, left his daughter nothing. Although Mandelson's salary increased when he briefly served in the Cabinet, the gap between income and outgoings remains dizzying and unexplored. Only the English can dismiss the need to ask searching questions of a politician who is consuming conspicuously without visible means of support as puritanical and tasteless.) The terms of the loan from Robinson were known only to Mandelson, Robinson and their solicitors. Unless one of them talked, *The Guardian*'s inquiries were liable to be fruitless. Mandelson decided on a pre-emptive strike. He told *The Guardian* in the week before Christmas what Routledge had found, hoping that after a few days' fuss, the fire-curtain of the holiday would fall and his name would be old news when normal media service resumed.

This, too, was a miscalculation by the grand manipulator. As his power slipped away, opinion-formers wheeled and squawked. For 24 hours, friendly journalists stuck to Mandelson's script and tried to deflect attention onto Brown; they then covered Mandelson's resignation with wistful predictions of his return. Routledge added to the bonhomie by saying he was considering abandoning the life of a rude hack. If his manuscript had not been stolen, he would have cut the passage about the loan from his book. He knew that Whelan would be blamed for leaking it to him (he was) and would have to resign (he did).

The *Sun*, the soul of New Labour, said the affair 'stank', and its condemnation of Mandelson helped push him out of the Cabinet. Within three weeks, the editor's nose had cleared. He hired Benjamin Wegg-Prosser, Mandelson's spin doctor, as a political consultant to write in the leader columns hymns in praise of his once and future king. The paper was repeating a giddy pattern set in the autumn. On 28 October Matthew Parris, the politician turned journalist, said in passing to Jeremy Paxman on *Newsnight* that Mandelson was gay. He wasn't breaking a confidence: the *News of the World* had outed the minister in the Eighties. But there had been no public reference to his sexuality since in the mainstream media. Mandelson thought that he must and could keep the conversation away from sex, in tabloid Britain, of all places, because he believed the public would never accept a gay Prime Minister. (Hubris is Routledge's favourite noun in this book, and you can see why.) Parris unwittingly provided the excuse for an ersatz scandal filled with exclusive revelations of what was already known. The red-blooded and red-necked *Sun* began its contribution with a uniquely tolerant leader. Mandelson was 'a talented politician' with 'a brilliant mind'. 'We say to Mandelson: Tell the truth. You will win respect for your honesty.' On 9 November it reversed its U-turn and applied the most shop-worn tactic of anti-Semitism to sexual politics. A covert pink conspiracy was secretly pulling the levers of government, media and monarchy, it reported under the front page headline: 'Tell us the truth Tony: Are we being run by a gay Mafia?' Three days later the paper decided that, after all, we weren't and reversed the reversal of its U-turn. The *Sun* would be nice from now on, ignore grubby trivia about politicians' sex lives and get on with covering 'what really matters in life'. To show he meant business, the editor called Parris, who had a column in the paper, and fired him. The editor, whose name need not detain you, explained he was happy with the coverage his flip-flops had received because he wanted the *Sun* 'to make a noise'. The only noise that could be heard was the sound of mocking laughter.

Rupert Murdoch, owner of the *Sun*, three other national newspapers and the BSkyB satellite network, will keep up the bullying and flattery for as long as Mandelson has the ear of the Prime Minister. Murdoch's bid to buy Manchester United was referred to the DTI in September, when Mandelson was Trade Secretary. Alastair Campbell, Blair's spokesman and Britain's unelected minister of propaganda, worried that the takeover would expose the contradictions in the ruling ideology of elite populism. (On the one hand, New Labour is Murdoch's facilitator. On the other, the supporters of the most fêted club in the country expected the government to stop Murdoch getting his hands on their team.) Campbell phoned Tim Allan, director of corporate communications at BSkyB, to find out what was happening. He didn't have to introduce himself. Allan was Campbell's deputy at the Downing Street press office until he took a well-padded chair in a Murdoch office. Campbell then called Rosie Boycott, the editor of the *Express*, and turned down a lunch invitation. (In April 1998 Boycott had given Routledge the political editorship of her newspaper, only to snatch it away after senior Blairites informed her that *they* decided who should write about politics in the free press – and Routledge's views were not to their liking.) Campbell was agitated because Boycott had invited him to lunch with Elisabeth Murdoch, who had been given control of BSkyB by her fiercely meritocratic father. Murdoch jr is a friend and dancing partner of Mandelson's. Campbell didn't want to encourage cynical rumours by being seen in her company at a delicate moment.

The Express Group is owned by Lord Hollick, a New Labour peer and government adviser, who retains the services of Philip Gould, Tony Blair's private pollster and focus group organiser. As the pundits wrestled with the pseudo-ethical pseudo-problem of Parris's repetition of old news, and reached no clear conclusion, Amanda Platell, editor of the *Express on Sunday*, received a picture of a male friend of Mandelson's and decided to run it. Mandelson lobbied everyone he could think of to stop the story appearing. He ordered the Press Complaints Commission to censor the paper, and when he was told it had no power to intervene, he threatened to abolish it. The item appeared, hacked back and underplayed, on an inside page. Mandelson said he could not understand why *Express* staff had not been disciplined. All Platell's friends who had backed her decision to publish suddenly found pressing reasons to avoid talking to her. She was sacked in January.

Jeremy Paxman, supposedly the meanest interviewer in Britain, was mortified by Parris's aside in the October edition of *Newsnight*. He rushed from the BBC studios to Notting Hill and posted a handwritten apology at midnight through Mandelson's door. Mandelson refused to accept his regrets and said Paxman had conspired with Parris to embarrass him. The Editorial Policy Unit of the BBC (which staff know by the suitably Orwellian title of 'Editpol') sought to assuage his anger. 'Please will all programmes note that under no circumstances whatsoever should the allegations about the private life of Peter Mandelson be repeated or referred to on any broadcast,' it instructed the controllers of all the radio and television stations in the world's largest network.

Journalists protested and Mandelson's Cabinet colleagues accused the BBC of giving him privileged treatment. Their conspiracy theories were dismissed as fantasy by a BBC spokesman ('we would take the same action for anyone'). As he was speaking, Glyn Mathias, a BBC political correspondent, was screaming, 'Are you gay?' at Ron Davies, the Secretary of State for Wales, who had resigned after being caught searching for the comfort of strangers on Clapham Common.

The Director-General of the BBC, Sir John Birt, who was knighted by Tony Blair, worked with and befriended Mandelson at London Weekend Television in the early Eighties. LWT executives became millionaires when a share option lottery in 1993 fell well for them. Among the lucky LWT managers were Melvyn Bragg, Barry Cox and Greg Dyke. They provided most of the £79,000 Tony Blair spent on his campaign to become Labour leader. Bragg was ennobled by New Labour, Cox is a senior executive in the ITV network and Dyke's contributions to Labour funds are not likely to hinder his chances of becoming the next director-general of the BBC.

Mandelson was condemned to watch his friends prosper with a minimum of effort while he received a lower-middle-class salary working a 60-hour week for the Labour Party. Like the Prime Minister, he had come to move in circles where excessive wealth is the norm and, because self-pity is the defining vice of the metropolitan rich, is seen as barely adequate to cover the costs of thieving tradesmen, children who want it all and nannies who are little better than extortionists in Peter Jones aprons. Labour, Mandelson said just before his fall, was 'intensely relaxed about people becoming filthy rich'.

When the *Guardian* story broke and Mandelson thought he was still managing the news, he was confident it would be sufficient to say that Robinson thought 'it important for me to get settled in a home base in London if I was going to be effective as a minister'. He didn't appear to grasp that his explanation would not satisfy 95 per cent of Londoners and 100 per cent of Hartlepool voters who had settled for more modest home bases. You don't need to be a sociologist of genius to trace the links between environment and consciousness in this affair.

After Mandelson resigned, Lady Carla Powell wailed publicly about the traumatic treatment of her confidant and soul mate. Mandelson had stayed with her while his Notting Hill base was redesigned. Her husband,

Sir Charles Powell, was Margaret Thatcher's foreign policy adviser. One of Powell's brothers, Jonathan, is Tony Blair's chief of staff; a second, Chris, manages the Labour advertising account. Mandelson is friends with Tory MPs; Prince Charles; Drue Heinz, widow of a baked bean billionaire; Linda Wachner, an American underwear tycoon who had him flown across the Atlantic in her private jet; and the owner of the Ministry of Sound, who provided him with a free chauffeur and limousine before the election – 'we are a professional, mobile team and the days of relying on a penny farthing machine are over,' Mandelson told those who questioned the propriety of the gift. Along with George Robinson, Mo Mowlam and Chris Smith, he was trained by the fascinating and secretive British-American Project for a Successor Generation, which instructs young and friendly natives, who look likely to climb the provincial ladder of power, on the advantages of following the American way.

Do you begin to see the outline of a political class? A bickering and faintly risible elite, whose ranks are filled with old Thatcherites, downsizing executives, ageing media monopolists and New Labour modernisers smelling slightly stale after less than two years in power; an establishment at odds with itself over Europe and sexual freedom, but one that can compute the value of favours given and received in an instant and is aware that, if perceptions can be managed, interests need not conflict in Tony's One Nation Britain.

Routledge is impressed by the absurdity of it all. Mandelson's 'hubris prevents him from seeing that the Mandy network, assembled so ingeniously over decades, is incapable of delivering the leadership,' he writes. 'The New Establishment – even assuming it holds together for more than the New Labour salad days – is an audience, not an electorate.' Many of those he interviews agree. Mandelson has a fatal flaw for a politician: the knack of making implacable enemies. He doesn't merely defeat opponents, but tries to destroy them and ensure, as he told a Labour press officer who crossed him, that they will never work again. Time and again his victims, invariably former friends, repeat that they've been betrayed by an electoral calculating machine without a principle or policy he wouldn't drop if a focus group told him to recant. 'The result of the Mandelsonisation of the Labour Party is that we seem to stand for nothing positive and clear whatsoever,' Ken Livingstone said in a speech Chris Patten repeated with approval when he was Conservative Party Chairman. Brian Sedgemore, a left-wing Labour MP, has said that the hatred of Mandelson 'is consistent throughout every geographical area and cuts across gender, class, social background and occupation'.

Yet in a suicidally frank interview given in the autumn, Mandelson presented himself as the antithesis of a poll-watching office-seeker and sneered at the gutless pygmies who surrounded him in government. 'They're always sitting on the fence. At the first sign of controversy they run for cover. They're always there, sort of creeping about in the undergrowth in order to maintain their positions and keep their place in the Cabinet. Well, they are the majority. The minority are the people [with] the strong personalities, strong views who are not cowards, who are risk-takers. You' – he said, addressing his interviewer, Michael Portillo – 'have paid the price for being a risk-taker, and so have I.'

Note the facility with which he appropriates the cant of *Wall Street Journal* PR for buccaneering executives as the highest praise a democratic politician could wish for. (A senior Murdoch executive said he had realised New Labour would cause him few problems after seeing Mandelson stare like a 'star-fucker' at executives at a corporate party.) The recklessness that comes from belonging to a faction without significant opposition in party or country is as startling as the familiar self-pity and the imaginative failure to realise that many members of this Cabinet creep and fence-sit because dissent in New Labour is a sackable offence. Mandelson makes himself an easy target for derision – the phrase Notting Hill Nietzsche springs to mind – yet the question remains: if he sees himself as a risk-taker, who has he been taking risks for?

I won't bore you by discussing the abandoned pledges to redistribute wealth, end American control of foreign policy and renationalise the utilities. We have all been told that these were impossible and, on mature reflection, undesirable notions that Mandelson was right to fight. Yet even if we make life easy, and examine his career from the point of view of a New Labour idealist, Mandelson has acted decisively to undermine the mildest hopes. Blair's promise lay in his commitment to open up public life and devolve power. Mandelson has helped him retain control and devolve administration instead. He dismissed the need for a strong Freedom of Information Act and the measure was neutered. (He first voiced his opposition to glasnost in 1996, a year before Labour's election victory, so clichés about the corruption of power do not apply.) As pretty much everyone is in favour of freedom of information, you cannot accuse Mandelson of being a tool of focus groups in this case. A minimum wage is just as easy to sell in a conservative country: even the Americans have one. It rewards work rather than idleness and doesn't cost taxpayers a penny. Mandelson lobbied to give a lower rate to young workers and nothing at all to teenagers aged 17 and under. Whether he was opposing the naming and shaming of firms that wanted to sell arms to dictators or making the votes for trade union recognition in workplaces the most difficult ballots to win in Europe, he was consistently prepared to risk unpopularity if conservative goals demanded it.

At all times he knew he could rely on the eager approval of Blair. I hesitate to criticise Routledge, who has indeed done a great public service, but when he says the Mandy network has failed to give Mandelson the power-base he requires to become an unflinchingly conservative 'Labour' Prime Minister, he forgets that it does not need to: it already has Tony Blair.

London Review of Books February 1999

INDEX